AVENUES TO UNDERSTANDING

THE CENTURY PSYCHOLOGY SERIES

Kenneth MacCorquodale, Gardner Lindzey,
and Kenneth E. Clark, *Editors*

AVENUES TO UNDERSTANDING

The Dynamics
of Therapeutic
Interactions

by WILLIAM J. MUELLER

Michigan State University

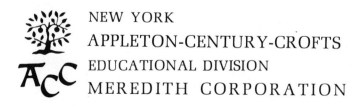

NEW YORK
APPLETON-CENTURY-CROFTS
EDUCATIONAL DIVISION
MEREDITH CORPORATION

TO LOUISE

Preface

This book is about psychotherapy. It is about the processes that define it, that give it substance, and that differentiate it from other human relationships and ventures. To understand the propositions advanced in this book about the processes through which behavioral change is effected, one must understand something of the character of the social group that generated the theses and the interpersonal community in which they reside.

The proposals about how and why behavioral change occurs during therapy were developed from more than a decade of work with young adults of university age and status. A university is by nature a thriving community that provides a cross-section of values and a good sampling of the various ways that people tend to behave with each other in order to contain their anxiety. Such a broadly based community provides rich material for studying conflict in human interactions. And the students populating that community who turn to a therapist for help reflect the full range of human conflict. They present a range of problems with degrees of severity as diverse as their backgrounds. Some are mildly troubled; others reveal long histories of conflict that was deeply ingrained in the home and reinforced many times by unsatisfying interpersonal relationships.

By education and disposition clients who are university students often times have good verbal facility, are psychologically minded, and in many cases are curious about their own inner processes. Their communications are often complex, their conflicts being conveyed at a number of symbolic levels simultaneously. They are often impatient to learn. And as a group they tend to move rapidly in therapy and the therapist might find himself amazed at their progress.

Almost by definition, university students are in process. Many of them are in the process of shaping their careers and that search for a vocational identity is often representative of their own internal struggles to find themselves, it reflects their state of flux, and it is symbolic of their efforts to come to grips with their own identities. That condition makes them vulnerable. Their conflicts are many times active. They often live with a good deal of anxiety. And conflicts which might have lain dormant for years under other circumstances are sometimes exacerbated by the stresses of university life and the diversity of values represented in that community.

That is not to imply that clients who are university students are always easy to help. In some cases the clients' defenses are strong and impenetrable and they have learned ways of hiding behind their verbal facility and turning their psychological mindedness to advantage in warding off the therapist. But it is more often true that their conflicts are not overlaid with many defensive layers and that their defenses are fluid, providing relatively easy access to underlying motivation and sources of anxiety.

In this book, a number of proposals about the processes which facilitate or inhibit change in working with such a population of clients are advanced and applied to therapeutic practice. The book is divided into two parts. In the first section, the foundations for change during therapy are introduced. In those chapters, the many sources which provide the basis for a therapist's understanding of his client's emotional life are surveyed. Particular emphasis is given to those sources of understanding that are intrinsic to therapy and are generated by the intricate interplay of those conditions that are unique to the therapeutic situation.

Consideration of the sources of data unique to therapy and generated by the dynamics of therapeutic interactions interlocks with and leads to the introduction of critical features of process. The change process is considered from the perspective of the dynamic forces which actuate, underlie, and shape those processes by which constructive change is facilitated or inhibited. Throughout the first section, case materials are introduced to illustrate the richness of some sources of data and to demonstrate the underlying interlocking effects and synthetic potential of different avenues to understanding, thereby providing a brief prospective glimpse into the dynamics of therapeutic interactions.

Whereas in the first part of the book case material is introduced mainly to underwrite a concept, to convey an idea, or to support a proposition, case material receives much more prominence in the second part. In the second section, the perspective is altered and a conceptual framework is derived inductively from analysis of the dynamics of therapeutic interactions. The concepts, propositions, and many ways of understanding introduced in earlier parts of the book are reintroduced as they naturally occur and bear on the work of the therapist.

In presenting case material, particularly in the second section, where more extensive sojourns are made into the emotional lives of clients, the cases are used to provide a basis for generating hypotheses, to sort out dynamic issues, or to illustrate principles. As such, fidelity to a particular case was neither intended nor considered desirable. Compressions, modifications, and elaborations drawn from dynamically similar cases have been variously utilized in order to insure anonymity as well as to bring underlying dynamic issues into bold relief.

Those who engage in the work of helping emotionally troubled young adults in face-to-face therapeutic relationships might find the concepts and applications presented in the following pages useful in their own training and professional practice and in the training of their students. The ideas were developed from study of dyadic interactions with young adults. Whether and which concepts apply beyond the parameters defined by that population and setting only the reader can determine as he compares what is said with his own practice. The book can also be read from a second perspective and might be of interest to students of personality. In many chapters, particularly during the second part of the book, the etiology, development, and current interpersonal expression of conflict is detailed with some care.

I feel a deep sense of gratitude to the clients who over the past ten years of my work at the Counseling Center at Michigan State University have allowed me the privilege of entering their emotional lives and searching with them for the sources of their anxiety. From them I have learned about the pleasures, anxiety, excitement, and challenge of therapy. With them I have often lived out much of what I eventually have come to conceptualize as significant to the process of change during therapy. My appreciation for help in understanding the change process extends well beyond the clients whom I have known personally. Over the years, many, many clients and their therapists have permitted the course of their therapy to be followed closely, providing much rich diagnostic and interview material for the study of the psychotherapeutic process. Those data have been a very helpful resource in writing this book.

I have been taught much about the work of a therapist from the interns and practicum students whose work I have supervised over the years. The person being supervised often does not grasp the full impact of himself as the teacher of his supervisor. In revealing his innermost feelings and thoughts as he works with different clients, in his innovativeness, and in providing his supervisor with a running account of his continuing cases, the supervisee allows his supervisor to observe, study, and learn about process in ways that just are not otherwise possible.

I have learned much from my colleagues at the Counseling Center. Those who work in an agency with a major investment in service know the importance of colleagues—to listen at times, to share anxiety as well as ideas, and often to act as an observer of a colleague-therapist's own internal process when relationships reach impasse. Among my colleagues, I am particularly indebted to Dr. Bill Kell. My association with Bill as a friend, colleague, consultant, and collaborator has been a deeply rewarding one and a continuing source of stimulation for my professional work. Bill Kell and I collaborated in writing two books, *Impact and Change* and *Coping with Conflict*. Those books, inquiries into the processes which characterize therapeutic interactions and supervisory relationships, have already been published by Appleton-Century-Crofts. The many hours we spent together sharing ideas and feelings have deeply influenced my thinking about the way that a relationship comes to be a therapeutic one. I am also grateful to Bill for his careful reading of this manuscript.

I have also been influenced by and learned from many others as well, who have struggled with some of the same issues that have stirred my interest. Those influences are reflected in the bibliographic section but of especial importance to me have been the clinical insights, therapeutic skillfulness, and developmental concepts of Harry Stack Sullivan, Franz Alexander, Erik H. Erikson, Frieda Fromm-Reichmann, Erich Fromm, and Carl R. Rogers.

I would also like to acknowledge those who helped in the preparation of this book during its many stages. Nancy Bossenbroek, Lynn Hayes, Marilyn Hinderer, and Sue Smith spent many hours in the exacting work of typing, retyping, and proofreading the manuscript. Finally, my thanks to the editorial staff of my publisher for helping me to clarify what I wanted to communicate with sensitivity to my meaning.

W. J. M.

Contents

Part I

THE FOUNDATIONS
FOR CHANGE
THROUGH THERAPY

1

Avenues to Understanding:
An Introduction

When a client turns to a therapist for help, he has often struggled alone for a long time to understand what he feels and fears. In the hope that understanding might bring control and relief, the client might have undertaken extensive introspective sojourns in an attempt to grasp the meaning of what is troubling him. Yet, despite his efforts to understand himself, the client is likely to have found his search to be unrewarding and frustrating rather than enlightening and liberating.

A client's frustration often interlocks with heightening anxiety, confusion, and fears that his life situation is worsening. As his fright increases, a client might find that his fears are compounded and generalizing; actions, spontaneity, and creativity seem to give way to inaction, apathy, and withdrawal. In his anxiety the client might find that he doesn't approach new situations with curiosity and a sense of experimentation, but rather with fear and restraint, knowing only that he feels a sense of danger to himself. Panic might then lead to further withdrawal, not because he enjoys solitude, but because he fears the company of others.

For reasons unknown to himself, the client might find that forgotten impulses begin to make a reappearance with a power that is frightening. The more that he struggles to control his poorly understood impulses, the more they seem to be gaining control of him. He might feel that he is crazy or fears going crazy. Or disturbing feelings might intrude into a client's work and distract him into daydreams that violate his moral code, yet daydreams that he finds himself enjoying just the same.

A client might turn to a therapist because he is unable to understand what has happened to his zest for life. Whereas at one time he might have faced the future with optimism, that optimism has been dulled by disappointment and tinged with cynicism. For him, confidence, certainty, concerted study, and planning have become overshadowed with self-doubt.

Still another client might feel burdened and overwhelmed by the demands of others, yet feel helpless to free himself. It might seem to him that he will never break free of his home and family. For reasons that baffle him, he is drawn back into the family despite his conscious wish to be independent of them. Feelings of indebtedness, guilt, anger, and resentment characterize his thoughts about family relationships. He might not know whether he loves or hates his parents; all that he knows is that when in their presence he experiences an overriding fear of becoming entangled in a suffocating web that leaves him anxious and helpless.

The client who enters therapy might have found that the harder he has tried to grasp the meaning of his life, to make sense of his feelings and behavior, the more he seems to lose grip of himself. And all he might feel he has gained from his research into the sources of his unwanted feelings and behavior is a disconnected array of memories about persons and events that he knows are somehow significant, but those insights seem to make little difference to his ability to change his feelings, stifle his fantasies, and modify his behavior.

A client who turns to a therapist realizes only vaguely, if at all, that his efforts on his own behalf have been unproductive because the avenues to understanding himself have been blocked by anxiety and covered by years of carefully constructed ways and means of protecting himself from knowing about the very things that could provide him with the freedom he seeks. The anxieties which set the conflict into motion and the conscious experiences of and reactions to that conflict, along with an intricate defensive and signal system, all work against the client's recovery of those experiences and his understanding of them.

Until the meaning of the anxiety is traced to its source, it will continue to operate in unhampered and destructive ways in the life of the client. For anxiety can bring a client up short immediately before a major achievement. It can take the joy out of life and replace it with apathy. It can drive a person into the therapist's office and it can drive him right back out again. It can choke off feeling what is experienced, and knowing what is felt. It can retard development, blot out memories of what was felt or fantasized, and lead to the development of elaborate systems for protecting oneself. Its effects can be seen in the bubbly, "chattery" character of one person or in the depression of another. It can attack in a crowd or in the privacy of an enclosed room. It can lead one person to act like a joker because he fears being taken seriously and another to act seriously because he fears being ridiculed. It can attach itself to something specific which can be avoided, or it can fill a man's insides with a vague, undifferentiated fear, uneasiness, and foreboding.

THE CONDITION OF ANXIOUSNESS—
OPENING THE AVENUES TO UNDERSTANDING

Whereas anxiety has blocked the client's understanding of himself and frustrated his own efforts, it provides the key that the therapist and client must learn to use to break the client free of whatever binds him. The therapist knows that the anxiety and sense of discomfort that brings the client to his office sets the stage for learning since it provides the drive which impels the client to reveal himself and his motivations insofar as he understands them.

The therapist clearly understands that anxiety provides the opportunity for change and that change cannot occur without it. Although the therapist understands that clearly, the client who enters therapy has often only experienced the destructive, maiming effects of anxiety. He cannot know of his own potential for overpowering anxiety, for taming it, and for turning it to his own uses. How he can use his anxiety as a vehicle for learning is what the therapeutic process will teach him.

Whereas the client views his anxiety with pessimism, the therapist's optimism about anxiety emanates also from what he knows about human conflict. The client's anxiety means that his conflicts are still active, that he hasn't wiped the slate clean, resolved the conflict. It means the client is still fighting and his voluntary entrance into a therapeutic relationship is evidence that he is approaching rather than avoiding those situations, persons, and relationships that provoke anxiety.

The condition of anxiousness, then, provides the opportunity for change and is the basis on which a therapeutic relationship is built. From that base, the therapist and client can get a clear look around the emotional life of the client that would otherwise not be available to them. Knowing that anxiety points to conflict, the therapist can use the heightening and reduction of anxiety as a guide to whether his search with the client is moving along productive lines. Provided that he uses the client's feelings of anxiety adroitly, sensitively, and constructively, the avenues to understanding the client will remain open. If the therapist activates too much anxiety, if the client feels diffusely anxious or overwhelmed by fear, then the client will begin to respond to the anxiety and forget the search. In this way, anxiety provides the potential for learning.

But anxiety has an even more useful function in the therapy of a client. Whereas initial anxiety sets the stage and points to conflict, once the therapist has helped the client to encounter and resolve some initial problem, anxiety takes on a new and more mature function in the relationship. For it now no longer is simply the therapist's tool to assess conflict areas and facilitate learning; it becomes the client's tool for his own learning.

When the client who has been anxious comes to know himself better as a result of hanging onto his anxiety long enough to see what it means, he will be deeply gratified and it will provide the desire to search deeper for greater freedom. More importantly the client will begin to experience the manageability of his own anxiety. Further, he will have his first sense of its usefulness to him since it has stimulated the search back and forth in his mental process. What has been a roadblock to freedom then can become the client's source of strength in liberating himself. For anxiety is the vehicle for rechanneling energy and strengthening ego functions so that the client's life can move along in an ever broadening, spiraling enriched experience for him.

The anxiety that confines a client is the very factor of his mental processes that can liberate him. The therapeutic task is to use the anxiety as a signal and guide for the search into those factors in the client's emotional life that are causing trouble and to teach the client the means at his disposal by which he can continue the search beyond the termination of therapy. The ways in which the therapist undertakes to teach the client how to search effectively constitutes a major phase of the mature therapeutic work.

During the course of therapy, the client must be taught the searching process that the therapist has learned if he is an effective therapist. When the therapist becomes anxious during a therapeutic session, he uses his anxiety as an internal yardstick to trouble in the relationship and begins a search, using his own associational processes to conduct the search back and forth within himself in relation to the client and to what transpired between the two of them. The emotional insights that accrue from that search provide the therapist with the understanding that he can then convey to the client which provides the basis for the emotional experience in the client. The interlocking effects of this process of experiencing anxiety, associating, and understanding in the therapist and its effects on the ensuing emotional experience and eventual insights of the client will be taken up later.

For purposes of this general introduction, suffice it to say that the client must be taught by the therapist how to undertake that search, else a major goal of therapy will be left unfinished and the client will always be dependent on the therapist for understanding himself and growing. That process of the therapist's helping the client to utilize his own resources in expanding his understanding of his own emotional life is what is meant by the teaching function in therapy and constitutes its major usefulness in the life of the client.

Some clients never go beyond the initial phase of therapy, that is, they never learn to use their own resources to track their anxiety. They enter therapy because they are anxious and in their anxiety they allow the therapist freedom to look into their lives, but they never learn to take over the search themselves. Those clients constitute the group who often report situational anxiety which, when sufficiently reduced to get them functional again, leave therapy to return again when another crisis looms on the horizon.

But many clients have the capacity to learn how to continue beyond termination to channel and utilize their own resources to develop still greater resources. At the outset of therapy, the client might enter the relationship with the feeling that he has no control over himself, over what he does, or what he feels. At the termination of successful therapy, what had been a compulsion becomes a probability. A declarative becomes a subjunctive, what "must be" becomes what "could be" if a search isn't undertaken into the causes of unrest.

And the client feels that he has control over that search, that the opportunity for changing his condition resides within himself. The client's anxiety doesn't so much block thinking as it aids thinking. Whereas at the outset of therapy, anxiety, because of its frightening character, instituted defenses with a rapidity that precluded the search, at termination it is felt as a motivating force—a creative force—that institutes a search and not simply a defensive disabling reaction.

Knowing the productive use to which anxiety can be put is what provides the therapist with his optimism in working with conflicted clients. Knowing that anxiety means that conflict is active, that disabling resolutions have not been accomplished, that the stage is set for learning, that anxiety can be utilized as a guide to whether the search is moving along productive lines and that eventually it can be tamed and become a useful vehicle for growth enables the therapist to live with a client during anxious times without working to reduce it prematurely. Above all, the therapist realizes that anxiety opens the avenues to understanding and that so long as those avenues remain open change can occur.

SOME PRELIMINARY CONDITIONS FOR THERAPY: A FRAMEWORK FOR UNDERSTANDING

Anxiety in the client, then, is one of the conditions that will determine in part the unique character of the relationship and processes that define therapy. Before the impact of a client's anxiousness in setting certain dynamic processes in motion can be fully understood, however, several other interlocking influences which give shape and uniqueness to the relationship and process of therapy must be introduced.

First of all, the life experiences of the participants influence the potential for understanding and change that can characterize the therapeutic relationship. Those experiences also provide a rough approximation of the potential boundaries and course of the relationship. Second, the purposes of therapy—its intent and its method—set some unique dynamic processes into motion. Last, the therapeutic agreement itself—the commitment to help and the negotiations that surround it—trigger emotional reactions in a client that are dynamically important to the processes that are set into motion.

All of those conditions will influence the course of the relationship that is to develop. Each will provide the therapist with opportunities to understand the emotional life of his client. Together they will interact so as to set a process into motion that is dynamically unique. In the last section anxiety was described. In this section, the influence of the experiences of the participants, the intent of therapy, and the therapeutic contract will be discussed separately. And then in the next chapter, a first approximation of the dynamics generated by the interplay of those conditions and their effects in providing the therapist with rich avenues for understanding his client will be discussed.

Experiences of the Participants: Influences on Understanding

A therapeutic relationship begins, as does any human relationship, with the meeting of two strangers. When a client enters therapy, neither he nor the therapist who has offered to help him knows what lies ahead for them or whether their relationship will develop and survive the troubles that they most assuredly will encounter along the way. Although the course of the relationship is unknown, although neither participant has information about how this specific relationship will develop, both the therapist and client have lived through many other relationships; and those encounters will have left deeply imprinted attitudes on both about the nature, course, and outcome of human relationships.

Hopefully the therapist's previous human encounters will have been deeply satisfying to him. In fact, the residual effects of those relationships and the gains that he has experienced from previous encounters in large measure have probably provided the stimulation for the therapist's commitment to professional practice. In his encounters with other clients, the therapist has probably met some success in helping those in trouble to resolve their emotional conflicts; otherwise he probably would not find practice rewarding enough to compensate for its frustrations.

Based on his previous experiences, the therapist will be reasonably confident that he can help the next client who seeks his help but whether he can and in the way that he can remain unknown to him at the time of their first meeting. Despite his previous successes, the therapist will be able to recall vividly the struggles, conflicts, and anxiety that were generated in those previous relationships during the course of their development. He will remember how close at times he and other clients came to disappointment and failure. He will particularly remember the moments when his own anxiety intensified and generated conflicts about whether to approach material that threatened his own feelings of well-being.

During his initial contact with a client the therapist will recall times when another client's behavior brushed against his own values and he had the impulse to moralize rather than to understand. He will recall clearly how at times he became confused, and how his own welfare—his needs to reduce his own anxiety—interfered with his concern about a client. But he will also remember that he and his other clients survived those troubled sessions and that they were a necessary prelude to his client's changing; so as the therapist plans to enter a new relationship he will do so with some anxiety but also with optimism and with some awareness that his motivation to help is genuine.

In the same way that the therapist's previous experiences in relationships and particularly in therapeutic relationships have helped to shape his beliefs, attitudes, and anticipations, so also do the client's memories, fantasies, and feelings generated in past relationships condition his attitudes and expectations for the relationship that he contemplates. The residual effects of other relationships—the attitudes that have accrued and the internal interpretation of previous experiences—provide the client with the perceptual framework that he brings to the relationship. The learned ways of blocking out anxiety-provoking experiences and of distorting those experiences in consciousness so as to make them more acceptable will provide the client with his defensive armor.

The client's sense of who he is, what he wants in a relationship, how people help each other or damage each other will provide him with the backlog of experiences that he trails along with him. The pleasures, disappointments, and frustrations that have characterized other experiences will be all he can know of the benefits and risks of human relationships. The deeply imprinted attitudes derived from other relationships, in other words, will provide the client with the only means available to him out of which he will conceptualize himself and others, the framework from which he will interpret events, and the defenses he will institute to avoid injury.

Previous experiences might have taken their toll in the client's optimism about whether he can understand his emotional life and he might enter therapy with little confidence that help will be offered or that he will be able to accept that help. Whether the conflicts will become too intense to face, whether anxiety will disable the relationship, whether fears will overshadow the wish to break free of those conflicts, only time will tell. How pervasive the conflicts are in the life of the client, how much they interpenetrate every part of his existence, how overwhelmed he feels by the conflicts, and how consistently damaging prior relationships during his developmental years have been will all combine to determine how much the client is able to tolerate anxiety and how long he will be able to struggle with his ambiguity before needing to reach an emotional decision. At times a client is willing to settle for any solution to the problem. If the client has been bitterly disappointed in the past, if his optimism about his ability to relate, to develop, and to change has been badly damaged, then he might not be able to struggle long before he might need to retreat behind his defenses.

On the other hand, how able and willing the therapist is to help this particular client, how much this particular client will trigger feelings and associations in the therapist that reduce his effectiveness, how disabling the therapist will find this particular client, neither the therapist nor the client know at the outset of therapy. What *might* transpire is based upon the backlog of experiences that both parties bring to the interaction. What *will* transpire in the relationship will be a function of how much the anxiety of either party interferes with bringing into awareness without distortion the feelings and thoughts that must become conscious during the experience if the client is to free himself of what disables him.

The encounters in previous relationships—the disappointments, losses, the futile attempts at interaction, the anger, frustration, and resentment—are experiences that stimulate doubt and ambivalence in the mind of the client as he sits with the therapist. His hopes for therapy are mixed with fears and those fears are based on the imagined consequences of an intense encounter with this stranger. The assumptions and predictions that he holds about this as yet unknown venture provide the basis from which the participants will need to struggle if the relationship is to survive. But both the client and his therapist have some sense that previous experiences have been sufficiently satisfying to the client to keep the fantasy alive that he can resolve his emotional conflicts;

otherwise he wouldn't be risking another relationship no matter how tentatively he does so. That fact provides the therapist with hope that he might be able to help.

In addition, the clients who often frequent the therapist's office are amazingly resilient people. They have often struggled a long time with their conflicts and despite a vast number of disabling experiences, they continue to fight back. If professional practice teaches anything well, it is to respect the resiliency and integrating capacity of persons in conflict. Despite struggles that have developed over long periods of time, clients continue to attempt to relate to others, to fight isolation, loneliness, and despair.

Those who traverse serious conflicts and survive have a strength about them that might be unknown to those who have not suffered traumas or extended periods of deprivation. They also have a sense of humanness and compassion that seems to be born out of the suffering they have undergone. No therapist sits long in his office without experiencing this strength of a human being, the urgency to have human contact, the constructive ever self-correcting factors in human existence, the wish to affiliate and to love rather than to hate and reject. A therapist has only to follow the progress of some client filled with hostility, anger, and resentment to soon see the underlying flattened positive affect emerge. No matter how repetitive and unwholesome a client's interactions—how destructive and self-defeating—the spark of drives to reconstruct, to relearn, to reexperience life in different or more satisfying ways undergirds them.

Even in situations where the destructive, devastating characteristics have been so well set that the client seems unreachable, the therapist might be amazed at the resiliency and the need of the person to try to reconstruct again. That resiliency of clients also provides the therapist with the optimism and freedom to work with difficult clients, for the therapist recognizes that even if he errs, even if he approaches things at times insensitively and incompetently, the strength of the clients' needs for human relationships is such that they will recover and give the therapist another chance to help.

The Therapeutic Effort: Its Focus on Anxiety

The experience of anxiety in the client as he approaches the therapeutic relationship and the previous life experiences of both participants provide two of the conditions which interact to provide the relationship which is to develop with some of its unique characteristics. Interacting with those conditions to heighten the anxiety of the client and further distinguish therapy from other relationships and processes is its purpose.

Although the strength of a therapeutic relationship resides in its humanness, the therapeutic relationship differs from other human experiences along a significant dimension. In many relationships, people can run from their anxiety, they can conceal it, or deny it. They can cover what they experience with defenses and succeed in maintaining the relationship. They can pretend. In fact in some human relationships, the association is nurtured by the ability of the participants to cover the tracks of their conflicts with each other, by their capacity to feed the neurosis of the other, by their mutual pact to avoid, deny, and confuse. In some relationships, the anxiety of the two persons interlocks and they work together to prevent mutual disturbances.

Therapy differs from other relationships in this regard. Therapy focuses on conflict, on human motivation, and on the ways in which people defend against experiencing what would be damaging to them. The sole purpose of therapy is to meet and struggle with conflict, to defeat it so that needs can be met. In other relationships, conflict might occur but it is incidental to the relationship. Conflict is a normal consequence of human interaction but it is not the impelling motive for bringing two people together. In the course of all relationships conflicts emerge, but the intention of most relationships is not to bring conflict into bold relief for constructive purposes.

In therapy the main reason for the people coming together is to cope with the conflicts of the client who seeks out the therapist for assistance. The therapeutic task is one of examining the defenses that are erected to achieve satisfaction by circuitous routes, to learn of the effects of those defenses in their toll on human energy and on self-deception, and to break through the roadblocks they create which prevent development, maturity, and greater satisfaction. In therapy, conflict cannot be avoided. If the intent of therapy—to explore conflict and study human motivation surrounding it so that feelings and behavior can change—is frustrated, then the therapeutic relationship loses its purpose for existing. Once the needs that brought the people together are thwarted, the relationship will be meaningless.

The Commitment: Setting the Process into Motion

To the conditions which influence and differentiate a therapeutic relationship must be added one more: the effect of the therapist's verbal offer to help. The "offer to help" in itself seems to set into motion a series of emotional reactions in a client that are astonishing in what they reveal of the dynamics of human conflict and the character of defenses. The "offer to help" probably does so because at some level the client vaguely recognizes the demand on his emotional life that a commitment implies.

No matter how tentatively the offer to help is given or accepted, it implies a commitment to change. And that commitment is a first reality step toward changing. Until the offer has been given and accepted, the notion of changing has been a fantasy which like many other fantasies might be "fun to fool around with" so long as it doesn't become real. Once, however, some reality is attached to a fantasy, a client's unconscious will do some rather interesting things to reincorporate the fantasy so that an imbalance does not occur in the client's emotional life.

The client's anxiousness about a commitment also stems from other implications of the therapist's offer. The therapist's offer to help is generally given in terms of an agreement "that he will work with" the client to effect change. The nature of the proposed relationship that is implied in the offer to help activates additional anxiety since the client realizes that he and the therapist are proposing a joint venture. The client turned to the therapist because he was searching for someone to help him with understanding his motivations, conflicts, and anxiety. But, again, the reality factors impinge on the fantasy because the client realizes with sudden clarity that an honest relationship necessitates giving to another person access to hidden motivations. And the client also realizes that the therapist, as a trained professional, is likely to be perceptive about areas of conflict. What the client has no way of knowing at the time of the initial commitment is whether the therapist will use his perceptiveness sensitively. That question is likely to be a very real one for the client since he would probably be in less need of a therapist if others had been more sensitive to his feelings. And so, when the risks involved in a commitment filter through a client's unconscious, he, like any good human being who fears for his survival, will react with fervor.

The offer to help affects different clients in varying ways depending upon their underlying motivation and method of coping with stress. For some clients, the offer acts as an instant escape valve and there is a flood of affect that apparently has been held back by crumbling defenses. Others recoil in dramatic ways. For those clients, it is as though, until the help was offered, only one side of the client's needs was showing, the side that was in pain. The case for help might have been presented plaintively and fervently. Once, however, the therapist agrees to work with the client, the client seems almost with premeditation to "break out his bag of tricks." Defensive operations and perceptual distortions occur with a flourish and rapidity that is unbelievable. Problems get reconceptualized in less dramatic ways in some and become more dramatic in others. It seems that the client's unconscious strikes out aggressively to drive unwanted intruders from tampering with a well-known pattern of life.

Regardless of what those initial moments of contact and the transactions that surround them stimulate in the client and therapist, the point is that during that initial interaction, a relationship is seeded which can be potentially therapeutic or destructive. From the moment of their first encounter, the dynamic processes that characterize therapy are activated. From the moment that the therapist has offered to help the client without knowing how and in what ways he can be helpful until the time that the client and therapist by mutual agreement or otherwise terminate that relationship, everything that transpires will be an experience that is potentially useful in providing for therapeutic help.

The relationship will expand, deepen, and provide the opportunity for change, or it will be dampened, attenuated, and restricting, depending upon the willingness and ability of both parties to utilize fully the emotional experiences that are generated in and occur as a consequence of their interaction. How limiting or liberating therapy can become, how limited or extensive the potential for change is, how significant that relationship will be in the life of the client and how far-reaching its consequences will be, those dimensions of therapy have their genesis in those first few moments of contact.

2

The Uniqueness of Therapy:
Dimensions for Understanding

To understand a client, a therapist must understand many things about the way that anxiety has intruded in the life of a client to frustrate his goals, turn his interpersonal relationships into unrewarding associations, and create inner conflicts which preclude the satisfaction of needs. As therapy progresses from moment to moment, the therapist's opportunities for understanding his client expand. With each encounter, with each new association, experience, memory, and insight, the therapist's sense of who his client is deepens. In a continuing, deepening spiral the therapist's understanding increases and becomes more specific to the client who is seated with him.

With each moment of therapy, understanding increases; and with each new understanding, the opportunity for still deeper understanding is awakened. In many cases the therapist's understanding is the stimulus for the client's succeeding experiences. If assisted by the therapist, each moment of experience during therapy provides the basis in the client for potential insight and growth. And each new insight provides the opportunity for expanding and deepening experience. As will be seen in this and succeeding chapters, the cycling of experiencing and understanding continues to flow along throughout therapy, each feeding the other and providing the basis for continually opening new channels for growth.

In the last chapter, several characteristics of therapy were described which distinguish it from other human endeavors. It was proposed that those characteristics provide therapy with the basis for a unique relationship and processes. It was proposed further that insofar as the therapist grasps the meaning of the dynamics generated by the interplay of those characteristics, he has at his disposal rich avenues to understanding the emotional life of his client.

13

In this chapter, the sources and dimensions for understanding clients will be surveyed in some detail. In a sense, the development of this chapter parallels the way in which a therapist expands and deepens his understanding of his client. In his initial contacts, a therapist's understanding is most superficial; it is generic in nature. It happens to apply to a particular client but it could apply as well to many other persons. As therapy progresses, new and more complex dimensions for understanding make their appearance as the relationship deepens and as the therapist's understanding becomes increasingly specific to his interactions with a particular individual.

As this chapter develops, our survey of the various dimensions for understanding will follow that same sequence. At the outset of the chapter, those sources of understanding that are important but not unique to a therapeutic relationship will be discussed. And then, as the chapter progresses, the dimensions for understanding that are unique to therapy—those that are embedded in and generated by the therapeutic interaction—will be introduced. As each new dimension for understanding is introduced, it will complicate the picture but it will also enlarge and enrich the potential for understanding the avenues already considered.

SOURCES OF UNDERSTANDING:
AN INTRODUCTION

During therapy, a therapist learns many things about a client. Some of what the therapist learns is more critical to therapeutic progress than other material. Operationally, the value of any knowledge in the therapist consists of its potential for awakening channels of communication between therapist and client and in deepening understanding so that the client can become aware of connections between his conscious conflicts and the unconscious processes that motivate his disabling behavior. Unless the information can be used to link anxiety and conflict in that way, its relevance is questionable.

A therapist's initial assessments of a client often are first impressions of a client's cognitive and affective functioning and of the developmental antecedents which apparently have influenced those mental processes. A therapist listens closely to what and how the client perceives, how he conceptualizes his problems, how he interacts with others, what he seeks in his relationships, and where anxiety seems to intrude to prevent gratification.

Each of those features of a client's personality becomes a part of the therapist's understanding of him. The therapist's understanding of the client is based upon the constant interplay between what the client says and does and how the therapist internally organizes that information and makes it sensible to himself. Much of what a therapist mentally processes during his first contacts is often compared and evaluated by him in terms of his previous experiences and his theoretical understanding of the nature of conflict. At the outset of therapy, when assessment is in its most generalized form, those initial speculations are often closest to theory.

Although a therapist's grasp of theory cannot be equated with effectiveness, theoretical understanding is an essential requisite to being effective. A therapist understands and organizes information about clients in terms of his own interpretations of theory about the development of conflict. Those understandings of people that are a function of a therapist's prior professional experience, his training, his grasp of human conflict and the dynamics of behavior—those understandings are probably most useful to the therapist as a means for getting therapy underway. They are the generalizations about behavior which permit the therapist to make some first approximations about conflict areas; they heighten his perceptiveness and they stimulate trust as a client senses the therapist's competence. But it is only as generalizations drop off, as theoretical understandings fade into the background, as the uniqueness of the client and his individuality emerge, that the opportunities for significant change in the client increase.

Anxiety Revisited: Opening the Way for Understanding

The effects of anxiety were discussed earlier, but one aspect of anxiety—its effects on bringing the emotional life of a client into the open—should be reconsidered here in terms of its potential for providing understanding. Because of the nature of the therapeutic situation with its emphasis on anxiety, it acts to trigger even greater anxiety since a client will be frightened of what he can only vaguely foretell about the relationship and the risks involved.

That anxiety, however, increases a client's vulnerability and provides a therapist with the means to help him. Anxiety implies an intensification in internal pressure and thereby takes on an additional function which is critical for therapeutic progress. Anxiety blunts a client's censor, forcing into the open the client's inner interpretation of his life experiences, thus making them available to the therapist in his efforts to understand the client.

Under conditions of heightened stress, a client's ability to monitor his reactions and defend against revealing his feelings is weakened; he will project, distort, and react in the present with feelings that belong to the past. Anxiety works to heighten mood swings; it provides the opportunity to observe otherwise hidden, disguised, or attenuated reactions. The person reveals himself and his motivations both directly and indirectly. When a person labors under stress, perceptual distortions are more likely to occur. Dynamics can be inferred with greater ease because the behavioral reactions are clearer. Efforts to ward off the breakthrough of impulses are redoubled and, through his strident efforts, the client reveals himself.

SOURCES OF UNDERSTANDING:
THE CLIENT'S SELF-REVELATIONS

Anxiety, therefore, brings out critical features of a person's emotional life. And, as such, it serves to heighten understanding of some of the dynamic processes at work underlying conflict. Because of the internal pressure of anxiety, the client might in initial sessions reveal much of the content of his previous and current interactions that he feels interfere with his sense of well-being. Those revelations of what transpires during his interactions and what has occurred in interactions with parents, siblings, and other significant figures in the past can be very useful to a therapist.

In some cases, the content of the interactions reported by the client often provides the therapist with some insights into the developmental patterns in the family and more generally in the life of the client. Some of the interactions reported by the client might be experiences that have a direct connection to the client's distressed feelings. If so, the significance of those occurrences is probably only sensed by the client because the actual experience is likely to be stripped of associated affect.

The content of those interactions will predictably recur with some regularity and prominence later during therapy. At each time that they are reintroduced, their significance will be felt more keenly by the client as the feelings that have been severed by anxiety begin to emerge. And only as those feelings are worked through and the experience fully integrated will their recurrence fade from prominence in therapeutic sessions.

At other times, the usefulness of the client's reports might consist of what they reveal about the layers of defensive material that overlay the disabling experiences rather than in the insights they provide as a direct pipeline to problem interactions. Some of the interactions reported might be fantasies, they might be attempts to project blame, or they might be downright lies. In some cases, the memories of a client might reflect only one side of an interaction. In reporting critical incidents, it often happens that only those facets of the interaction are immediately remembered that tell the client's side of the story. They reveal the ways in which the client feels that he has been battered and misused. And the chances are that the client has been misused but not for the reasons he believes. His own motivations and collusions are often concealed wittingly or otherwise. The submerged dimensions of the interaction only become available later as the client becomes more trusting and has gotten some of the anger out of his system.

The question that the therapist must always ask himself is why the client has selected out the incidents and episodes that he has. The point is not that the client's care in selecting the interactions he reports makes those reports less significant. On the contrary their significance resides in what they reveal of the client's motivations and the way he interprets his experiences, what they reveal of his defensive modes, what they reveal of how he wants the therapist to view him and his problems, and what they reveal of how the client conceptualizes his experiences and the nature and development of his conflicts.

Not only do the client's deviousness, his caution, and his rationalizations make therapy more interesting, but paradoxically they provide the therapist with the knowledge that his client is healthier than another client who might not approach therapy with caution. The client who proceeds to reveal all of his innermost secrets in initial contacts with a therapist is suspect. The person who immediately and with no reservation reveals what one would surmise are supposedly well-guarded wishes and fears, who during initial sessions spills out his innermost thoughts with abandon is likely to have badly damaged reality testing or to be using the "flooding" of the therapist with intense material for dynamic purposes that will probably only become clear at a later time during therapy.

It is only after therapy has developed to the point where a client feels that the therapist is trustworthy enough and tolerant enough to use the information constructively that he will begin to reveal some of what he consciously hides. There are a number of reasons why that is so. First of all, the right to privacy is one of man's most carefully guarded possessions. The right is cherished because a person's private thoughts, feelings, attitudes, wishes, and fears together comprise what the person experiences as making him what he is. So there is a need to retain consistency or the personality is in danger of being badly damaged. There is danger, in other words, to jarring the emotional balance.

Secondly, the person who has spent a considerable amount of time in guarding some secrets probably has little sense of validation for some of his feelings and the secrets that he holds. He is a loner with regard to sharing feelings. Chances are that he fears that revelation will lead to negative evaluation, rejection, and further isolation from the human community. And, of course, in most cases, a client simply does not know what secrets he is guarding. In actuality, it is often his own motivations that he fears learning about and those are not available to him. If he could become aware of them without intense anxiety he would not be in need of a therapist. Such a client provides the therapist with what he does believe of himself and what he thinks might be relevant.

None of the foregoing reasons detract in any way from the vital importance that a therapist must attach to the self-revelations of a client. The therapist can rest assured that the content of the interactions that are reported will reemerge again later in therapy at which time their dynamic character might become clearer in terms of what the therapist then knows about the emotional life of the client. In some cases, as stated earlier, they will reemerge accompanied by the appropriate affect which was initially absent; at other times they might be reintroduced with insights into their defensive value or with a sense of the motivations underlying the interactions.

The point is simply that their importance might not so much reside in the face validity of the client's reports as it does in what they reveal of the client's motivational system and in his perceptual processes. That process of interpreting and processing material internally as revealed through the client's perceptions and conceptualizations is another avenue to understanding a client that the therapist learns about directly from his client's reactions to him and indirectly from the way that a client interprets the meaning of his other interactions. But before turning to those sources of understanding, some comments would seem to be inappropriate about the ways in which a client's interpersonal behavior provides the therapist with some reference points for understanding his emotional maturity.

Interpersonal Behavior: Context for
Understanding Emotional Development

From what the therapist learns of the behavioral interactions of a client, he can begin to speculate about the client's emotional maturity. Productive therapeutic work is contingent on the accuracy of the therapist's speculations about the developmental stages in which major amounts of a client's emotional energy are invested. And so, a therapist listens carefully to what a client selects out and responds to in his relationships with others.

By putting his ear to the dynamics of those interactions as reported by the client, the therapist can get some sense of where the client is developmentally. A client will reveal those developmental stages where emotional energy is bound by how he interprets his interactions, what arouses anxiety, what pleases him, and what angers him. From the way the client relates to others, from what he seems to seek in his relationships, and from what he fails to get, the therapist begins to sense where the client was pushed too hard during his development, where he was held back, and what he still needs.

If a client has not managed to cope with the crises which differentiate various stages of development, he will continue to invest energy in attempting to meet those psychological demands and satisfy the needs unique to those developmental periods. As a client reveals his interactions with peers, with younger and older persons, with those perceived to be in positions of authority or subject to the client's authority, he will reveal much of where he is developmentally by how he copes in those situations.

When the client relates to peers, the therapist notes whether he does so as a child relating to a parent, as a peer, as a superior—aloof and supercilious—or as an inferior—submissive and ingratiating. Under scrutiny, a client's interactions are often not what they might appear to be at a superficial level. To assume, for example, that a client who introduces a peer relationship into his discussion is experiencing the other as a peer simply because they are of the same chronological age is to miss the whole point. One of the "peers" might actually be a substitute parent. If those roles are unconsciously unacceptable to the participants, conflict will be generated between the participants because of the disparity in the needs that the two persons are attempting to meet through their relationship.

For example, one partner in a heterosexual relationship might be seeking a mature partnership whereas the other is attempting to satisfy childhood or adolescent needs through it. One might be searching for a marriage partner while the other is using the relationship to bolster up his ego, to chalk up another conquest, or to be mothered or fathered. One might find his sexual needs frustrated because his partner is still fantasizing relationships in idealized, platonic, and childlike terms.

Such relationships are likely to be frustrating and mutually terminated since the needs of neither are gratified. More often than not relationships that appear superficially to be mutually unrewarding continue because a collusion exists below the surface and less conscious needs are being met. In such cases, the relationship continues, characterized on the surface by anger, conflict, and bickering but with intense anxiety generated in both parties at the thought of a potential rupture in the relationship.

A therapist constantly compares the needs being expressed by his client through his reported interpersonal behavior against his own internalized continuum of what the crises and needs of the various developmental periods are. Through such a comparison, the therapist is in a position to evaluate areas of client growth, note points of fixation, and assess the meaning of regressive behavior. That process of continually comparing a client's interactions against the critical features of different stages of emotional development continues throughout therapy and provides the therapist with an ongoing guideline for therapeutic progress.

SOURCES OF UNDERSTANDING:
INFERRED INTERNAL PROCESSES

As a client begins to reveal material that he believes is relevant to his concerns, he will reveal much about himself indirectly by the way he perceives, what he anticipates, and how he conceptualizes. As he talks, sits, listens, or lapses into silence, his moods, affect changes, and physiological reactions will reflect the flow of his inner processes and suggest his internal reactions and experiences to what he expresses.

Some of the internal processes in a client can be inferred from the way a client perceives events, situations, and relationships; from the quality of his percepts; from the way in which those percepts are organized into a conceptual framework; and from the way in which the essence of those concepts is compressed and expressed obliquely through symbolic means. Each of those cognitive processes represents the experience of the client and the aftereffects of those experiences in cognitive functioning.

The Perceptual Process

The perceptual process of a client provides the therapist with an important avenue to understanding the client. The way in which the client sees the world, what he sees, what he anticipates, and what he attributes to those with whom he relates are all important considerations for the emotional life of a client. Perception, as an external reflector of significant internal processes, provides the therapist with the means to hypothesize about potential conflict areas. The perceptual process is distorted, molded, shaped, and denied in terms of the inner conflicts and press of the needs of clients. Clients perceive what they need to perceive in order to maintain some semblance of unity without suffering undue anxiety. A client sees what he wants to see, what he needs to see, and he avoids seeing those things that he can't afford to see because they are too dangerous.

The client's perceptions provide a window to his internal press, to the needs he experiences, to those he attempts to meet, and to those he can't afford to meet. At each session, the therapist is conscious of what the client is looking for, how he sees it, what happened during the week that is important for him to remember, what he recalls, how he frames the meaning of what he recalls, and how he interprets his experience during the week. Those perceptions tell the therapist much about where the client is emotionally.

A therapist is not only concerned with how a client views the world outside the therapy hour, he is even more interested in how the client perceives the events that transpire within therapy and particularly as they relate to the person of the therapist. Those perceptions are the most critical since the therapist can compare the client's perceptions of what has transpired with his own experience of those events, with his own feelings and intentions. That comparison provides the therapist with critical information about "what" and "how" the client distorts, paving the way for the time when the therapist can begin to understand "why" the client distorts as he does.

A person perceives others in terms of what his own experiences with those person types have been in the past. And the client's initial perceptions of his therapist will be based upon his previous experiences with "therapist types." A client's repertoire about therapist types will be based on what he has learned from his relationships with others who have contended they were interested in helping him. If his prior experiences with people who said they intended to help did not do so, or if they confused helping with some other emotional experiences, such as smothering, punitiveness, curiosity, or deceitfulness, then, when "help" is offered by a therapist, it will trigger vigorous emotional reactions since it connotes anything but "benefit."

A client, therefore, will be hypersensitive to certain matters. What those matters are will vary from client to client. In any case, that sensitivity is a function of a massive amount of collected evidence about how that particular characteristic, those matters, or that relationship will affect him. Those are the client's internal predictions about affairs and they become a vital part of the therapeutic process as we will see later.

Clients predict all the time from evidence that they have gathered over the years. Some of the evidence is real; some imagined. But one area of sensitivity that is common to many clients is their internal processing of what people "really mean" when they say thus and so. That is why the behavior of a therapist, instead of his words, takes precedence. A client is very sensitive to what a therapist is experiencing from a whole lifetime of needing to be sensitive to the feelings and attitudes that underlie words rather than to the words themselves.

Incidentally, the adage that you can "fool some of the people some of the time" must be modified for a therapist. A therapist is *never* able to fool a client about his own underlying attitudes, anxieties, motives, and values. A therapist's anxiety in particular affects a client deeply. When a client finds that a therapist's underlying attitudes differ from his words or when he senses a therapist's anxiety about whether he can help pull the client out of his "muddle," the client will flee the scene much the worse for wear.

The client's perceptions of situations—what he picks out to respond to in the relationship, what he is most sensitive about, what he exaggerates and what he minimizes in their interaction—provide the therapist with clues to understanding the emotional life of his client. That perceptual process, as will be seen later, becomes even more important to the therapeutic process when consideration is given to the way in which those perceptions affect and are affected by the therapeutic interaction.

Conceptualizations, Compressions and Symbolism

A client reveals much of himself to a therapist by the way he conceptualizes matters, by the way he has compressed certain emotional experiences, and from the way he represents critical aspects of his conflicts obliquely in symbolic language. The client's conceptualizations, abstractions, compressions, symbolism, and his idiomatic language all reflect attempts at integration and cognitive control over emotional matters. Analyzing, abstracting, synthesizing, and labeling of emotional matters are essential ego functions which provide the basis for integration and growth. The question with regard to those processes in a client is how useful and productive those attempts at integration and control have been in providing the client with the basis for continued growth.

The way in which a client conceptualizes phenomena is closely associated with the perceptual mechanism. The client's conceptual framework with regard to emotional matters is the end-product of an extensive synthesizing process of the commonalities among discrete perceptions. The way in which the client conceptualizes people and relationships is based on a process of noting over time and through continued human interactions those characteristics of his relationships that affect him in emotionally similar ways, abstracting the similarities, and organizing them into some relatively firm concepts that make some psychological sense to a client.

Against those conceptualizations, then, the client can compare new perceptions, altering conceptualizations as new information necessitates modification. Those concepts which are most easily modifiable, most potentially expansive, which lend themselves to growth and change, have generally been learned within the context of positive emotional conditions. On the other hand, conceptualizations that tend toward rigidity and are less accessible to change are often those that have developed within an emotional milieu that was consistently destructive and traumatic.

Perhaps the way in which a client reacts to "authority" and "authority figures" might provide some insight into how conceptualizations can affect therapy and be a useful vehicle for understanding a client and being therapeutic with him. From his contacts with parents, teachers, and others, the client will have abstracted certain common emotional experiences from his relationships with them. The common emotional conditions—the context—of those interactions will provide the client with the material for constructing his concept of authority, and that conception will be an operational definition in terms of the consequences of those interactions on the client's sense of well-being, their emotional impact on him.

The therapeutic situation is a "natural" for activating reactions to a therapist that are emotionally similar to a client's reactions to significant persons in authority during his developmental years. Several elements in a therapeutic situation are dynamically similar to the emotional conditions that the client experienced during childhood when he was helpless and when authority figures were most significant to him.

First of all, the nature of a therapeutic relationship is a dependent one. The client needs help, he can't manage by himself, and so he must rely on the therapist for assistance. In addition, the client often feels that his knowledge of himself is limited and he perceives the therapist as someone with superior understanding who has control over how much assistance he will render. The fact that the therapist actually controls what and how much he will give might be reinforced early in the relationship during the initial negotiations surrounding the therapeutic agreement.

Those elements of being dependent on another for help and of being unable to control the source of help are dynamically similar to the conditions which characterize a child's relationship to the adult world. The child is helpless to fend for himself and his survival is contingent on the good graces of those in authority who tend him, particularly his parents. For a client, then, the sense of being placed in a dependent role, of being needy, and of relying on another person for assistance provokes reactions in him toward the therapist and leads to the expectation of reactions that are dynamically similar to what actually transpired in the client's earlier encounters with parents and other authorities during his formative years.

The tremendous therapeutic value to which those projections and the transfer of such feelings can be put by a therapist for purposes of helping the client will be taken up extensively in the next section and in later chapters. The point at this time is simply that the perceived similarities set reactions into motion which provide the therapist with an opportunity to understand the client better.

Insofar as those earlier contacts with authority have been problematic for a client, his experience of the similarity of those emotional conditions in the therapeutic situation will activate intense anxiety and heighten the potential for irrational, distorted reactions. Whereas the client's perception of the similarity in the conditions of being dependent, needy, and unable to control the source of supplies heightens the potential for projection, it does not determine the character of the projections.

The character of those projections is contingent on the concomitant emotional conditions which provided the broader emotional context in which the interactions with prior authority figures occurred. In themselves, the conditions of being dependent and relying on those in authority for assistance are neutral conditions—they are natural to a child-parent relationship—and as such they do not provide the client with the perceptual material which contributes to his positive or negative conceptualization about authority. Whether a client is attracted to authority or repulsed by it is determined by how his parents and other adults *used that authority*. Those additional elements, the context in which help was rendered or withheld, provide the basis for the emotional charge that the client attaches to those in authority. And it is that emotional charge which determines the character of what is projected.

The client's perception of the similarity of certain conditions in therapy and in his earlier development is accurate. He is in a dependent position, he is needy, and he cannot control the emotional life of the therapist. But the similarity hopefully stops there. What the client assumes and what determines the character of his projections is that the concomitant emotional conditions which characterized his interactions with other authority figures also will characterize his relationship to the therapist. And it is precisely at the point of providing the client with a different emotional context that the therapeutic work centers. If the therapist, through his own reactions to the client's projections, through his own responsiveness to the client's emotional needs, begins to alter the emotional context in which the original learning occurred, then the potential is available for relearning and growth.

Perhaps a couple of brief examples of the way in which differing concomitant emotional conditions provide the basis for a client's projections might be useful. How the client reacts to the therapist will reveal much of what his sum total of experiences with people in authority have been. If the client's conceptualization has arisen out of negative conditions, such as withholding, punitiveness, and criticalness, then "authority" will be walled in with a highly charged negative emotional reaction to anyone who is perceived as an authority.

In some such cases, authority might connote coldness and distance. From such a background, a client's expectations for therapy must be that he will be treated with coldness and disdain, constantly living under the threat of rejection. The client might wish for warmth and expect coldness. And within the confines of his own conceptualization of the relationship, the client will initially perceive coldness even when warmth was intended.

Even in the face of mounting evidence to the contrary based upon his actual interactions with the therapist, the client might continue to perceive the therapist's behavior in terms of what the behavior of the authority figures has been. It is dynamically determined that the client would need to do so for several reasons. In the first place, no conceptualization is maintained in isolation; an entire complex of related conceptualizations are also affected.

More importantly, the conceptualization was founded in anxiety-provoking experiences and its reworking necessitates reopening old wounds. It often occurs that the moment in therapy where a client allows in, emotionally experiences the actual conditions of the relationship which he is resisting, denying, or misperceiving, he experiences a traumatic reaction. For that awareness releases affect in the present that has been pent up from the past. The experience is relieving and yet painful. At the moment of his awareness of the emotional conditions that have been walled out by anxiety, it is as though the unconscious simultaneously releases the emotionally charged memories that have been bound by the perceptual distortions.

Essentially what seems to happen is that the client's anxiety is counterbalanced by intense need. And at the moment the scales are tripped in favor of the need, the full impact of the need reaches awareness. The moment of release is simultaneously an experience in the present and a reexperiencing of the past. The client's *experience of the need in awareness immediately changes the need.* Because of its experience in the presence of the therapist, it is by that fact already partially gratified. That moment of release is also the awareness of memories of the emotional conditions which have bound the initial generic experiences. Those memories flood into consciousness.

At such times, the client is often highly emotional; memories tumble out, each with pain but with a growing sense of release and relief. At such times, the client is very close to the therapist, feeling his warmth and presence keenly, feeling gratified for his help and therefore nurturant of him. The sense of relief the client experiences provides him with the basis for a deeply warm, affiliative relationship with the therapist and activates a desire to identify with the therapist and learn from him. And, at such times, the therapist feels as keenly the presence of his client. He feels his anxiety, his release, and his responsivity. And in his turn, the therapist feels—for reasons that probably have little to do with his professional training or with his notions about objectivity—very warm and responsive to the client. At that moment of their relationship the therapist has both understood his client and is beginning to understand his client. At that moment, therapy has both occurred and begun.

In another example, the parents of a client might have "bound" him in relationships with them that were confusing to the client. If the parents proffered warmth and, in responding to their warmth, the client found himself enmeshed and restrained, then he will expect that a therapist might also set honey traps for him. Until he learns more about his client, it might be confusing to a therapist who reacts in nurturant ways to a client to note that his nurturance is met with hostility or intense anxiety. Such clients are very conscious of strings being attached to gifts and they tend to search carefully under words, carpets, and in closets for hidden meanings and subtle traps. When he enters therapy, a client whose heritage has included entrapping parents tends to want to be very clear with the therapist that he sees him as an objective, professional, and impersonal listener.

At any time that the therapist becomes subjective or reacts in personal ways, the client will become anxious and attempt to introduce material that reestablishes safe distance. Anxiety about the therapist's becoming involved is a clear indication of the overinvolvement of others. Often such a client has been in interactions with parents whose motives have been significantly at odds with their verbalizations. So the client doesn't listen well to words; he senses attitudes and he understands behavior.

The histories of clients who fear emotional involvements turn out to be replete with incidents in which some significant person maneuvered the client into anxious situations by playing on the client's guilt, by overwhelming the client with the "right" words for the wrong reasons, by subterfuge, and by deceit. Some parents can be unusually adroit at satisfying their needs through their children with little regard for what the effects on the emotional life of the child will be. As a child, the client might not have sensed the full impact of what the parent was up to; as a child the client might have only known the vague, diffuse sense of anxiousness he experienced in the presence of such a person. As an adult, that same client will be uncommonly sensitive to anything resembling parallel emotional conditions in his interactions with others. And the client in later life will become an intuitive expert at noting those times when the conditions are ripe for recreating the initial trauma and in devising ways to disengage himself.

If the therapist becomes disgruntled at being defined as an impersonal observer of his client, he might begin to debate the value of emotional closeness, pointing out the interpersonal method of therapy; or he might lash out at the client for holding him off. Such arguments are fodder for driving the client out of therapy. Not only do they serve to set up anxiety in the client, but if the therapist contemplates his reactions he will note that he has taken recourse to using intellectual arguments as an avenue to reducing emotional distance, a rather untenable dynamic hypothesis!

One good reason why a therapist might undertake such an untenable position is to keep from knowing that he and his client are not so different regarding their assumptions about the dangers of closeness. And of course if the client catches on to the usefulness of arguing with the therapist as a means for maintaining distance, he and his therapist might successfully continue to cover their anxiety for many sessions.

Interlocking Effects of Cognitive and Affective Processes

The initial observations and inferences of a therapist about the cognitive functioning of his client can provide him with some useful understandings. In addition, a therapist learns about the emotional life of his client from his client's moods and the cycling of affective states, from his emotional reactions (particularly anxiety), from his characteristic interpersonal modes, and the structure and brittleness of his defenses. No therapist studies any one process in isolation. He observes their interaction and their total impact on the client. Insofar as the therapist is able to synthesize the different aspects of the mental processes of a client, he is able to view the client as a human being whose functioning is limited rather than as a "problem" that happens to have a person attached to it.

Studying the effects in the person of the interaction of those different processes is complex, but it is their complexity that provides the therapist with the opportunity to deepen his understanding of the client. Cognitive processes are obviously tightly woven with the affective functioning of a client. The symbolic representation of conflict, intellectual defenses, and rationalizations exemplify the intricate interlocking of affective and cognitive processes. The function that perception serves to maintain internal consistency and stave off anxiety provides another such example. Perceptions not only provide a pathway to the client's inner emotional life, to his fantasies, and to his affective reactivity but they act as a safeguard against emotional trauma.

A client, for example, will paint the world around him with the colors of his moods. For some, the world is seen in grays, reflecting the drabness of their outlook. For those clients their hopes may have been dulled, the edges taken off their creativity, their affect flattened, and feelings attenuated by unfeeling and fearful parents and other adults whom they encountered during their developmental years.

Other clients might never see the gray; they are consistently bright, enthusiastic, bubbling, and cheerful. They fear negative affect in the same way that the other clients fear any affect. Their bright, even friendliness is often envied at first by those they meet, but the envy soon turns to irritation and then to sympathy as it dawns on others that the person is shallow and basically very frightened and that his interpersonal mode serves to ward off intense encounters or close emotional involvement.

And here again the disabling effects of anxiety have made their appearance and taken their toll. For it soon becomes apparent to a therapist that both the cheerless and cheerful clients have cut out a piece of experience in their lives. Their perceptual processes are badly delimited to only a few affective experiences. In effect, they perceive the world with blinders, recognizing, allowing in to consciousness only a small fragment of what is actually happening to them.

Not only does anxiety open the way to understanding, but it activates defenses against understanding, and those defensive maneuvers of a client are an important consideration in the therapist's efforts to understand him. A therapist notices, for example, a client's method of coping with anxious moments, his modes of approaching conflict and warding it off, his way of anticipating danger and protecting himself from it. A client reveals areas of concern by what he recalls of the past, how he recalls it, how he interprets those experiences, what he forgets, what incidents stand out, and what interactions seem important.

Not only from what the client *says* makes him anxious, but also from those times that he *avoids* focusing on certain topics does the therapist note areas of concern. He learns of his client's emotional life from what the client doesn't hear in their relationship as well as from what he distorts. He begins to understand his client as he observes his client deny events that have occurred in his presence. He learns of his client's anxiety from his inability to recall what transpired in the previous sessions. And, in particular, the therapist notes those times that the client reverts to symbolic language or avoids talking about events in concrete ways. At any of those times, a therapist begins to sense sore spots in the life of the client and pinpoints areas where anxiety intrudes in the client's life.

It is only as therapy develops that the therapist has the opportunity to understand his client's defenses in terms other than their general usefulness in handling anxiety. For example, at the outset of therapy when a therapist notes his client's sudden discomfort, he makes an inference that the client is struggling with some inner conflict. That information is a meaningless generalization, however, unless the therapist can eventually relate that information in meaningful ways to this client, to his problems, and to what those problems might mean in the client's total life pattern. Otherwise the information is piecemeal, fragmented, and if relayed to the client leaves him feeling empty. It is only later that the therapist can become increasingly specific about what is blocked out, for what purpose, and to accomplish what tasks. That process of attempting to determine the unique purposes that a client's defenses serve—the specific needs, impulses, and motivations that underlie and trigger anxiety—begins at the time of the therapist's first contact with his client and continues throughout the therapy.

THE ASSOCIATIONAL PROCESS: VEHICLE FOR UNDERSTANDING

In the example cited above, the client's discomfort was construed as reflecting some internal struggle in reaction to what was transpiring in therapy. In essence, when the therapist noted the client's reaction, he made an assumption that there was some dynamic internal connection between the stimulus value of their verbal exchange and the client's behavioral response of becoming uneasy. That assumption is based on a more generally held premise that all behavior is meaningfully related and that even the apparently random thoughts of the client—or of the therapist himself—are in fact dynamically associated.

Once the therapist takes the position that the flow of a client's thoughts, his reactions, and his perceptions, no matter how apparently unrelated, are in fact psychologically associated, then he provides himself with a most crucial vehicle for understanding the emotional life of the client. Under those circumstances, a therapist doesn't permit any apparently unrelated pieces of data to bypass his scrutiny. And under scrutiny he will often find that subsumed by the most disjunctive thoughts of a client are dynamic connections that are at the roots of the client's conflict.

From the point of view of the therapeutic work, it is also a generally held premise that if those dynamic links subsuming seemingly irrelevant fragments of data, whether thoughts or reactions, can be made explicit, they will have a significant effect on unraveling the sources of conflict which inhibit the client. To help the client to provide the relevant links and to facilitate bringing into awareness the emotional experiences subsumed by them, the therapist must allow his own associations and creative processes to work on what the client says and does as well as to expect that the client will spontaneously provide the therapist with associative material.

When the client associates, either because he is directed to by the therapist or because he spontaneously introduces in seemingly random order those things that have affected him during the week, he reveals the process of his psychological thinking, the process of his conflicts, and the critical features of those conflicts. Through the apparently illogical but spontaneous order in which events of importance to the client are presented, the therapist is provided with some of his finest contextual clues for understanding the emotional life of his client.

The value of the associational process resides in the way in which it links together the different facets of the client's emotional life. Associations link together the present with the past. They link together what transpires during a therapy hour with what occurs outside the session. They link the therapist, the parent, the spouse, and the peer together in terms of what are the most important dynamic characteristics of those people in the life of the client, and they provide evidence for what stimulates the client to react positively, negatively, and with anxiety to those features.

When the client introduces two apparently disparate thoughts, the therapist wonders what internal process provides the continuity. He wonders what dynamic purpose is served by the client's linking together those events and those persons as he does. He wonders what feelings, censorship, anxiety, and modifications have occurred in the mind of the client between an observation, a statement, or reaction and the client's succeeding observation. He wonders what motivates the client to introduce a particular topic at that moment during therapy. In essence, he wonders what moment-to-moment activity within the client saw some psychological link between the apparently irrelevant thoughts and observations.

Associations Link the Present with the Past

Some associations of the client link together the emotional experiences of his current life with some still unresolved conflicts from his past. A young adult male client, for example, reported that he felt increasingly attracted to a friend's fiancee; yet he hesitated to make his feelings known to the girl for the fear of hurting his friend. Further, he feared that if his friend discovered his attraction there would be a confrontation and a physical altercation which he wished to avoid. The client had the fantasy that he could subdue his friend physically and could win the girl, but the fantasy of winning was overshadowed with feelings of guilt. Even in discussing the matter during the therapeutic session, the client manifested intense anxiety.

Immediately on the heels of reporting those fantasies and the anxious feelings they evoked, the client spontaneously shifted to discussing some prior conflict laden interactions between himself and his father. If the therapist assumed that the client had simply changed the topic in order to avoid anxiety or to deflect the therapist from focusing on the current conflict, he would have missed the dynamic connection between the two events. If the therapist assumed that the client was simply rambling on about various points of conflict in his life that were insulated from each other, he would have missed a crucial opportunity to uncover a central aspect of the client's conflicts.

For those two events, the ongoing current interaction with his male friend and his previous encounters with his father were far from isolated and insulated episodes. It is true that those events were separated along a temporal dimension by many years. Psychologically, however, those two events were intricately interwoven; they represented different facets of the same conflict. The client's ongoing interaction with his male friend and his earlier encounters with his father were parallel emotional experiences, and both were manifestations of deeper conflict that was embedded in the generic relationship with the father.

The temporal dimension between the sequential thoughts of a client might deceive the therapist into believing that they are unrelated. In addition, the apparently unrelated content of successive thoughts might be deceptive but the therapist must constantly be aware of the fact that if a client spontaneously shifts from one idea to another, an underlying and unifying emotional theme links those thoughts together.

Although seemingly unrelated in content, a female client's unsolicited spontaneous flow of thoughts were found upon exploration to be highly relevant to her conflicts about men. This client reported to her male therapist that she was conflicted in her relationship with her boyfriend. On the one hand, she wanted to make their relationship into a permanent arrangement; yet she feared that if she did she would tend to shackle the man. She felt that no man wanted to be restrained in a permanent relationship and that a man's response to such restraint was to become hostile and resentful. She couldn't pin down her fears to any events in her relationship which supported her predictions; yet she felt them just the same.

The client was caught between wanting to be close to the man, wanting to marry, wanting to rear a family, and yet fearing that in doing so she would limit the man's freedom, that she would tie him to the house, and that he would resent it, eventuating in the relationship's breaking up. Having expressed her thoughts, fantasies, and predictions with a great deal of emotion, the client, after regaining composure, almost casually mentioned that she had telephoned her father during the week to talk with him.

When asked about the phone call, she simply said that she had turned to her father for lack of someone else to talk with. The therapist pointed out that there might be a connection between her feelings about her boyfriend and some residual feelings related to her father. And the client was asked to talk freely about her relationship with her father and her feelings about him. Immediately, the client became emotional again. She felt that her father had been at one time an active, aggressive man with many interesting ideas, but that through the years he had become passive, resentful, and cynical. Further exploration of the matter revealed that she felt that her mother had been a limiting factor in his spontaneity; that her mother had essentially shackled him to the home; and that her father had reacted in resentful, hostile ways toward her mother. The client observed that the relationship between her parents had grown more distant over time and for all practical purposes was nonexistent. And, from the attitudes of both parents, the client inferred that they remained together for the sake of the children.

The point in presenting this case fragment is not to examine how the therapist might work with the client to help her gain eventual insight into the way in which her predictions about her current relationships were based in her observations of her family pattern. Nor is it intended through this example to suggest that the client's fantasies and deeper emotional attachments with regard to her father and negative feelings about her mother were not generating some of the client's anxiety. Emotional insights about such matters are essential to liberate the client to engage in a more mature relationship with her boyfriend without fears of recapitulating the family history. But the important point for present considerations is that what can appear to be disconnected thoughts or what could be construed by the therapist as the client's attempts to change topics in order to avoid discussing conflict laden material are in fact often dynamically linked thoughts, which when expanded provide a path to the heart of a client's emotional conflicts.

Associations Connect the Therapeutic Hour with Life in General

When a client, in discussing an ongoing, conflictual relationship in his life outside of therapy, suddenly changes topics and begins to talk about some events that have transpired during a therapeutic hour, that sudden switch in topics is not a random event in the life of the client. Similarly, if the client, in discussing some aspect of his work with the therapist, spontaneously introduces for no apparent reason some facet of an ongoing extratherapeutic relationship, that spontaneous association must be construed as an index of some psychological link between the emotional conditions of those two relationships.

When a client switches topics in that way, the therapist must assume that some relevant internal process has gone on in the client that has linked together that moment of the therapeutic hour with the client's life outside; and if that associative link can be unearthed, it will act as an explanatory concept for the apparent discontinuity of the client's thoughts. Through his associations, the client essentially strips the two relationships of their differences and reacts to some facet of those relationships that he perceives as dynamically similar. Insofar as the therapist can uncover that linkage and bring into awareness the nature of that similarity, he will have substantially increased his understanding of his client and provided the basis for perceptual modification and growth.

Unearthing the links that stimulate a client to associate the therapeutic relationship with some extratherapeutic encounter is often not a difficult task. There are several factors that contribute to facilitating the uncovery of those links. The most crucial point is that the therapist is a participant in one of the relationships. As such, the therapist has an experiential basis for comparing and interpreting the meaning of the client's reactions. In addition, when the client shifts from a discussion of one relationship to another he often unwittingly provides the therapist with clues to the emotional conditions that link those two relationships together.

The client does so by the often clear and explicit way in which he elaborates on the emotional experiences of the associated relationship. In listening to those experiences, the therapist is often able to discern that the emotional tone of the interactions in the extratherapeutic relationship is a thinly disguised symbolic representation of feelings and reactions that the client might actually be experiencing toward the therapist. Although not conscious, those feelings are often near the surface. Their indirection and submerged character reflects the potential threat of such direct expression. By directing those feelings toward someone other than the therapist, the client essentially experiences some release without accompanying threat of rejection for what is being experienced or expressed.

Often with some minor help from the therapist, the client is able to redirect those feelings toward their true target, the therapist. Perhaps an example would help to demonstrate how a client's sudden recall of events in another relationship at a crucial moment during therapy provided her with a means for deflecting her feelings from the therapist to a boyfriend. That displacement served the dynamic purpose of defending against the threat of rejection.

In this case the client was an undergraduate woman who was being seen by a male therapist in a university setting. Because of the forthcoming spring recess, her therapist informed her that he would be vacationing during break and would be unable to see her for several weeks. His client accepted the fact passively, was agreeable, pleasant, and the matter seemed closed.

After a pause of a few moments, however, the client introduced a seemingly unrelated topic. During the week, her fiance, someone to whom she had become quite attached and whom she relied on, "ditched" her. The client proceeded to relate the incident of being scorned with a great deal of emotion. She was angry and threatened to retaliate against the boyfriend; essentially she was considering ways of hurting him in return.

Unless the therapist's anxiety was activated by some unconscious reaction to the client's hostility, he is likely to assume that there is a considerable probability that the client's thoughts and reactions are not so much directed at the boyfriend as they are directed toward him. In this case, the client's exboyfriend is feeling the brunt of the client's anger that was actually stimulated by the therapist's plans to be away for several weeks. Unless the therapist sees that potential associative link between those two events, he has lost a valuable source of information which could provide him and his client with the opportunity to work through those feelings directly toward him instead of being displaced and expressed indirectly via the subterfuge of a disagreeable boyfriend.

The fact of the matter is that the client was "ditched" and she is likely to be angry about that. But the client's association at the particular moment in therapy when the therapist informed her that he would be vacationing strongly suggests that the client perceived the therapist's vacation as a serious attack on her "ego," and at a deeper level, as a threat of being abandoned. The challenging feature of a client's association at such moments in therapy consists of the fact that there is always validity to the client's story. There are reality features to the story, and those reality features tend, and might be "intended," to distract the therapist from investigating the deeper and more anxiety-provoking possibilities that the client's attack is personal. And in this case that possibility is that the client is enraged at the therapist because she fears being abandoned.

The therapist can test the hypothesis that his client's anger is directed at him by reopening the topic and implying that there are submerged feelings about his vacation that are still unexplored. The therapist might note further that the feelings that the client is expressing toward her boyfriend are displaced and safer for her than confronting him directly about his plans.

Whether a client sees such an association is irrelevant. A client is able to "see" an association only after it is no longer charged with affect, and the therapist is a critical factor in that neutralizing process. What is initially important is whether the client is able to redirect and experience whatever feelings have been submerged, deflected, or symbolically represented. Once those feelings are accurately experienced and the therapist acts constructively on them, then the client's pent-up affect will be released, and the client's feelings about the therapist will simultaneously change.

Then, and only then, might the client spontaneously see the associative link between her thoughts about her boyfriend and the therapist. At the point where the client gains insight into the associative connections between her thoughts, she has made a discovery about her own internal processes that provides the basis for her being able to expand those processes and to begin to make minute connections herself and to need less help from the therapist. At the moment when the client begins to work on her own associations, a critical hurdle in therapy has been overcome. Two beneficial effects accrue. From that point on, not only does the client begin to manage herself better but she is simultaneously liberated to provide the therapist with deeper and richer associations.

Longer Sequences of Spontaneous Associations

When the client spontaneously moves from topic to topic during a session, the flow of the client's thoughts often provide the therapist with an increased opportunity to understand what the critical links are that connect the complex of seemingly unrelated thoughts. As the therapist listens to the flow of thoughts of his client, he can often glean some major recurrent emotional themes that pervade the thoughts and link them together. Although the therapist notes the content of the client's associations, he listens mainly with an ear to the emotional themes that pervade the various encounters, memories, insights, and conflicts that characterize the client's life between sessions.

The more involved the client is and the more freely he talks about the things that are important to him, the more he provides his therapist with the opportunity of helping him discover the sources of his conflict. One client, for example, became increasingly anxious during the week between sessions. As the session began, she talked immediately about her recent visit home. While at home, she noted that her father was very depressed and was behaving in rather maudlin, self-depreciating ways, contending that he had very little left to give to his wife or daughter. The father's increasingly weakened position in the home was very threatening to the mother who had always leaned rather heavily on the father, didn't work outside the home, and had always been rather helpless when the father was away on business.

The client next mentioned that during her visit home one of her chores was to clean the basement, and in doing so she noticed that the foundation had become quite brittle and was cracking in spots. For some reason that observation made her very anxious. Then the client recalled that she had seen a television performance during the week in which an executive was no longer able to compete in the business world and was being edged out by a younger man. The show left her feeling shaken. With each report of different events that occurred during the week, the client's anxiety heightened. Lastly, the client rather incidentally mentioned the fact that she and her fiancé had finally set a date for their marriage. She then turned to the therapist and rather bluntly inquired about whether she could invite her boyfriend to the next session; she wanted the therapist to meet him.

If the therapist had listened with an ear to the recurrent emotional content underlying the configuration of events that were presented to him, if he had assumed that some central dynamic theme connected those events in some meaningful way for the client, then the therapist would be in a position to undertake a fruitful exploration of the meaning of the client's anxiety. On the other hand, if the therapist selected out one or the other facet of what the client related as though it were emotionally insulated from the remainder of the configuration, then he would have missed the motivating force of the anxiety—and might be left wondering why the client suddenly wanted him to meet her boyfriend.

From analysis of the configuration, the therapist noted an interesting progression in anxiety that centered around reactions to impotence in a significant male figure. At a time in her life when the client was contemplating marriage to an apparently substantial male, her observations of her father's impotent behavior and her mother's reactions could have been traumatizing. The client had always regarded her father as a pillar of strength; his collapse and its effects in her mother's anxiety and insecurity could have triggered her own sense of insecurity and doubts about her fiancé's potency.

The intensity of the client's anxiety reaction was evident from the way in which it intruded in and affected her perceptions of everything that transpired during the week. The client's observation and concomitant anxiety about the "weakened foundation" while cleaning the basement of her family home was an apparent symbolic representation of her father's collapse and her mother's insecurity. The television program reflected and further aggravated her feelings of insecurity and reactions to eventual male impotence.

As the therapist searches for some unifying emotional theme, many questions would cross his mind. He would wonder whether the client fears that her boyfriend would eventually break down, leaving her to go through what her mother is experiencing. He would wonder whether the client fears that the strength she sees in her boyfriend is actually a cover for weakness. He would wonder whether the client wants the therapist to meet the boyfriend to assess that strength, to confirm the validity of her appraisal of his substance.

At a deeper level, the therapist would wonder what residual attachments toward the father are influencing her reactions. Does she unconsciously associate her marriage to her boyfriend with her father's depressed state? Does she fear that her marriage would be destructive to her relationship and fantasies about her father? Was her anxiety about the television production generated by some inner association that her boyfriend was "edging out" her father?

The therapist would also wonder about the client's identification with her mother. He would especially wonder how symbiotic that relationship was. The mother's anxiety and insecurity seem in some respects to be directly incorporated by the client and experienced as her own. If the intense anxiety and need for a "pillar of strength" that characterized the mother's relationship with the father is also an unconscious motivating force in the client's relationship to men, then that unconscious need raises additional questions about the "unstable foundation" on which the client's own marriage might be built.

As that thought occurs to the therapist, he "sees" the possibility that the client's anxiety about the weakened foundation in the home was multidetermined and connects the numerous emotional stresses in her current life situation with still unmet needs from the past. Not only was the client's perception of the cracking foundation possibly triggered by her father's behavior and her unconscious identification with her mother's insecurity but it was probably also determined by constructive ego-centered reactions to the potential destructive effects of attempting to use a marriage to meet her childlike strivings.

Of course, the therapist doesn't "know" whether his own associations and hypotheses about the central theme are correct. But he doesn't need to "know" the specific dynamics which are generating anxiety. What the therapist does need to do is to "have a feel" for the continuity undergirding the client's thoughts and to note some general recurrent theme on which he can act in a tentative way. By playing back a possible general theme that he senses underlies the configuration, the therapist effects several purposes. He calls the client's attention to the "configuration," thus paving the way for insight into how the associational process works; and he provides the client with some generalized and projective stimulus for reaction and exploration. If the therapist's response is to a general pervasive theme, if it is tentative, and if it is projective, then the client will be free to expand on whatever aspects of the events are most dynamically urgent to him and to the dynamics generating anxiety.

The Therapist's Own Associations

As the client talks on, it is the emotional content that the therapist hears when he puts his ear to what the client says. As the therapist listens he becomes curious, he internally questions, and most of all he always wonders "why." And as he listens, the therapist observes; he observes the client's reactions at points in his discussion, he notes the client's agitation, and he senses the client's relief. And as the therapist listens and observes he associates. And it is the therapist's own associations to what and how the client behaves and reacts that provide him with an additional source of understanding.

The therapist's associations to his own internal reactions during sessions provide him with unique opportunities to understand the stimulus value of his client. When the therapist experiences some internal reaction during a therapeutic session which seems irrelevant to his contact with his client, that seeming irrelevance ought to act as a signal to the therapist that there is probably much about his thoughts and reactions that is in fact highly relevant to the emotional conditions of the relationship. Insofar as the therapist can creatively bring into awareness the associative links between those apparently disconnected reactions, he might find that they reveal much to him about his relationship to his client that he had only intuitively sensed before.

If a male therapist, for example, in a session with an adult male client suddenly recalls with some anxiety that he has agreed to lead a discussion about a controversial topic at a forthcoming convention, the intrusion of that thought at the particular moment in therapy where it occurred might have much to do with what just transpired between therapist and client. A number of possibilities might be cited to explain its occurrence. It might be that the client was "rattling on" in order to distract the therapist from getting down to the hard work of therapy; and the therapist, becoming bored, allowed his thoughts to wander over matters of some importance to himself.

A more compelling and interesting possibility, however, is that the male client was competitive and was introducing material that was stirring up the therapist's own competitiveness. Perhaps the client had been bragging of his achievements or said or did something that was intended to "put down" the therapist. Whatever the motivating events, the therapist's reaction was to become anxious and to recall a forthcoming potentially competitive encounter in which he was "ego" involved. That recall was both an index of the therapist's own competitive feelings toward the client and a measure of the threat he experienced at that moment.

The client's behavior, in other words, acted as a stimulus for the therapist's own anxiety and activated compensatory behavior on his part. But the client's competitiveness was not experienced directly by the therapist; it was experienced simply as a reference to a discussion he was planning to lead. If, however, the therapist is able to associate his fantasy to the appropriate stimulation in the interview, then he has learned a number of significant things about his relationship to the client, about the client's stimulus value, his evocative powers, and most importantly, he has gained some insights into his client's emotional life. And the therapist might actually end up being pleased that he felt as he did; *for through his own threat reactions he has personally validated his intuitive sense of his client's potency*!

It is not intended in this section to describe the way in which the therapist might put his understanding to use in the relationship. It is intended only to point out that a therapist's random thoughts during a session are no more random than are his client's thoughts. And unless the therapist can accurately represent what he experiences and associate it to the events in the relationship that stimulated his reactions, he has lost a valuable source of understanding his client. Further, it is proposed that if the therapist knows himself, knows what evokes the feelings that he experiences in relation to given stimuli, then that knowledge provides him with inferential data about the client's emotional life.

At times, a therapist might be unable to see the relevance of his own thoughts and reactions or those of his client to what has transpired in his session. One of the critical reasons for such inability to make dynamic connections is that the therapist is defending against some experience in that relationship. To cite a brief example, an attractive female client was behaving in seductive ways toward her therapist. At the level of manifest content, the session was centered on an intellectual debate about some apparently irrelevant matter. Despite the nature of the content, the client managed to intersperse it with sexual innuendos. The client's voice, posture, and dress provided an emotional undercurrent that was consistent with the sexual message and confirmed the seductive intent of the client.

The therapist, however, didn't see the seduction! But he did experience anxiety in relation to the client and felt that progress was limited. The therapist openly discussed some of his concerns about progress with the client and suggested to the client that he use some of their recorded sessions to review the case with a colleague. The client readily assented. In listening to the sessions, to the therapist's description of his client's behavior, and to the therapist's interpretations, the colleague noted the therapist's anxiousness and defensiveness and was able to help the therapist to associate his feelings to the rather blatant seductive features of the interviews.

The rather amusing aspect of the case for consideration here is that during one of the sessions being reviewed the therapist's colleague noted that the client, when she had finally exhausted her repertoire of seductive entrees, suddenly changed the topic and angrily commented on the fact that she had a rather dull, uninteresting, and inept boyfriend. The sudden shift in topics baffled the therapist. But the colleague who saw the seduction also saw the irony of the client's comment. For the therapist, in being unable to connect her comment about a dull boyfriend to himself and his own defensive reactions to her seduction, had behaviorally confirmed her feelings about him as dull, uninteresting, and inept.

THE UNIQUENESS OF THERAPY: AN INTRODUCTION

Thus far, a number of avenues by which a therapist learns about the emotional life of his client have been surveyed. The client's usual life styles and cognitive and affective functioning—the way in which he perceives, conceptualizes, defends, reacts, and interacts—are potential sources of understanding. In addition, anxiety works to exaggerate and clarify some emotional processes in ways not otherwise available, thus providing additional opportunities to understand. Finally, the client's associations provide access to the underlying emotional themes which link together seemingly unrelated thoughts and act as explanatory mechanisms for discrete perceptions.

Those sources of understanding are significant. Through a study of the cognitive functioning, affective reactions, associational processes, and defensive maneuvers, an observer such as a therapist, is able to learn much of the emotional life of another person. The therapist who listens and observes is able to make significant connections between a client's behavior and underlying conflict by comparing his observations of the client with those internalized norms he uses to make behavior sensible to himself. Through such a comparison, a therapist can make reasonable assessments of the degree and kinds of emotional disturbance, note signposts of trouble, and hazard educated guesses about the sources of trouble.

But the importance of a therapist's observations and inferences for the therapeutic work remains hypothetical until the therapist goes beyond assessment. Unless he can do so, the therapist has learned nothing that could not have been discovered by others. In fact, other observers of human behavior, through similar or different means, can make assessments about the emotional functioning of a person that might surpass in accuracy those of the therapist.

There is nothing intrinsic in the character of the sources of understanding that have been considered to this point that makes them unique to therapy. Those sources of understanding are essential to therapy, but they are not differentiating. Other observers, as was pointed out above, can make some of the same observations about the emotional life of a client that the therapist can. The dimensions for understanding unique to therapy have a partial basis in the essential differences between the motivations of a therapist and those of other observers. Those differences have their roots in the observation that it is *what the therapist does with his knowledge, what he intends, and how he goes about his work* that differentiates him from others.

But the motivation of the therapist is just one facet of the complex of characteristics that differentiate therapy from other human encounters and provide the basis for deepening understanding, for generating new dimensions for understanding, and for paving the way for therapeutic gains. In the introductory chapter, consideration was given to the conditions preliminary to and surrounding the inception of therapy which were unique to it, which defined it, and which differentiated it from other human endeavors.

At that time, it was pointed out that the condition of anxiety in the client and dissatisfaction with his life set the stage for learning. In addition, the historical development of the particular, concrete emotional conditions which limited the client's growth were considered to affect the nature of the client's perceptions, his reactions to help, and the extent to which he might reasonably profit from therapy. Similarly, it was proposed that the personal and professional experiences of a therapist affect his perceptions and capacity to help different clients depending upon how much his own anxiety and experiences affect whether he can provide the experiential basis for his client to relearn and gratify his frustrated needs.

It was also suggested that the purposes of therapy—to focus on anxiety for constructive purposes—and its interpersonal method—to participate with the client in the search for the sources of anxiety so as to alleviate them—further differentiated therapy from other human endeavors. It was then proposed that when the intent and method of therapy are coupled to the condition of anxiety in the client—whether that anxiety is manifestly present or latent as evidenced by the experience of unrest and dissatisfaction—the interplay of those conditions will act to trigger greater anxiety. That anxiety will heighten the potential for uncensored reactions and projections which will provide significant information about how anxiety has worked in the client's life to preclude the satisfaction of needs.

Lastly, it was pointed out that those reactions manifest themselves at the moment of the therapist's first contact with the client during the initial negotiations surrounding the therapeutic agreement. Those reactions continue to intensify and generalize throughout the progress of therapy, constantly providing opportunity for deepening understanding. Those conditions, in other words, set the stage for a relationship and concomitant processes, the dynamics of which, if properly understood, can provide the therapist with unique sources of understanding and an experiential base for his being therapeutic with his client.

THE THERAPEUTIC RELATIONSHIP: NEW DIMENSIONS FOR UNDERSTANDING

A therapist doesn't simply take a history; he doesn't listen for purposes of developing a generic understanding of human behavior. Nor does the client who seeks his services expect that he will do so. The client expects help to modify facets of his life that are troublesome. That process of changing is set into motion *when the therapist, a trained professional, reacts to what the client says and does for purposes of helping the client to effect constructive change.* At that moment, new dimensions are added to the potential for understanding. New avenues to understanding are opened, deeper layers to understanding are available, and a unique dynamic interaction takes place as the participants progress to deeper layers.

When the therapist reacts, he opens the door to allowing the client to use him for purposes of changing. The therapist's participation and intent complicates the equation between observation and understanding but it adds dimensions to understanding that provide the experiential base for what is truly therapeutic. When the therapist reacts he makes a commitment; he puts all of his personal and professional resources at the disposal of the client, forming the basis for a relationship that will both attract and threaten the client.

In a sense, the therapist through his offer to help makes concrete and real what the client was fantasizing—someone to whom he could turn for assistance in changing himself. But that potential relationship is highly charged with both positive and negative emotional valences for the client. On the one hand, the relationship holds promise; it is potentially rewarding and integrating and the client senses those possibilities. But on the other hand the potency of the relationship is also threatening and understandably so. And that threat becomes very real for the client in short order.

The Client's Ambivalence and Resistance

The work of the therapist, particularly as he is perceptive about areas of conflict, necessarily threatens the client. When the therapist reacts to the different sides of the client, the client's fantasies about changing are no longer potential. The first reality step toward change has been taken. Once that step has been taken, once the commitment is recognized and the risks are experienced as anxiety, then the client's defenses are activated and he is thrown into a conflict situation which he experiences as ambivalence.

At that moment, the client is threatened by the therapist as well as attracted to him. And that peculiar combination of attitudes in the client accounts substantially for the many phenomena which complicate therapy and provide the basis for its uniqueness. In one respect, the therapeutic intent is clearly at odds with the client's need to avoid pain. In such a relationship, hypersensitivity to the nuances of the relationship, particularly to the emotional conditions which can intensify conflicts and contribute to feelings of loss of well-being become weighed against the potential for gain. In effect, the client's motivation to change becomes countered by the wish to avoid greater anxiety.

The client's anxiety and his developing fears are understandable because he fears what underlies his behavior. The client might begin to feel that his behavior, although constraining, might be safer than the risks involved in changing. He might begin to feel uncertain about where therapy is going. His current emotional state might be more comfortable than the premonition of anxiety that is stirring in him. The client might begin to feel that hidden by his inhibitions are thoughts, memories, feelings, and fantasies that are better left hidden. He might sense that forbidden thoughts and feelings and impulses will emerge and that old battles will be refought. He might fear losing the semblance of control that he has and acting without restraint. His concerns might mount that the therapist is unable to control him, is unable to help him, or might reject him.

The client might also sense that feelings are emerging which will be destructive to the fantasies that he cherishes. He might fear that he will lose more than he will gain. He might fear that he will now have to live his life with awareness but with no relief. His greatest fear might be getting reenmeshed in old webs with his last state worse than the first. His past is a carefully charted course; he fears the uncharted future.

At such times, a client will want to hide behind whatever defenses characterized his ways of coping with his conflicts in the past. And at such times, the client will begin to resist the therapeutic efforts. He will use whatever means are at his disposal to prevent the emergence of his poorly understood feelings. In his anxiety, the client might lash out at the therapist. Often at such times the client in his anxiety might ask if that is all there is to therapy. He might say that he has gotten some insights but they provide him with no relief. He might say that he knows why he behaves as he does but it doesn't get him out of the muddle. He might say that his feelings haven't changed and he sees no value to therapy. He might threaten to break the relationship. At such times, the client's motivation to change is in balance with his wish to avoid greater anxiety.

The client's initial ambivalence, his angry reactions, and his resistant efforts are the behavioral representations of anxiety; more precisely they reflect the internal counterbalancing of anxiety against needs. In early sessions, those reactions of the client which he experiences as ambivalence and expresses in doubts, uncertainties, and fears are likely to represent his direct reaction to the premonition of anxiety and, as such, they tend to inhibit learning. Later in therapy, however, the nature of the client's resistant behavior is more likely to be dynamically linked to the character of the therapeutic interaction, particularly as those interactions reflect the client's distortions of the therapist in terms of his needs.

At those times, a client's resistance doesn't reflect a bifurcation of needs and anxiety; it represents the vestiges of former significant interactions as they are distorted in relation to the therapist. When the client's resistance in later therapy is a function of his reacting to the therapist as a representative of previous significant figures, then those reactions suggest much about the nature of the client's unmet needs. And at that time, the client's efforts to counter the therapist, to render him ineffective, to stimulate anxiety in him, and to thwart his efforts reflect significant central features of the client's neurosis.

If a therapist views a client's ambivalence, his resistance, and his negative reactions as *blocks to his understanding of a client*, he will have missed a most critical avenue to understanding. Instead of viewing his client's maneuvers as blocking his understanding, the therapist ought to consider the behavior as an entree for developing a deeper understanding of the client. If the therapist observes carefully the ways in which the client reacts and notes what triggers particular reactions, he will soon be able to reconstruct the emotional context in which anxiety was experienced and the potential for learning was inhibited. Through his reactions, the client furnishes a potent source of material for hypotheses about the nature of the needs that seek gratification, the ways in which gratification is denied or delayed, and the alternative means by which the client attempts to achieve partial satisfaction.

The Client's Irrational Premises
and Transference Reactions

When the client enters therapy, considerable emotional energy might remain encapsulated within the context of some prior life experiences. Continually throughout later life, the client might tend to rework those experiences in fantasy and given the appropriate emotional milieu, he will tend to reestablish those conditions and to project onto others those characteristics that are the emotionally charged vestiges of his prior problematic relationships.

What the client projects and attempts to recreate is contingent on his underlying motivations and that varies in accord with differing generic experiences. A client might recreate certain emotional conditions in an effort to complete a fantasy, to achieve satisfaction for some need, to reduce anxiety, or to resolve some conflict and break free of the inhibiting past.

The tendency of a client to recreate the emotional conditions of the past in the present in order to resolve conflict or complete fantasies is not limited to the client's interactions with his therapist. On the contrary, those tendencies interpenetrate many of a client's interpersonal relationships. If the therapist listens carefully he can often hear the past reconstructed time and again in his client's ongoing relationships. And, in the final chapter of this book, those generalized tendencies to recreate the emotional conditions of the past in the present, their effects in a client's ongoing interpersonal relationships, and their therapeutic usefulness will be spelled out in some detail.

There are, however, features of a therapeutic relationship which aggravate those tendencies and which stimulate the reexperiencing of and reworking of past conflict in the present in relation to the therapist. The motivating forces for those irrational reactions during therapy, their effects in the relationship, and their usefulness for facilitating change will be taken up more extensively in the next and later chapters. Suffice it to say at this time that a complex of conditions unique to the therapeutic situations *heightens* the potential for the client's irrational reactions. And, as will be seen, those irrational reactions provide the therapist with a unique opportunity to help the client to change.

Through his projections and irrational reactions to the therapist that have been generated by inadequate emotional learning, the client places at the disposal of the therapist one of the therapist's richest avenues to understanding him. Once the client begins to react to the therapist as he has reacted to other significant persons in the past, then the therapist becomes part of the equation between observation and understanding.

The client's shaping the therapist to fit his unmet needs and then reacting to the therapist he has created adds an experiential base to the therapist's understanding. From the meanings the client reads into the therapist's behavior when those meanings differ from what the therapist intended or felt, the therapist begins to sense what, how, and why the client distorts. Those distortions reflect the disturbances that characterized the client's other relationships. Those projections represent most clearly the emotional consequences of the client's interactions in other relationships.

What he could only understand before from his client's reactions to and perceptions of others, the therapist can now experience directly in relation to the client for the entire sequence of conflict might be reenacted in his presence, thus opening the avenue for the therapist to use his own feelings and reactions as a guide to what is distorted and for what reasons. That reenactment of conflict in his presence is a crucial source of understanding. What makes therapy unique is the way in which the flow of feelings, memories, and eventual insights occur because of and in relation to the client's feelings and thoughts about the therapist. What makes those understandings so critical is the fact that the therapist, as a participant in the client's struggles, has the potential for reacting to the client's feelings directly, thus providing the basis for juxtaposing and eventually modifying the client's experiential framework.

The essential power of that relearning derives from the fact that at times when conflict is reenacted in his presence, the therapist—so far as the client's emotional life is concerned—is the embodiment of past significant figures. At such times during therapy, the interaction of client and therapist has reached an emotional crescendo that is as powerful for the client as the initial disabling experience. And it is precisely because the therapeutic interaction has reached comparability in power with the generic experiences that the potential for substituting new learning occurs.

Once the client begins to react to the therapist as he has to other significant persons out of his past, then the introduction of material by a client takes on new meaning. For now, the therapist can ask additional questions about the client's motivation for introducing what he does, not only in terms of what the generic conflict might have been, but in terms *of what it would mean for the client to do so with him, his therapist.*

The Therapist's Personal Experience in the Relationship

The therapeutic interaction is further complicated, and its uniqueness highlighted, when the implications of the therapeutic relationship are considered from another point of view. When the therapist reacts, when he places his resources at the disposal of the client, when he commits himself to the therapeutic relationship, he opens the door to anxiety, conflict, and ambivalence in himself. The therapist's own personality becomes a part of the equation between observation and understanding.

Understanding a client is not based solely in the knowledge of human dynamics and motivation. Nor does understanding of general theory provide a therapist with the resources to effect change in a client. Having a good theoretical understanding is essential but such understanding does not necessarily imply that it can be applied and utilized effectively. Theory can be learned from a book; its application involves using all of one's personal resources within the context of an interpersonal relationship. And the interpersonal dimension, the human interaction that is essential to change—with all that implies about human conflict—is at the heart of what is potentially therapeutic.

When the therapist reacts to his client, he participates in the client's search for the meaning of the conflicts that inhibit him. As a participant in the emotional life of the client, the therapist's personal dynamics play an essential role in what he can permit himself to understand. Unless the therapist has the internal freedom to do so because he is unhampered by his own conflicts and anxiety, he might be unable to listen to the client and help him to make sense of his experiences. And unless he can help the client to utilize what he experiences, to bring it into his awareness, the opportunity for the client's becoming more human is lost.

As the client begins to react to the therapist, as he attempts to use the therapist to work out his problems, as he makes the therapist into many different persons to project and satisfy his needs, as he lashes out at the therapist in anger and out of anxiety, as he distorts what the therapist says to suit himself, as he ambivalently tries to change and then attacks the therapist for helping, as his usual modes of defending go into operation during the therapeutic hour, he will stimulate emotional reactions in the therapist.

If the therapist understands the interpersonal dimension of therapy in its fullest sense, then he will recognize that there is a very high probability that whatever he experiences during an interview is determined *to some extent* by the behavior of his client. Such a premise necessitates that the therapist never slough off any of his emotional reactions during an interview without carefully scrutinizing the source of stimulation. To state the premise operationally, if a therapist becomes inattentive during some phase of his relationship to a client and begins to contemplate matters that seem to have little relevance to the client, he needs to consider several possibilities. In the first place, of course, the therapist could have entered the interview preoccupied with personal matters which divert his attention and have little to do with the client's stimulation.

The more likely probability, however, is that the therapist's preoccupation is directly connected in a dynamic way to the ongoing emotional conditions of his relationship to the client. That latter possibility cannot be dismissed until it is carefully explored. Whether the content of the therapist's fantasies at such a time is also related in some way to the events in the relationship is a more complex issue. But the possibility must be left open that the nature of the fantasies themselves during the reverie period is in fact also related dynamically to the client's stimulation.

The therapist's own emotional reactions can afford him one of his most powerful vehicles for learning about a client and being therapeutic with him. The therapist's own emotional responsivity broadens the experiential base for therapy; all other experiences in relation to the client have an inferential quality to them. The usefulness of that primary avenue to understanding is, however, contingent on several considerations. First of all, the potential value of the therapist's experience is founded in the therapist's capacity to interpret accurately the meaning of his experience in relation to the client. Insofar as the therapist can represent what he experiences in relation to the client accurately in his own awareness—whether warmth, anger, anxiety, or whatever—his ability to help is expanded.

Insofar as the therapist must distort his experience in relation to the client, he limits his ability to help. The therapist can't help a client to know what an experience is or means if he fears that experience in himself. It is dynamically impossible for a therapist to understand or help a client to examine areas of concern that he can't permit himself to experience or that he needs to distort. In areas where experiences are blocked from his own awareness, the therapist becomes impotent; and, at every point where such blocks occur, at every point where the therapist fears to explore areas because of his own emotional limitations, he will attempt to control the relationship, to divert the client, or to misconstrue the intended meaning so as to avoid the experience of anxiety in himself.

The therapist's own reactions, then, if properly understood by him provide an unusual opportunity for learning about a client and being therapeutic. Conversely, the extent to which experiences must be distorted by a therapist is a vital index of how limited will be his potential usefulness as a therapeutic agent.

If the therapist's experience must be denied or distorted by him, the emotional consequences of that distortion in the client will be to reinforce old patterns, confirm suspicions about people, and firm up defenses against changing.

A second contingency on the usefulness of the therapist's own reactions consists of his effectiveness in associating those reactions to the emotional conditions that stimulate them. It should be pointed out that it is insufficient for the therapist to simply "know," that is, to represent his reactions accurately in awareness. The therapist must be able to use that "knowing" therapeutically, and to do so he must be able to bridge the gap between his reaction and the events in the relationship that are associated to it.

Once the therapist accurately represents his experience, he begins a search back and forth in himself, in the relationship, and in the dynamics of the interaction to determine what triggered those responses. The associational process that the therapist goes through often reveals much to him about where his client is emotionally, what the client tends to and perhaps intends to evoke in other persons, and how the client goes about negotiating his relationships so as to maintain his internal consistency and resist changing.

The major point is that unless the therapist construes his reactions accurately and can relate them to the sources of stimulation and to their effects in the relationship, the usefulness of those experiences as a vehicle for understanding his client is lost. The intricacies of how the therapist goes about the process of reflecting, associating, analyzing, synthesizing, and working back and forth between his experience and understanding as a guide to understanding the client and being therapeutic with him is more directly related to the therapeutic process proper and as such will be the content of later chapters.

THE UNIQUENESS OF THERAPY IN RETROSPECT AND PROSPECT

In this chapter, the various ways in which a therapist learns about the emotional life of his client were surveyed. In developing the chapter, an attempt was made to move from generalized sources of understanding to those that were specific to the therapeutic situation. In earlier sections, the observations and inferences of a therapist which are essential to understanding but are not inherent in and specific to the therapeutic situation were reviewed. In later sections, those sources of understanding that are intrinsic to therapy and are generated by the interplay of the unique conditions that define therapy and differentiate it from other human endeavors were described.

Although the purposes of this chapter were limited by intent to delineating the sources of understanding, clarification of specific issues and the meaningful evaluation of sources dictated expansion beyond simply cataloguing material. In particular, as those sources of data intrinsic to therapy and generated by the uniqueness of the therapeutic situation were introduced, a natural convergence with therapeutic applications occurred. Case fragments were introduced to illustrate the richness of some data and to demonstrate the underlying interlocking effects and synthetic potential of different avenues to understanding. At such times, the data of this chapter provided some brief prospective glimpses into therapeutic processes.

In later chapters, the therapist's understanding, derived from the many sources considered in this chapter, will be reintroduced from the perspective of how those understandings interlock with process, reflect and affect the relationship, and provide a vehicle for effecting constructive change in the lives of clients. What had been in this chapter a brief prospective glimpse of therapeutic work itself will be expanded in later chapters to become the center of attention. But before turning to the actual therapeutic work, it is necessary to explore in some depth the critical features of process which provide the unique foundations on which therapy is built.

3

The Processes of Therapy:
Foundations for Change

In previous chapters, a number of factors which differentiate therapy from other human endeavors have been considered. In particular, it has been proposed that the goals of therapy and the complex of antecedent and concomitant conditions surrounding the inception of therapy set into motion processes unique to the accomplishment of those goals. The characteristics of those processes have been tangentially alluded to and repeatedly implied in the content of the last two chapters. In this chapter, the dynamics of the change processes will be more carefully delineated.

The processes of therapy by which constructive change is effected are complex. They are complex because the conflicts which bring the client to the therapist's office often represent the end product of many unsuccessful efforts at resolution, and, as such, they are intricately interwoven into the total personality. The process of conflict resolution can be no simpler than the intricate patterning of the conflict itself. To understand the dimensions and the process of change, therefore, the determinants of conflict must be first understood.

FOUNDATIONS FOR CHANGE:
DETERMINANTS OF CONFLICT

The client's experience of conflict and attendant anxiety represent the still viable strivings of the client which cannot for whatever reasons be adequately satisfied and incorporated into the total functioning personality. The client's conflicts reflect the outcome of prior emotional experiences which were in some way traumatic, overpowering, frustrating, or inhibiting. Essentially, the experi-

47

ence of anxiety cut off or truncated the potential for normal development in certain regards. And so for the client to achieve satisfaction in conflict-laden areas, he must distort, delay, or satisfy those needs in very circuitous ways. So long as the conflict remains active, the strivings must either go unmet or be indirectly satisfied; but in either case they cannot be integrated into the total personality and contribute to the client's continuing development. But more optimistically, it can also be said that so long as the conflict remains viable, the potential for change and growth exists.

When the client enters therapy, the original experiences that generated conflict are overlaid with defenses against reexperiencing those same emotional conditions. And, if the client has survived to adulthood, the therapist can rest assured that the client has developed some interesting and intricate ways of protecting himself against the recurrence of those painful situations. The complexity of the client's protective system is a measure of the intense danger that those experiences represent to the client. And, if the client's personality is a fairly well integrated one, the defensive system is likely to have worked reasonably well for him and become over the years an integral part of his way of reacting and relating so as to achieve some gains without undue anxiety.

Often when the client enters therapy the process of defending against the recurrence of some life experiences has become a well-established pattern in his life. In addition, for the client to be reasonably functioning, he must have found alternative, although devious, circuitous, and energy-expending routes to satisfy needs without experiencing the need directly as such. And so the process of resolving conflict requires an intricate reworking through or around the defensive system and often requires extensive work in countering the client's learned modes of coping to avoid certain affective experiences. Only then, can the disabling emotional experience itself actually be encountered, coped with, and modified.

The complexity of resolving conflict is heightened by other facets of a client's ingenuity. As mentioned above, the client will have found alternative routes for partial need satisfaction in order to maintain some semblance of internal emotional balance. In addition, clients are often emotionally astute enough to find rather interesting, however unconscious, ways of putting their neurosis to work for them in solving some internal dynamic issues. Some clients, for example, while denying themselves the conscious comfort of being dependent, often find ways of becoming massively dependent without ever experiencing the dependency in awareness.

Those secondary gains and partial satisfactions tend to work against the client's changing since they provide the client with some motivation to maintain his present state of equilibrium. If the client changes, he might actually have to sacrifice his immature ways of achieving satisfaction. The prospect of maturity and the abrogation of some rather pleasant infantile behavior might activate some second thoughts in the client about changing. At any rate, those partial satisfactions and secondary gains tend to activate a client's ambivalence, tend to diminish his motivation to change, and counter the constructive therapeutic processes.

In other cases, clients sometimes attempt to achieve satisfaction, to complete some cherished fantasy, or to rework again and again some old conflicts by actually living out their conflicts with others. Unless such clients get relief through therapy, they might spend their lifetimes in creating relationships that parallel along significant dimensions some of the interactions that they have lived through or fantasized living through with important persons in their past. In those cases the neurotic character of those relationships is evident from the client's continuing frustrating efforts to achieve satisfaction through those relationships.

As will be pointed out later, the parallel elements in those relationships might be dimensions that are projected into the relationship by the client because of his needs; they might be fabricated conditions; or those relationships might actually contain reality elements that are magnified by the client because of his needs. In any case, the transference components of those relationships in which early fantasies or actual interactions are replayed in the present with those who happen to be available in the client's environment provide the therapist with a very useful vehicle for understanding the client's conflicts and assisting him to effect change.

At the same time that those relationships provide the therapist with a useful vehicle for understanding the client by bringing the broad outlines of conflict into bold relief, those relationships set up a very difficult hurdle for the therapist to overcome. A number of facets of those relationships work against the client's changing. In the first place, a client might achieve significant satisfaction in those relationships and as such they tend to reduce tension sufficiently so that the client's motivation to examine them is diminished.

More importantly, however, there are often enough reality elements to those relationships, however minute they might be, which parallel some significant earlier relationships so that the client invests a tremendous amount of emotional energy in those relationships. Because of the energy invested in those relationships, the client often cannot be persuaded to "see" the parallel elements. The needs of the client are often strong enough and the relationship is convenient enough so that it provokes an almost compulsive reaction in the client to attempt resolution of conflict through the relationship rather than to "see" the relationship as a repeat performance of prior ones in his life. And the compulsive character of the client's intent to work out his needs through those relationships makes distracting the client difficult and increases the difficulty of conflict resolution.

Lastly, the conflicts of clients have often been triggered by experiences early in their lives. Those experiences often set a pattern into motion in which future experiences act to reinforce the early experience, to complicate it, or distort and confuse it so that the dimensions of the generic conflict are difficult to assess. In addition, anxiety works to blot out memories of the situations which generated conflict, thus reducing the client's and therapist's potential access to them.

FOUNDATIONS FOR CHANGE:
AN INTRODUCTION TO PROCESS

So the process of change is complicated by the complexity of the conflict itself, by the extensive history of conflict, by forgetting, by distorting, by diffusing and merging of one conflict with another, by an overlay of defensive operations, and by the interlocking of fantasy and reality. Those components of conflict are intricately interwoven into the personality over time, and the process of change is a challenging task of reworking back through time, linking present conflict with past experiences, separating fantasy from reality, and differentiating between the irrational and rational until the anxiety is attached to the experiences that triggered it and set the conflict into motion.

Throughout therapy there is a continual recycling of anxiety, experiencing, remembering, emotional insight, and integration. That process continues to recycle throughout therapy, but with each recycling there is an expanding, deepening, spiraling into the personality and into the sources of conflict. With each recycling there is a regression in the client. But there is also a progression. Each deepening spiral links the present to the past as the conflicts of the day and the hour are found to have their sources in the past.

With each cycling, the experience of anxiety heightens and is followed by some painful experiences, but those experiences release pent up affect, open memories, and provide emotional insight and eventual integration. That progressive recycling process is difficult and risky for the client, however, since regression precedes progression. And in that regression the client is most vulnerable. With each regression, the intensity of the situation heightens, the significance of the therapist increases, and the basis is laid for a closer revisitation to some of the significant events that have either been pushed out of consciousness or have been divested of their emotional components.

The build up of anxiety during therapy heralds the emergence into awareness of warded-off feelings, needs, attitudes, and experiences. That experiencing in awareness of what was warded off is at the heart of change. It is accompanied by memories and emotional insight into the dynamics of the conflict itself. For effective therapeutic gains, the conditions which stimulate conflict must be emotionally understood in relation to present conflict as well as to the generic causes of conflict. Unless that two-pronged flow of insight into current conflict and its generic stimulus are both experienced by the client, there is a potential recycling of anxiety until the related aspects of the generic conflict are also emotionally grasped.

Once that two-pronged emotional insight occurs, integration, progression in therapy, and personal growth spontaneously occur. With integration, the recycling of anxiety and experiencing might recur as new facets of conflict are introduced and other conflicts emerge. The emergence of different facets of conflict are not to be viewed with pessimism; they are a necessary progressive feature of therapy. The personality is unified and the various facets of conflict are simply contingencies which reflect the dynamic interplay of facets of personality.

Progress in therapy is evident from the increased optimism with which the client might undertake the continued and deeper exploration of himself. Progress is evident from the increased capacity of the client to utilize previous gains in deepening his search. Progress is evident from the way in which the client's anxiety becomes more directed and less diffuse. Progress is evident from the way in which the client begins to rely on his own resources, to assess with increasing accuracy the meaning of his conflicts, to see his own dynamics at work in his interactions, to gain insight into how his own associational and symbolic processes signal areas of potential conflict. And most importantly, progress is evident and termination is in sight when the client begins to sense how he can find ways and means of self-correcting those conditions which restrict personal growth.

FOUNDATIONS FOR CHANGE: DIMENSIONS OF PROCESS

In a general way, the processes of therapy by which constructive change is effected can be conceptualized in terms of three underlying and interlocking dynamic processes. Those processes, centering around learning and its inhibition, provide a dynamic basis for organizing and interpreting much of what transpires during therapy. The process by which the client reexperiences, gains emotional insight, and emotionally reorganizes is complemented by the process of acquiring and integrating new and growth producing learnings. Those two processes create the basis for effecting constructive change through therapy. A third general process, however, which on the one hand motivates learning can also act to counter the growth force. That process is activated by the intrusion of intense anxiety into the learning experience. Intense anxiety can set contradictory defensive processes into motion which inhibit change and tend to frustrate the therapeutic goals.

The processes by which inappropriate behavior patterns are modified and new patterns are assimilated or frustrated by the intrusion of intense anxiety characterize in varying degrees every therapeutic relationship. In some respects, therapy contributes mainly to the modification of ineffective behavior patterns since the growth process proceeds to a considerable extent under its own power once the anxiety that frustrates growth is blunted. The processes of relearning and the work of thwarting the inhibiting influences of anxiety therefore constitute a significant and essential phase of the therapeutic effort. But therapy reaches a point suitable for termination only when the process of integration and experimentation with more productive reactions has proceeded to the point where the client has sufficiently consolidated his resources so that he can continue to build beyond termination upon a solid emotional foundation.

In the following sections, the process of change will be considered from the perspective of the dynamic forces which actuate the change process and which underlie the processes by which constructive change is facilitated or inhibited. In order to understand the power of therapy to effect constructive change, it is of particular importance that the impact of several interlocking sources of influence on the change process be understood.

Those sources which influence process consist of some considerations about the client, the therapist, and the interpersonal character of the therapeutic situation. Although those influences have been described elsewhere, they will be reintroduced and expanded throughout the coming sections in the context of how they shape process and provide the basis for a unique learning situation. Throughout the following sections, it will be pointed out in different ways that no one of those influences in itself adequately explains the change process; to understand the process of change, the impact of the configuration of those influences on the change process must be understood.

DIMENSIONS OF PROCESS THAT FACILITATE CONSTRUCTIVE CHANGE

When the client enters therapy, he might be manifestly anxious; he might experience conflict in significant features of his life; or the anxiety might be latent and the expenditure of energy that is utilized in internal battling might be evidenced only through unrest or dissatisfaction. But at any rate, the client is dissatisfied with aspects of his life situation and that dissatisfaction motivates the client to seek help. The client's conscious motivation to change provides one of the bases for setting into motion the change process since the client's vulnerability leads him to reveal aspects of his life that he would not otherwise do and thus makes changing potential.

The counterpart to the client's motivation to change and the primary force which actuates the change process occurs when the therapist reacts constructively to what the client says and does. When the therapist reacts, he sets an interpersonal process into motion. The conflicts which bring the client to the therapist were engendered in an interpersonal context and their resolution necessitates a relationship whose significance reaches an emotional level comparable in power to the conditions of the initial disabling experiences. The first step in the direction of achieving that significance occurs with the therapist's constructive reaction to the client's presentation of himself.

If the therapist is motivated to help the client, is genuinely interested in the client, can listen to what the client says and does without needing to distort, and can react constructively, he sets the change process into motion. Those conditions of the relationship, principally the trustworthiness and competence of the therapist, provide the basis for the client's willingness to expand and deepen his exploration. For those conditions in turn activate the client's confidence in the therapist and his trust of him. And that trust is based in the reality conditions of the relationship. It is communicated by the therapist, not through his contention that he is trustworthy, but rather in his behavioral reactions to the client.

The client's sense of trust is based on those early—perhaps minute—but for the client very significant ways in which the therapist might provide the client with some optimism that he can help. That trust might be based on the ways in which the therapist makes some initial associations that are helpful. That trust might be based on some slight gesture of interest in the client or some expression of regard for the client's individuality. But, at any rate, the trustworthiness of the therapist, his interest, competence, and motivation to help must be behaviorally communicated and cannot be contended or implied by the good offices of the therapist's position.

Those conditions of the relationship provide the interpersonal context in which the client will open himself to anxiety and potential change. Whereas in earlier relationships, the client's resentment and anger toward those in authority might have precluded learning, the reality of the conditions of the therapeutic relationship, insofar as they differ, open the avenue to learning. Those conditions tend to activate natural growth forces in the client; they stimulate his curiosity and creativity; and they provide a basis for his willingness to risk questioning, investigating, and experimenting.

Those reality factors of the relationship provide one basis for the client's positive feelings about the therapist. And, to some extent, they provide a partial explanation for the client's dependency, identification with the therapist, and eventual growth. It is because the therapist is in fact interested in him that the client expands his inner life. It is because the therapist is in fact competent as evidenced by the way he helps the client to use his anxiety to associate it to its generating sources that the client feels gratified for some real help and relief in his life. It is because the therapist uses what the client provides him in constructive ways—rather than as a basis for punitive, hostile, depreciating, or moralizing reactions—that the client experiences strong positive feelings about the therapist and is willing to learn from him. And those conditions of the relationship provide solid reasons for the client's changing feelings and growth through therapy.

As important as those conditions are, however, they provide only a partial explanation for the significant change that is characteristic of therapy. Those conditions of the relationship set the stage for still other processes through which reorganization occurs in the emotional life of the client during therapy. In a sense those conditions of the relationship provide a foothold for the client's deeper search into himself. And as that search is undertaken, the client will begin to react irrationally to the therapist for a number of reasons to be cited later. But those irrational reactions which provide another avenue to change would not occur, the client would not risk the anxiety and involvement which foster such reactions, unless the conditions of the relationship provided a sound emotional basis in trust for his willingness to do so.

The client soon finds as therapy gets underway that the work of the therapist tends to activate and intensify anxiety in the client. The client's heightened anxiety works both to deepen the relationship and to set additional more complex change processes into motion. Not only does heightened anxiety set additional facilitative processes into motion, but it also activates counter processes which inhibit the change process. Those processes activated by anxiety which contradict growth will be taken up at a later time. At this time, the potential of anxiety for complicating the therapeutic processes and providing additional bases for significant change will be considered.

The client's anxiety, unless it becomes too diffuse, serves a most useful therapeutic purpose, for it sets into motion some irrational processes which are significant determinants of the client's eventual changing behavior. Anxiety increases the likelihood that the client will project, will distort, will misperceive, and generally behave in irrational ways toward the therapist. And *in those irrational reactions the foundations are laid for deeper and more significant change than would be otherwise possible.* The constructive use to which the therapist can put those irrational reactions will be introduced later. But first, the motivating forces which actuate the irrational processes that characterize therapy will be taken up.

Motivating Forces for the Irrational Processes

In the first place, as was suggested above, anxiety, as it intensifies tends to inhibit censorship and the client is more likely to project into the relationship, distort features of it, and anticipate reactions from the therapist that are based on his own subjective experiences rather than on the reality of the therapist's behavior, expectations, or feelings. A further explanation for the client's increased tendency to react irrationally at times of anxiety is based on considerations about the dynamic function that anxiety serves. Anxiety serves to mobilize the person, to alert him, to signal danger. When anxiety heightens during therapy, it signals proximity to the experiences that underlie and generate conflict.

Anxiety reflects the increased internal pressure of needs, impulses, feelings, and reactions that would be dangerous to experience or express. For the client, anxiety warns of dangerous territory. For the therapist, the client's anxiety alerts him to increase his sensitivity to what is projected at such times, what is reenacted, or to what is anticipated for those reactions of the client at times of heightened stress will reflect the character of the unmet needs.

Anxiety, therefore, is a hypothetical construct that provides a partial explanation for the client's irrational reactions. But anxiety provides only a partial explanation for the tendency of the client to project and behave irrationally. To understand the tendency more fully, anxiety must be viewed in relation to several additional considerations about the interpersonal character of the client's unmet needs and about the therapeutic situation.

The client's conflicts were engendered by the emotional conditions of some previously significant interpersonal relationships. As the therapist and client converge on the awakening of needs, impulses, or feelings that have been endangered by the behavior of others, the client's anticipation is that the experience of those needs will provoke the same reaction in the therapist. He has no experiential basis for predicting otherwise. Thus, he anticipates that the therapist will react as other significant persons have done and those predictions are expressed as projections onto the therapist *and as reactions to* what he anticipates.

An additional prominent feature in the client's tendency to react irrationally to the therapist is that inadequate or destructive interpersonal relationships tend to fixate a client emotionally at certain developmental stages in which the inhibiting experiences occurred. Those unmet needs and strivings often remain attached in fantasy to the past significant figures who provided the emotional context in which the needs were experienced and either were unsatisfied, distorted, gratified inappropriately, or were endangered. In later life, the client might continue to invest his energy in well-worn fantasies about those periods of life and in automatically setting up those emotional conditions in relation to others so as to resolve the conflicts, master the anxiety, complete the fantasies, or alter the initial disabling experiences.

The still unmet needs of the client, then, aggravate the tendency to react irrationally. But they do not explain the character of the client's projections or the nature of what is transferred. The character of the projections and the misperceptions and the specifics of the restaging of the conflict are a function of what the specific emotional conditions were that triggered the anxiety. They are determined by the nature of the unmet needs and by the way in which the specific strivings were experienced and were later distorted. The character of those earlier interactions also determines to some extent the nature of what the client will ward off, resist, and attempt to avoid experiencing.

The nature of the therapeutic situation itself provides an additional partial explanation for the client's tendency to react irrationally and for the development of transference reactions to the therapist. When the client enters therapy, he is anxious and in need of help. He feels that he cannot make it on his own, which is a variant of the experience of helplessness that is felt by the child. The therapist who offers help is accurately perceived as someone who is an authority and is more knowledgeable about psychological processes than the client is. In addition, the client often assumes that the therapist knows more about the client's own processes than he himself does. And it is often true that a client feels and actually is very unsophisticated about the workings of his own emotional life.

In addition, during the negotiations surrounding the initial contacts, the therapist might specify some of the conditions for therapy. Even if the therapist were to specify nothing more than the frequency of sessions, he will have communicated to a hypersensitive client that he controls to some extent the nature and limitations of the help that he can and will render. What the client does with those negotiations varies with the needs and conflicts of particular clients. But in some, the condition of needing to rely on another person whose emotional life the client can no more control than he could control the source of his supplies when he was a child exacerbates the sense of dependency and helplessness that the client already feels.

Those conditions in the therapeutic situation—the client's neediness, his inability to master his own situation or control the source of help, and his perception of the therapist as an authority who is more knowledgeable about the client's emotional processes than the client himself is—recapitulate along significant dimensions some of the conditions that the client must have experienced during his developmental years when the original conflicts that bring him to the therapist were engendered. As such those parallel conditions set the stage for transference reactions.

The Usefulness of the Irrational
Processes: General Considerations

That tendency of a client to recreate or to anticipate the recreation of the emotional conditions in the present with those with whom he interacts, which are based on his unresolved conflicts of the past, carries over into therapy, is exacerbated by the conditions of therapy, and becomes a significant feature of the therapeutic process. The irrational processes which are actuated by the complex of conditions described above provide the therapist with a powerful means for effecting change. And the significance of that vehicle for change resides in the fact that when the client reacts to the therapist as he has to the significant figures in the past he provides the therapist with a unique experiential basis for participating in the change process.

Although noted in the last chapter, it is worth repeating that when the client projects feelings onto the therapist that arise from the client's subjective experience rather than from any accurate representation of what the therapist is experiencing, the therapist's base for understanding his client is immensely expanded. The therapist's own feelings and experience can guide his understanding and participation. Through his client's attributions, the therapist begins to sense the character of the experiences that the client needs to distort and the avenue is opened to understanding why those distortions are necessary.

Further, when the client behaves in ways that are irrational with regard to the reality conditions of the relationship—when the client projects traits onto the therapist and then reacts to the therapist as he has to persons in his past who embodied those traits; when he begins to feel toward the therapist emotions that he experienced toward others who were significant factors in why he has become conflicted and confused; when the therapist becomes the figurative embodiment of those characteristics which reflect and stimulate conflict; when the client projects into the relationship the conditions of the interpersonal context in which some facet of his problem had its roots; when a conflict situation is reenacted in the therapist's presence with the therapist as a principal or the target of the reenactment—then the therapist and therapy have reached a level of emotional significance to the client comparable in power and parallel in context to the experience in which conflict was generated. And in that comparability in emotional valence, the foundations are laid for significant change.

How the therapist reacts, what he does about the client's irrational premises and reactions as those reactions manifest themselves during therapy is a critical feature in the change process. The therapist might choose to ignore the client's irrational reactions, to circumvent them, to incorporate them productively into his own reaction patterns to the client, or to confront them directly and attempt to reattach the emotional experience to the generic source. Whatever means the therapist uses, so long as the therapist *acts in the full knowledge of the occurrence of the irrational reactions, then progress can still be made.*

The change process can be facilitated in many different ways dependent upon varying ways in which a therapist finds that he can be useful. If, however, the therapist denies, avoids, doesn't hear or see the client's reactions, or doesn't feel competent to cope with them; if the therapist, in other words, "tunes them out" *because to experience them or cope with them would be too threatening to him*, then that is quite a different matter and insofar as the therapist distorts, denies, or avoids for reasons of personal anxiety, the change process is limited.

The critical factor in whether the client's irrational reactions further the change process, then, rests not so much with the different theoretical formulations about "how to" react. Rather the determining factor is in whether the client's behavior must be denied. The reasons seem simple enough. To deny those factors distorts what the client is experiencing in the relationship; it cuts out a piece of the client's experience. Further, and most importantly, those facets of experience are excluded from the relationship because the therapist cannot tolerate their occurrence; he cannot cope with them. And those conditions of having his experiences distorted are likely to recapitulate with a high degree of emotional accuracy the interpersonal context of the generic conflict. The therapist, through his behavior, has reinforced the conflict, has reduced potential access to it, and sets counter processes into motion which tend to inhibit change.

DIMENSIONS OF PROCESS THAT CAN FACILITATE OR INHIBIT CONSTRUCTIVE CHANGE

Anxiety, on the one hand, heightens the potential for change and contributes to setting complex processes into motion which provide a powerful vehicle for effecting significant change. On the other hand, intense anxiety also tends to activate a client's defenses against changing. And, as such, anxiety sets a process into motion that counters the growth force. That contradictory process, activated by the intrusion of anxiety, tends toward inhibiting change and frustrating the therapeutic goals.

The Complex Effects of the Client's Anxiety on the Change Process

Perhaps the way in which anxiety can work both to facilitate and inhibit change can be clarified when viewed in terms of its effects on motivation. Anxiety, as was pointed out earlier, is one of the factors which motivates a client to want to change. It acts as the carrier wave for motivation. If anxiety becomes intense or diffuse, change is inhibited. If a modicum of anxiety is experienced, it facilitates change. If anxiety abates, motivation diminishes.

A client's motivation to change varies with and is a behavioral expression of the dynamic functions that are served by anxiety. If a client's motivation to change is minimal, it might be because the discomfort that he suffers is limited to particular situations which are well-insulated experiences. His anxiety might be situational, and once the events that trigger anxiety and threaten a well-established pattern of living are alleviated, the client's anxiety abates along with the resolution of the particulars of the situation. And the client's motivation to change diminishes. A client's anxiety might increase dramatically at times when previously effective coping styles for warding off the experience of deeper anxiety are suddenly rendered ineffective by a change in an interpersonal relationship. At those times, the client's motivation to change increases.

Some clients are able to profit more from therapy because they are able to tolerate anxiety and learn to convert it to good use. A client, for example, who has spent a good deal of his life in a conflict-ridden state and whose life has consisted of trying to wear a path between experiences of intensifying and diminishing anxiety might be highly motivated to change unless anxiety functions as an integral and necessary part of his life pattern. The therapy of such a client is more likely to follow the process model suggested in the introduction to this section of the chapter. He is more likely to tolerate anxiety to search, more likely to react irrationally and allow the therapist to assist him to use that irrationality to uncover and modify the inhibiting forces in his life.

He is more likely, in other words, to allow his anxiety to work for him, to maintain a sufficiently high level of anxiety during therapy so that his associational processes work for him, his symbolic processes emerge and become sensible, his dynamics can be understood, and integration can occur. He is more likely to be a "good client," which is simply another way of saying that the client has good resources and can live his life in a useful, functioning manner in the present while allowing himself to become disorganized enough to achieve a more integrated, more fully functioning personality.

In therapy, a certain level of anxiety is essential throughout its course in order to maintain access to dynamics. Appropriate levels of anxiety sufficiently blunt the client's censors so that he reveals himself and his motivations to the therapist. Appropriate levels of anxiety keep the client working to find new and more appropriate ways of reducing stress in his life. Appropriate levels of anxiety provide access, in other words, to the processes in the client which are those otherwise hidden and attenuated dynamic motivational forces which stimulate and maintain conflict.

Whether anxiety will continue to work for the client to maintain his motivation to change is contingent on the effectiveness with which the therapist can continually help the client to cycle through to integration as new facets of conflict emerge or as deeper conflict is uncovered with the resolution of more superficial manifestations of conflict. That process of maintaining motivation is most intricate, for the client must experience both relief and a thirst for greater integration as he proceeds through therapy. With each cycling of anxiety, experience, memories, insight, and integration, the client must be both gratified and yet motivated to continue the search.

Anxiety, then, if appropriately maintained during therapy works to facilitate change. On the other hand, if anxiety becomes diffuse, it is likely to inhibit the process of change. For, under those circumstances, the client is likely to react to the anxiety, to feel disorganized, and to have his capacity for seeing relationships seriously impaired. When anxiety is diffuse, the client experiences a sense of impending danger, fears disorganization, and loss of identity.

Those fears, as they mount, are experienced as feelings of panic. As panic builds, it serves to intensify the anxiety already present and sets into motion a process of erratic and random efforts at reducing anxiety at any cost. At those times, change is not only at a standstill, but the experience of intense anxiety tends to make the client shy from any possible recurrence of anxiety. At such times, the work of the therapist is particularly delicate since the anxiety must be sufficiently reduced and directed to its source so that the fears of its recurrence are balanced by some sense of gratification and relief; otherwise the client will institute defenses that make reaching him difficult.

On the one hand, then, anxiety is a motivating force for change. But when it becomes diffuse or intense, it acts to inhibit change. Similarly, when anxiety abates prematurely, the client's motivation to change is also likely to diminish. Interestingly enough, one of the most salient reasons why a motivated client's anxiety abates prematurely rests with the ineptness of the therapist.

If anxiety is generated by the work of the therapist, and the therapist cannot, for whatever reasons, trace it appropriately to the experiences that generate it, if that conflict is not worked through to integration, the client is unlikely to flush out of his unconscious again the conflict laden experience that generated anxiety for it is often simply too painful to do so.

A therapist's ineptness is a frightening experience for a vulnerable client. What guarantee does the client have that he might not be left in some disorganized state "on the next go around"? On this occasion, the client might have recovered from his anxiousness without the therapist's help, and most functioning young adults can do so. But the client might question his own resiliency to recover by himself the next time.

The responsibility for the premature abatement of anxiety does not always rest with the therapist. The client might simply find the search too difficult and prefer to go on with life as he has in the past. In other clients, where anxiety is situational, it often abates as soon as the stimulating influences have been reconnoitered. In still other clients, the premature abatement of anxiety might be a function of some "dynamic correction" in an interpersonal relationship that threatened an otherwise satisfying life-style.

Some clients enter therapy because their interpersonal relationships, interpenetrated with neurotic interactions, are suddenly threatened by a change in the pattern of their interpersonal relationships. The motivations of those clients to change are contingent on how compelling the secondary gains are that they experience in their relationships and how facile the clients are at reinstituting those patterns in their new relationships. The client's neurotic behavioral patterns are at once his source of satisfaction in life and his defense against anxiety. Those carefully elaborated interpersonal modes of coping serve to maintain the status quo and keep anxiety at a minimum. If such clients remain long in therapy, they make challenging clients.

The therapist might note that almost at the moment of their first contact, the client's anxiety abates. In its stead, the therapist might find himself being drawn into an interaction that is powerful and inhibiting. What has happened is that the client has immediately set into operation an interpersonal style of coping with people which is intended to incorporate them into a pattern that renders them ineffective and simultaneously provides the client with immensely satisfying, although highly neurotic gratifications.

One client, who had mastered the art of incorporating people into interpersonal relationships that were at once disabling, confusing, and highly controlling, entered therapy because her fiancé had decided to leave her. Despite a rather extensive repertoire of tricks to reensnare him, the client found that she failed to convince the male friend to behave the way "he was supposed to." Her sweetness failed; her threats failed; her seductiveness failed; her hostility failed. The man would have none of it. The client's anxiety mounted.

The client's anxiety mounted because her security was somehow based on the continuing compulsive need to manipulate men into doing what she wanted. So long as she could keep men in line and remain in control of the relationship, she felt integrated. Once that pattern was disrupted, anxiety flooded in. In her initial interview with a male therapist, the client was fearful that she was falling apart. Amidst many tears, she contended that she had never turned to a therapist for help before. She had always tried to figure out her problems on her own.

The therapist agreed to see her and worked out an appointment time for her. Immediately and dramatically, the tears dried up, the client's anxiety seemed to evaporate, the client was all "sweetness and light" and became a highly seductive, fetching young lady who related her life history in a graphic, amusing manner. And when the therapist attempted to open up areas of conflict with some brief comment about some minor facet of what the client had said, he experienced intense, cutting, and immobilizing hostility in the client's rejoinder to his comment.

The therapist couldn't at first understand the hostility and the complete abatement of anxiety. But in retrospect the dynamics seem obvious. Once the therapist had responded to the client's strident bids for help, he had acted as the boyfriend had not. Essentially, the client's pattern of interacting had been instantly reinstituted and she was underway at working on another man. From the point of view of the client's dynamics the therapist's agreement to work with the client was a behavioral validation for her continued ability to manipulate men.

Anxiety and Defensiveness

During the initial stages of therapy, the client's anxiety, if not manifest, soon becomes so as emotional material related to conflict begins to emerge. Initially, the client might experience his anxiety in diffuse ways. And diffuse anxiety, as was pointed out earlier, is particularly threatening since it is felt as a state of confusion. Although that state of confusion is a natural prelude to reorganization, the client can't possibly know that or the experience wouldn't be what it is.

What the client might experience is the threat of being totally disabled, of becoming disorganized, of losing his identity. That experience of being confused is heightened by the premonition of even greater anxiety. And those initial experiences in the client activate internal reactions to the therapist and therapy which are experienced by the client as ambivalence and expressed in various resistances to change.

At such times, the client will close up, provide little relevant material, react negatively to the therapist, become volatile, and might consider termination. The client's defensive reactions to the experience of anxiety and the threat of becoming disorganized continue in one form or another throughout much of therapy as new conflicts emerge and anxiety heightens during those times immediately preceding the client's experience in awareness of what has been denied, repressed, and suppressed.

As therapy proceeds, however, the client's anxiety becomes more directed and is not experienced as totally disabling. However, at moments where particularly dreaded emotions near awareness, there is a tendency to reexperience a disorganized state such as that experienced near the outset of therapy. But at those times, there is also often a more rapid-fire cycling through to integration than at first since the client is more familiar with the sensations of anxiety and their meaning. Essentially, the client can gain perspective faster on what is happening to himself internally.

If the client recoils from the experience of anxiety, he will tend to set into motion processes which are intended to thwart the therapist and to maintain the status quo. But despite the intent of the client's defensive system to work against change, it provides the therapist indirectly with a means for understanding his client's emotional life. The ways in which the client copes with stress, what he resists, and how he goes about attempting to alter conditions so as to avoid anxiety provide the therapist with clues to the sources of conflict.

As the client attempts to cope with his internal stress, he reveals much of himself by the way he defends, from what he anticipates, by what he distorts, and through the character of his projections. Through those processes the therapist learns much about how the client has interpreted his life experiences and the organizational framework against which the client compares new experiences. And insofar as the therapist can help the client in constructive ways to see the functions that those defenses serve, he can potentially turn those defenses into constructive processes for change.

Not all of the client's negative reactions or efforts at thwarting the therapist can be construed as defenses against changing. In later therapy, when the relationship has become significant to the client, the client's behavior must also be viewed in terms of whether that behavior represents a recapitulation of the emotional conditions which provided the context for the generic conflict. If so, those reactions must be viewed as a progressive working through of conflict rather than as resistance to changing. In one case, the client is living out his conflicts in relation to the therapist. In defensive behavior, the client is avoiding the experience of conflict.

The Complex Effects of the Therapist's
Anxiety on the Change Process

At times where the client does become defensive and resists working on his conflicts, the responsibility for impasse does not necessarily rest with the client. The therapist's attitudes about and reactions to the client, based in his own ambivalence and anxiety, play a significant explanatory role in understanding some client resistance. How creative a client can be and how extensive change can be depends to a large extent on the ability of the therapist to maintain awareness at all times of what he is experiencing in relation to the client.

Anxiety in the therapist can inhibit his potential to provide the conditions for change in the same way that anxiety in the client can inhibit change. After all, the client can become no less inhibited than his therapist is in areas of conflict that they mutually share outside awareness. The therapist is in a position to help the client insofar as the therapist experiences freedom in the relationship to experience what is transpiring and to utilize that experience constructively.

In order to determine the complex effects on the change process of the experience of anxiety in the therapist at any moment during therapy, its meaning must be evaluated along several interlocking dimensions. Those dimensions consist of considerations about the intensity of the experience of anxiety, sources which stimulated anxiety, the client's motivation in relation to the therapist's anxiety, the neurotic or therapeutic character of the therapist's reactions, and the client's ensuing reaction to the therapist. That complex of conditions surrounding the experience of anxiety must be taken into account if the effects of anxiety on the change process are to be fully appreciated.

To separate those conditions artificially for purposes of explication, it could be proposed in the first place that the intensity of the therapist's experience of anxiety must be evaluated in order to determine its effects on the ensuing relationship. Anxiety in the therapist as in the client can either facilitate or inhibit change. In itself, it is an indeterminate condition with regard to making predictions about its effects on the change process. The potential for predictions is enhanced, however, when several conditions of the experience are taken into account. Those conditions consist generally of considerations about the gradient of anxiety experienced and the therapist's reaction to his experience of anxiety.

In a general way, the more intense the experience of anxiety in the therapist, the more tenable is the hypothesis that events in the interaction have triggered conflict that is associatively linked to central dynamic features of the therapist's personality. Further, the more intense the anxiety, the more remote is the therapist's potential for sufficient recovery to make appropriate associations and note dynamic connections between the experience of anxiety and the antecedent conditions in the relationship and in the life of the client.

In addition to assessing the gradient of anxiety, the sources of its stimulation, the motivations of the client, and the interpersonal context in which anxiety was experienced must be considered if its effects are to be understood. With regard to those conditions, a series of sequential propositions such as the following could be established. At the outset of therapy, the therapist's anxiety is often understandable without reference to the stimulating effects of the client's behavior and its effects on the relationship are therefore indeterminate. Initially, the triggering of the therapist's anxiety might be associatively linked to his own internal concerns about his personal resources to cope with clients in general rather than being based in dynamic considerations that are linked to the specific behavioral reactions of a client. Such factors as the therapist's level of experience, his feelings about his competence, and certain reality based concerns about a client's emotional instability might trigger anxiety and influence the change process.

The therapist's anxiety and defensiveness might be a function of inexperience; an inexperienced therapist might become anxious and defensive because he has not yet demonstrated his competence; each new case is always a challenge to any therapist, but the challenge is experienced by a more mature therapist in ways which are reflected behaviorally in heightened perceptiveness, in aroused curiosity about whether he can help, and in an interest in the client and how the conflicts occurred and developed.

What anxiety the mature therapist experiences is usually converted by him into constructive purposes by activating his perceptiveness and his analytic and synthetic processes. For the beginning therapist, however, anxiety sometimes becomes intense enough so that it limits synthesis; it blinds the therapist to noting dynamic connections between events in the relationship; and it limits his ability to see associations between the client's behavior and the generic sources of conflict. What is experienced internally as doubting by the anxious therapist is often expressed behaviorally by overreacting, by talking too much, by overinterpreting, by attempting to reduce the client's anxiety prematurely, or by attempts to circumvent rather than traverse anxiety-provoking experiences. Through anxiety of this type, the therapist literally cuts off the relationship before it ever develops.

As therapy progresses, the anxiety of the therapist is increasingly a function of the stimulation of his client's behavior. The therapist's anxious reactions to that behavior, however, might be independent of his client's motivations underlying his stimulus behavior. A therapist might become anxious in the presence of hostility as a function of his own dynamics. The anxiety is a generalized reaction, and it cannot be assumed that the therapist's anxious reaction was intended by the client even though provoked by his behavior. That same reaction would have occurred in the therapist in relation to any other client that he was seeing. So the dynamics of the interaction, except in a most general way, have not influenced the therapist's anxiety. As such, the effects of the therapist's anxiety in the relationship are still indeterminate. The therapist's reactions, of course, will have a decided impact on the course of the relationship and will trigger significant reactions in the client, but those effects are not predictable.

The most viable hypothesis, however, during the mature phases of therapy is that the therapist's anxiety is not only stimulated by the client's behavior but that its occurrence is a function of the interlocking of certain therapist and client dynamics. At those times the therapist's anxiety is intricately interwoven into the interpersonal context of that relationship and into the dynamics underlying that interaction. As such, the therapist's anxiety has some dynamic value to the client. To assess its effects on the relationship, therefore, that anxiety must be viewed in the context of the interaction and in relation to the client's dynamics and motivations. If assessed in those regards, the therapist's reactions will have a determined, predictable impact on the relationship.

In its most extreme form, the therapist's and client's interaction might represent a neurotic interaction in which both client and therapist are engaged in living out together different but interlocking facets of the client's and therapist's conflicts. It could be hypothesized further in this regard that if the therapist's and client's interactions serve some mutually satisfying but neurotic dynamic purpose in which a minimum of anxiety is experienced, or if the anxiety that is experienced is utilized in the service of the neurotic interaction, then the likelihood of change is minimal. The relationship will continue to recycle through the same interpersonal reaction patterns with no relief.

Viewed from the perspective of the therapist's behavioral response to his experience of anxiety, the effects on the relationship are determined by the neurotic or therapeutic character of the therapist's reaction to the client following the stimulation of anxiety. Insofar as the therapist misrepresents the meaning of his anxiety or is unable to track it appropriately, his ensuing reactions are likely to be irrational responses to the client's stimulation. And, when the therapist's reaction is a neurotic one, questions must be raised about the extent to which the therapist and client are engaged in a neurotic interaction that is mutually satisfying.

If the therapist and client are locked into a neurotic interaction, then circularity in the relationship is predictable. With the activation of his irrational processes and countertransferring attitudes, the therapist has vacated the therapist's chair. Instead of *using his understanding as a guide to his participation*, the therapist has *substituted* participating for understanding. Further, that participation is based on the therapist's unconscious motivation to gratify his own unmet needs and to resolve his own conflicts through the relationship. Essentially, the therapist and client have become clients together without the services of anyone to bring the neurotic interaction under ego mastery.

The Effects of the Therapist's
Anxiety: Some Complex Issues

Some of the subtleties and complexities of the issues involved in how the therapist's anxious reactions can affect process might be demonstrated by a brief example. For illustrative purposes, suppose that after many sessions together, an attractive female client verbally assaults her male therapist for being incompetent. The client contends in an intensely feeling way that she feels no better than she did at the outset of therapy, that the therapist had indicated that he thought he could help her, that she had taken his "promise" to heart, and that she is now angry with herself for having been so credulous.

That emotional outburst of the client, despite its strong negative emotional valence, is in itself a neutral condition with regard to any predictions about how it will affect the therapeutic process. Whether that moment of experience in that therapeutic relationship will contribute to facilitating or inhibiting the growth of the client depends upon the therapist's reaction to the client's outburst.

A therapist will experience many internal affective and cognitive reactions to an outburst such as the one described, all of which will interact to provide the complex basis for determining whether the therapist's response to the client will be productive. In the next chapters, the complex effects of those many diverse experiences as they affect and are reflected in the dynamics of the interaction will be considered more fully. In this section, however, consideration is given mainly to the effects on the change process of the occurrence of anxiety in the therapist.

The Gradient of Anxiety

The therapist might be taken somewhat aback by the client's hostility. No one likes having his competence attacked and most therapists would be somewhat jarred by the experience. If they were not, one might question whether they were being therapeutic since to be unaffected by such an outburst must mean that the therapist's defenses against affect are working overtime. So the therapist, in his humanness, is apt to reflect his inner reaction with some outward sign of the attack's having registered.

As an aside, even that reaction is likely to have latent if not immediate effects on the therapeutic process depending upon the client's motivation underlying the outburst. If the client had perceived her therapist's behavior toward her as stereotyped and unfeeling and was motivated by curiosity about whether she or her therapist were human, the client, in her hypersensitivity, would note his slightest reactions. If the client, for example, had come from a long line of stone-faced, unresponsive parents and siblings, she might really not know whether she is able to influence people, whether she can affect a significant person. In that event, even the slightest gesture on the therapist's part that the attack had registered might provide the client with some optimism about her own humanness, which in itself might be a very therapeutic event for her.

But to return to the gradient of anxiety, if the client's behavior blocks the therapist's capacity to note dynamic connections between the outburst and the concomitant and antecedent conditions of the relationship and the more general dynamic processes at work in the client, then the therapist's anxiety is apt to inhibit progress. If the therapist reacts with more intense anxiety, he is apt to focus on his own internal processes and forget about the client. The therapist might, for example, react to his anxiety with fantasies about his competence or by becoming angry at the recalcitrant client. If the therapist does so, then processes are set into motion which alter the neutral conditions of the outburst in the direction of inhibiting change. As the therapist in fantasy reviews his successful cases, the client is apt to suffer. Preoccupied by his reverie, the therapist will be able neither to learn about what motivated his anxiety nor to observe the client.

While the therapist is "licking his wounds," the client is likely to be behaviorally and perhaps even verbally revealing significant information about her motivations for the assault and even more significant information about how she reacts to injured men. She might be apologizing, she might be posturing uncomfortably, she might be near tears, or she might be flashing with anger. She might be internally gloating or regretting. Unless the therapist can get back "into tune" fast with what is transpiring, he will have missed much that could otherwise provide a context for understanding and furthering the change process.

The therapist's anxiety, then, can lead to internal focusing and compensatory behavior which limits his capacity to observe and understand. Solely in terms of the gradient of anxiety experienced, a productive response to the client is inhibited in direct relation to the intensity of the experience of anxiety. Operationally, anxiety is facilitative insofar as it mobilizes the therapist's perceptiveness; it is inhibiting insofar as it interferes with his noting dynamic connections and causal relationships.

If anxiety heightens the therapist's perceptiveness, he is apt to attempt to understand his client's behavior by studying the convergence on that behavior of several tributaries which provide the dynamic basis for the client's response. Said another way, behavior is an expression of and a reaction to some inner experience. And a therapist always attempts to assess the meaning of any given behavior in terms of *the dynamic functions it serves* at the moment of its occurrence in the life of the client. That assessment necessitates studying the convergence on that behavior of a number of factors which contribute to its expression. From an assessment of those factors, the therapist is in a better position to understand the dynamic functions that the behavior serves.

The therapist will wonder, for example, what the behavior represents in terms of what is happening in the client's current life outside of therapy. He will wonder what the behavior means in terms of conflict in the client's longer history of interpersonal relationships. And, he will wonder what the behavior means in relation to him, the therapist. In that regard, the therapist will reflect on what has transpired in the session itself during the moments immediately preceding the client's reactions. And he will similarly reflect on the possible latent effects of interactions in previous sessions that might have contributed to the build up of the client's feelings.

In that assessment, the therapist will study the therapeutic interaction both as to its reality features and to the potential transference manifestations which might affect the client's reactions. Contrariwise, the therapist will reflect on his own conscious feelings about the client and will open himself to the question of whether his own feelings about and reactions to the client contain some irrational elements. In the main, he will question whether he and his client are locked into some neurotic interaction.

The Interlocking of Therapist
Anxiety and Client Motivation

Whether the therapist is able to conduct such a many faceted exploration into the meaning of his client's behavior is determined in part, then, by the intensity of the anxiety that he experiences in relation to his client's outbursts. But, as was already implied in the sample reactions presented, the client's motivation and life experiences interlock with a therapist's anxiety and contribute to the effects of that anxiety on the change process.

For example, suppose the client's remark caused the therapist to become unduly anxious because hostility makes him anxious; he is simply unable to cope with hostility. How that factor influences the relationship will vary depending upon a number of considerations about the motivational forces underlying the client's hostility, the conditions of the relationship that triggered it, and the client's general life experiences with men who become anxious in the face of her anger.

If the client had been in relationships before where people could not tolerate hostility, where it was suppressed or diverted into other feelings, then when the therapist becomes immobilized by her outburst, he might reinforce the client's feelings about the power of her anger. That is, the therapist's anxiousness might simply confirm what the client's earlier experiences have taught her. She might emotionally surmise that her anger is destructive and withdraw from open confrontation in the future.

In one such case, a client came from a family in which her father was a rather fragile man, both emotionally and physically. Apparently, he was unable to stand up to any of her feelings, anger being one of them. The client apparently had unconsciously associated her father's emotional fragility to his physical stature. For when she dated, she generally searched around for males who fell into the heavyweight class. She probably surmised that if the male was physically strong, he might be able to withstand the powerfulness of her feelings.

In that particular case, the angry outburst in the therapeutic session could have been motivated by wanting to test whether the therapist would react differently than her father did. Any client who feels the surge of intense feelings that are assumed to be destructive because he has been taught that his feelings are volatile, potent, and dangerous, needs to know that the therapist is strong enough to manage those feelings. Such a client must trust that the therapist can sustain himself and, if necessary, control the client because the feelings are experienced as explosive and uncontrollable.

Since the therapist collapsed under fire, it is unlikely that the client will retest the therapist. At future times, if the client continues in therapy, when she feels strongly toward the therapist she might need to blunt the edge of what she says, to alter somewhat the expression of what she is experiencing. That modification of expression doesn't occur because the client feels differently. Rather she withholds, denies, and remains frustrated because her feelings frighten others; they can't be tolerated and they must be excluded from her own interpersonal repertoire. Most importantly, the feelings of anger never get attached to their sources so they can't be incorporated into the total personality. The client is unable to test the limits of her own feelings or her controls. Her anger and other feelings are poorly understood and remain outside of ego control and, when frustrated, the client's feelings build up until they are expressed in explosive, volatile ways.

The complexity of the issues involved in predicting the effects of the therapist's anxious reactions in the relationship might be clarified by reviewing some of the conditions surrounding the occurrence of anxiety in the case just cited. In one respect, the therapist's anxiety to the client's behavior is generalizable beyond the client who was seated with him. Anger in women stimulates anxiety in the therapist; and his client happened to be an angry woman. Solely from the point of view of those dynamics, the effects of the therapist's reactions in the relationship are indeterminate. However, in this case, the therapist's dynamics and those of his client interlock *for the client intended the outburst as a test* of the therapist.

Once that motivation is included in the explanatory system, then predictions about outcome can be increased. For, when the therapist reacted as her father had done, it immediately set into motion processes which countered growth. The therapist's reaction reinforced the client's notions about men and she retreated from further testing. In order to explain the effects in the relationship, the therapist's reactions must be compared with the intentions of the client however unconscious the client's intentions might be is not the issue here. What the effects of a reaction will be, in other words, and how they can be utilized is contingent on some subtleties about the client's motivation underlying her outburst, about the therapist's relation to the client, and about what the therapist behaviorally does with the client's verbal assault.

The Interlocking of Therapist and Client Conflict

The picture becomes even more complicated when consideration is given to cases in which the therapist's anxious reactions are in fact dynamically determined reactions to the therapist's own unacceptable motivations, whether real or assumed, in working with the client. Assume, for example, that the client's verbal assault awakened anxiety in the therapist for reasons that are based in his unconscious seductive motivations with regard to his client.

Ignoring the client's motivation for a moment, suppose the therapist's behavior had been motivated in part by some unconscious need to seduce the client. The therapist might not have experienced his overt behavior as seductive; rather he experienced his efforts as attendant, solicitous, warm, and responsive. Laudatory reactions to a needy client! Yet outside awareness, the therapist was motivated by less altruistic motives. The therapist's relationship with the client was at least in part self-gratifying to some sexual fantasies.

In other but similar cases, the therapist's motivation might be more conscious and mixed. The therapist might want to help the client and might in fact have been doing a reasonably good job. But the therapist might also hold some gratifying conscious sexual fantasies about the client which he feels are inappropriate—unwisely and unrealistically it might be noted, considering his humanness and the therapeutic usefulness of such fantasies.

In either case, when the client verbally assaults the therapist for being unhelpful, for having made "promises" which he didn't keep, for not having followed through, and for her credulousness about men, that attack is certain to trigger anxiety. The attack and its language are simply associatively too close to the therapist's motivation and might be experienced by him simply as guilt or anxiety.

Solely from the point of view of the therapist's dynamics, the effects of the therapist's anxiety in the relationship will vary according to a number of contingencies. If the therapist's motivation was unconscious, the anxiety is likely to be disabling and reactivation might require the help of a colleague. If the motivation was mixed and conscious, then insofar as the therapist can grasp the meaning of his anxiety, he might recover sufficiently to explore the client's motivation for the assault on the therapist's intentions.

In either case, if those feelings activate in the therapist a tendency to respond inappropriately to the client so as to reduce his own anxiety, then he will inhibit progress. If the therapist, for example, attempts to placate or divert the client from exploring the source of her anger because he fears what he will discover about himself, then the therapist through his diversionary tactics inhibits the process of change.

Of course, thus far it has been assumed that the client had little to gain personally from the therapist's anxiousness, from his seduction, or from his immobilization. The fact of the matter is, however, that the therapist's reaction in many cases can be linked to the client's intentions. However unconsciously the client might do it, the intent often is to ensnare the therapist into an interaction which will contribute to inhibiting the exploration of the sources of anxiety and maintain the status quo. In order to examine the interaction of those processes and their more complicating effects on the relationship, it is necessary to reintroduce the way in which the neurotic interaction serves to minimize anxiety in both participants while providing some partial gratification of impulses.

The Neurotic Interaction
and the Recycling Process

At any moment during therapy, an interchange between a therapist and his client might represent one point in a neurotic interaction that has been recycling many times during the course of therapy with slight variations on the same theme. The neurotic interaction serves some useful dynamic functions since it permits the partial controlled expression and gratification of some needs without the experience of undue anxiety in their regard. In the interaction, each partner permits the other some gratification and yet controls the experience of anxiety by instituting behaviors that run counter to the fuller expression of the need, thus holding the partner's anxiety in check.

During the course of a neurotic interaction, it is not implied that the parties of the interaction do not experience anxiety. During the interaction, however, both parties collude in attaching the other's anxiety to inappropriate motivating forces which essentially immediately reduces the anxiety in favor of maintaining the neurotic interaction. So long as the collusion remains mutually satisfying, change will certainly not occur but neither will the relationship terminate. Change cannot occur because the therapist has become totally immersed as a participant and has lost his capacity to "see" what is happening to himself in relation to the client. He is living out his own conflicts through his client, and in those areas of conflict the therapist is as blind as is his client.

For illustrative purposes, let's assume that the client's angry outburst and the therapist's anxious reaction in the case just cited represent one such point in a neurotic interaction. If fully expanded, that interaction might be seen to cycle progressively through several interlocking phases. The client might have presented herself initially as submissive, suggestible, and vulnerable. The essential character of that part of the client's message is a challenge to the therapist as a man. She feels helpless and lets the therapist know that she needs a strong man to rescue her and care for her.

Coupled to that expression of need, however, is a more subtle seductive message which reinforces the challenge because the implication underlying the seduction is that the client tenders herself as the prize for the winner. That part of the message might be expressed obliquely through provocative dress and posturing. In addition, the content of the client's communication, although about matters of her distressed state, might be replete with graphic, symbolic language which betrays the seductive motivation and invites aggressive sexual fantasies in the listener.

That multiple communication might affect the therapist in various ways depending upon the power of his needs, his conflicts about sexuality, and his confusion about masculinity. In this case, let's assume that the therapist is highly susceptible to challenge by women. Dynamically that state of affairs might occur if the therapist holds the fantasy at some level that he can be a pretty masterful figure in the life of any woman. Perhaps he had a challenging mother who poked away at his potency in seductive ways and then backed off when he became responsive and he is acting out his fantasies of mastering her. The point here is not to explore the therapist's dynamics in any detail but simply to note how they might interlock with the client's dynamics and create conditions for the neurotic recycling process.

At any rate, the client's challenge might activate rescue fantasies in the therapist and he might behaviorally react to those fantasies in terms of "coming on as a strong man" in the life of the client. What the therapist is unfortunate enough not to realize at that moment in the interaction is that he has just set himself up for some game sport. Many clients present themselves as submissive and attempt to place the therapist on a pedestal. That, however, is the client's problem. But if the therapist himself *believes* that he is powerful enough to be set onto a pedestal, he will most assuredly be knocked off.

Most submissive clients have lived with pedestal dwellers for a good share of their lives and their anger about their submissive state is submerged and will be felt directly or indirectly in good time. And the therapist who entertains such brittle fantasies about his power over women is particularly vulnerable to the kind of challenge to his potency that the client in this case has set up. For the client, in presenting herself as submissive and needing a strong man is likely to be an iconoclast at heart.

In addition, those fantasies of meeting the client's challenge and providing her with a better life often provide a thin rationalization for the therapist's underlying feelings of power and his seductive motivations. The therapist dynamically can't afford to experience his underlying motives and that fact is what makes him so vulnerable. What the therapist consciously experiences is that he is someone who is about to provide a useful therapeutic experience for the client.

Once, however, the therapist behaviorally reacts to the client's state by being the potent male figure she expressed a need for, once his masculinity is "on the firing line," the client might immediately counter with unbelievably swift and intense hostility. And the therapist finds himself cut off his potent pedestal before he has had a chance to cast himself in bronze.

That phase of the cycle might be enacted with such rapidity that it increases the therapist's confusion about what has taken place. Since the therapist was motivated in part by his own unconscious seductive fantasies and in part by related feelings of power, he might simply experience the client's cutting remarks as anxiety and set about trying to placate his ruffled client.

In his anxiety, the therapist might behaviorally apologize in various ways to the client, thus assuring her through his behavior that he has been rendered appropriately impotent and that she is in control of the relationship. Up to that point in the interaction the client was probably experiencing some rather intense anxiety. But with the controls in her hands, that anxiety is relieved, and the client moves into the ascendance.

Assured that the therapist is impotent, the client might become gracious, submissive, in need of a strong male, and begin behaving seductively toward the therapist again, symbolically offering him his potency. If the therapist experiences relief at the client's recovery and does not challenge the client's motivation or at least recognize that his potency rests in her hands, the cycle will wind up again for a second time around.

During the cycle, both the therapist and client experienced anxiety, but in both cases, the anxiety was misrepresented and was reduced in favor of maintaining the neurotic interaction. By rendering the therapist impotent, the client helped the therapist to control his fantasies, thus relieving him of the burden of what might otherwise be fears about becoming too potent. And the therapist, because it is dynamically important for him to be kept in check, tends to be relieved. But, immediately, the other side of the dynamic kicks in, sets off renewed anxiety, and the therapist has to reprove that he is competent to meet the client's challenge.

On the second cycling, however, if the therapist experiences his castration at all, he might experience it only as anger toward his confusing client. And that anger might then be simply incorporated by him into more aggressive seductive fantasies toward the client, thus contributing to the recycling process. The therapist who continues to recycle with a client who juggles his potency might have had some interesting previous life experiences with seductive-castrating women and his efforts to master the anxiety associated with those experiences might be the motivating force which keeps him locked in with a client who exhibits some of those same characteristics.

THE FOUNDATIONS FOR CHANGE:
A SUMMARY AND PROSPECTUS

Thus far, a number of the dynamic forces which actuate and shape process and contribute to constructive change or its inhibition have been considered. In particular, it has been proposed in this chapter that to understand change, the impact on the change process of a complex of dynamic forces must be viewed in configuration.

It has been proposed that the client's dissatisfaction with his life situation and his experience of anxiety motivate the client to want to change and set the stage for learning. Those motivations, however, remain as fantasies about changing until the therapist reacts constructively to the client. With that reaction the interpersonal context is founded and certain reality dimensions to the relationship are established. Those conditions, based on the therapist's behavioral manifestations of his willingness, interest, and competence reinforce the client's motivation to expand his exploration; they create positive feelings about the therapist; and they provide a partial explanation for the processes of identifying, learning, and growth.

The therapist's competence, therefore, sets the change process into motion but as the exploration of the sources of conflict are undertaken the process is immediately complicated and expanded in new directions. As the exploration of conflict is expanded and deepened, past experiences that have been warded off begin to emerge and anxiety heightens. At that time certain irrational processes are set into motion which provide the basis in therapy for its uniqueness and for facilitating more extensive and more significant change than would be otherwise possible. At the same time that anxiety sets additional constructive processes into motion, however, the heightening of anxiety sets counter processes into motion which tend toward inhibiting change and frustrating the therapeutic goals. Those processes that contradict growth are experienced by the client initially as ambivalence about changing and are expressed behaviorally throughout the course of therapy in one form or another of resistance to the change process.

To explain the occurrence of the irrational processes during therapy, consideration was given to a complex of factors in the client, the therapist, and the therapeutic situation which tend to stimulate such reactions. From the point of view of the client, it was proposed that in respect to areas of conflict clients are still emotionally living in the past. Clients often remain emotionally fixated at the developmental periods where the significant experiences which generated conflict were engendered. And, they tend to have emotional energy attached in fantasy to the persons who provided the emotional context for the conflict laden experiences.

The nature of the exploration into the past interpersonal situations which engendered conflict creates conditions for unmet needs to restrive for expression and gratification. Anxiety reflects the internal pressure of needs whose experience or expression would endanger the client's sense of well-being. As those conflict situations are reawakened as a consequence of the therapeutic work, there is a tendency to relive those experiences in relation to the therapist, figuratively embodying him with the characteristics of past significant persons. At such times the client's tendency is to anticipate reactions from the therapist which are similar to those of significant past figures and to react to those anticipations on the basis of his past experiences.

An additional partial explanation for the activation of irrational processes during therapy was based on considerations about the nature of the therapeutic situation itself. Therapy, since it centers in conflict, is a natural interpersonal context for the reawakening, reexperiencing, and in some cases the reliving of some of those conflicts in relation to the therapist. In addition, the conditions of therapy and the negotiations surrounding it tend in varying degrees to exacerbate a client's sense of dependency and helplessness. And those feelings echo back to the emotional context in which conflict was engendered and further enhance the potential for transference manifestations.

The reawakening, recreation, and reliving of the emotional experiences of the past in the presence of a therapist provides him with a powerful vehicle for effecting constructive change. The manifestations of transference reactions signal proximity to dynamic issues which are central to the conflict. They signal the pressure of needs that are striving for expression. They signal the reworking of conflict situations. They signal efforts on the part of the client to complete fantasies or to master the anxiety that was generated in the initial situation. They alert the therapist to be hypersensitive to the nature of the client's interaction with him, to the dynamic forces that work in the client, and to the client's predictions about the outcome of the interaction.

The irrational components of the relationship and their importance in effecting change vary in manifestation and importance depending upon the nature of the conflict, the stage of therapy, and the extensiveness of the exploration necessary to free the client of his conflicts. But all conflict embodies elements of the past; so it might be expected that transference reactions will characterize in varying degrees all therapeutic relationships. The use to which a therapist puts those manifestations will vary with different theoretical orientations. In that regard, it was proposed that the principal consideration in determining whether those processes can be useful in effecting constructive change is based in whether the therapist acts in full knowledge of their occurrence or is unaware of their presence because of his own anxiety.

In this chapter, no attempt was made to study the way in which a therapist might utilize the irrational reactions of his client in ways which could provide a therapeutic experience for the client. The therapeutic usefulness of such irrational reactions and transference manifestations is significant enough so that a separate chapter will be devoted to expanding some of the features of those reactions as they are manifest in the therapeutic session as well as in the general life experiences of the client outside of therapy.

The purpose of this chapter was to delineate some of the critical components of the processes which provide therapy with a rich and unique foundation for effecting significant change. As in the last chapter, case material was introduced to highlight issues and at such points the reader was given a brief prospective glimpse of the process in action. But the introduction of such material was provided mainly to clarify more complex features of process. No concerted effort has been made thus far to study the way in which a therapist might set about providing his client with a therapeutic experience.

In succeeding chapters, that perspective will be inverted. Case material and the therapeutic interaction will become the natural focus for understanding the way in which a therapist attempts to provide his client with help in changing. The concepts presented in this chapter and preceding ones will be reintroduced as they bear on the therapeutic work and provide a framework for organizing material in order to understand the dynamics of the interaction. But, within those general organizational limits, the reasoning will as often be inductive, with hypotheses often generated from concrete analyses of the interaction itself.

Part II

THE DYNAMICS
OF THERAPEUTIC
INTERACTIONS

4

Guidelines to the Therapist's Participation in the Change Process

In previous chapters, consideration has been given to the foundations for change through therapy. In those chapters, some of the dimensions of therapy which provide the unique potential for effecting significant change have been viewed in broad outline. But, thus far, no concerted effort has been undertaken to convert that potential for change into action, to observe the client struggling with his conflicts, to follow the unfolding of conflict through therapy, or to study the work of the therapist as he interacts with a client in his efforts to help the client to effect constructive change in his life.

The material of this section will center in those struggles of the client and the work of the therapist as they negotiate a relationship that intends to be therapeutic for the client. Whereas the earlier part of the book centered in the components and bases for change through therapy, this section will focus on the dynamics of change. And the most natural focus for understanding the dynamics of change through therapy is the therapeutic interaction.

Case material will receive increasing prominence throughout this section since only through careful analysis of such material can the dynamics of therapeutic interactions be fully appreciated. When excerpts of cases were previously introduced, their introduction was more or less incidental to the clarification of concepts. Although case material will continue to serve that clarifying function, its introduction will often serve to generate hypotheses, principles, and guidelines about the processes by which therapeutic gains can be effected.

At times in this section, attention will be centered principally on the client. At other times, the therapist and his work will predominate. In some cases, brief excerpts of therapeutic interactions will often provide sufficient stimulation and act as a springboard for discussions about how conflict develops, is experienced, expressed, and resolved through the interpersonal context of a therapeutic relationship.

In other cases, more extensive excerpts or repeated intrusions into the therapeutic progress of particular clients will provide a better opportunity to abstract principles and clarify concepts. And, in either case, it will be necessary at times to undertake some extensive excursions into the family backgrounds and general life experience of clients in order to demonstrate the varying effects of those preconditions on the client's reactions to and anticipations about therapy.

In this chapter, an attempt will be made to observe the therapist as he searches for guidelines to his participation in the emotional life of his client. We will follow the therapist as he looks around the interview, studying where he looks and why he looks as he does; and we will note the ways that he acts on what he finds and some of the consequences of those actions. As we pursue his thought process, we will also follow his feelings, noting the way in which he utilizes his feelings and experiences for the client's benefit.

As we follow the therapist's thoughts in working with a client, we will take note of what he listens for, how he associates, analyzes, synthesizes, and when and why he interprets. As this chapter evolves, the many avenues to understanding clients that have been described earlier will be reintroduced, but they will be included as they naturally emerge and bear on the work of the therapist, influence the change process, and affect and are affected by the nature of the relationship and character of a particular client's conflicts.

The emphasis in this chapter will be on the general searching process that the therapist undertakes as he attempts to understand and help his client. Brief excerpts from an early and later interaction of a therapist and his client will provide a partial basis for generating some hypotheses and enunciating some of the principles which undergird and guide the searching process. Whereas in this chapter an attempt is made to provide an overview of the way that a therapist works, the content of the next chapter, a companion chapter, will consist of the careful expansion of several facets of that searching process. In particular, the material of the next chapter will be developed around the way in which the therapist searches for associations and behavioral parallels which link the therapeutic hour with the generating and sustaining sources of conflict as they are reflected in the client's past and current interpersonal relationships.

In the first part of this chapter, some general considerations which guide the therapist's searching process are briefly discussed. Following that brief introductory material, the dimensions of the searching process are clarified through a fairly extensive analysis of two brief fragments of case material taken from an initial and later therapeutic session with the same client. During the case analysis, the various avenues to understanding clients that were discussed in earlier chapters are reintroduced as they bear on and are reflected in the work of the therapist.

GUIDELINES TO THE THERAPIST'S
PARTICIPATION: AN INTRODUCTION

Throughout therapy, the therapist's understanding is his guide to participating. Understanding in this regard doesn't mean that the therapist knows what the client's conflicts are all about, how he got those conflicts, or how they can be resolved. At the outset of therapy, that understanding might be so simple as seeing some associative link in what the client says. At times the therapist's understanding means that he understands the feeling that the client is having. At other times the therapist's understanding might be much more complex. The therapist might be able to note an entire configuration of events from the client's earlier life that are being replayed in parallel fashion during his current interactions or within the therapeutic session.

At times the therapist's understanding is generic as might occur when he notes relationships between what the client says and what the therapist's professional experiences have taught him that such behavior is likely to represent. The therapist's understanding might arise from a good memory about the content of earlier interactions as they bear upon the client's experiences and interactions during later interviews. At times, the therapist reacts to some experiences with his client and only in retrospect understands them. At yet other times, the therapist's understanding precedes the client's experience and provides the stimulus for that experience.

The therapist doesn't develop an understanding of his client and then proceed "to do" therapy; rather understanding occurs if the relationship is developing. And as the relationship develops, the therapist conveys his understanding. Throughout therapy there is a constant flow between the therapist's experiencing, understanding, and participating. The therapist participates because he understands, and he experiences and understands because he has participated. His experience provides him with deepening understanding, and that understanding provides guidelines for participation at deeper levels. That interlocking process continues to spiral along throughout therapy and interlocks with the client's experiences, emotional insights, and growth. With each moment of interaction, with each experience with the client, the therapist deepens his understanding of the client. And that deepened understanding provides the therapist with the opportunity for participating with the client at a deeper and more idiosyncratic level.

THE SEARCHING PROCESS:
SOME GENERAL GUIDELINES

To participate meaningfully in the change process, the therapist must know how conflict is experienced and expressed in the current life of his client; he must know something of its origins and history of development, and he must know how it carries over and relates to the client's reactions in the therapeutic hour. Those are essential understandings which gradually develop over the course of therapy and provide the therapist with a sound basis for his continuing and deepening participation in the change process.

Throughout therapy, there is an intricate interlocking of the client's experiences in therapy with his experience and expression of conflict in his daily life and with the reawakening of earlier conflict-laden experiences. What the client reveals of himself and how and why he does so is influenced by his perceptions of the therapist and their relationship. In turn, what transpires in therapy influences the client's experience of conflict, generates intense feelings, and heightens anxiety in his daily life. As feelings build, past experiences are reawakened. And as they are awakened, they influence the client's reactions to and interactions with the therapist.

It is from an understanding of that dynamic interrelationship as it develops during therapy that the therapist is guided to participate in ways that tend to be therapeutic. Throughout therapy the therapist constantly looks at the communication of the client with several directions in mind. He looks at that communication in terms of what is going on currently in the life of the client as revealed by what he says, does, or fantasizes. He looks at what those emotional reactions reveal of his developmental history and the sources of conflict. And then he looks at what the client's communication means in relation to himself, the therapist, and most particularly, he wonders why the client reacted as he did at that moment during the session.

The therapist listens to the client's spontaneous associations, attempting to note links between what is transpiring in therapy, what transpired in the client's past, and what is transpiring outside of therapy. He looks for clues, for links, for causal relationships, for latent meanings which suggest the heightening of anxiety and feelings, and he constantly keeps in mind that the clues to the meaning of the communication can be determined only if they are approached in the context of their occurrence in the current session and in relation to other sessions that he has had with the client.

The client's communication to the therapist is often provided within the context of nonverbal behavior and symbolic meanings which complement or contradict the content of what is being discussed. To understand the client's communication, the therapist must look at it in terms of whether the client is "acting out" behaviorally some unsaid or unacceptable facet of conflict while denying the conflict verbally. And he must study the symbolic as well as the logical, syntactic meanings of the communication, noting the ways in which the client might through symbolization compress and wall out affect, thus permitting an anxiety-free representation of conflict.

In order to understand his client, the therapist moves freely between the client's present conflicts and their generic causes. As the therapist searches through the interview in an effort to understand his client, he looks for associative links between the client's past conflicts and his present interactions. And as he notes those links, the therapist searches for parallels in the emotional conditions of the interpersonal patterns of the client's current interactions as compared to those of the past. Those parallels often reveal points where emotional energy is still bound up with significant past figures. Not only do those parallel features of conflict suggest the emotional reliving of the past but they provide the therapist with foresight into the potential later reenactment of those conflicts in his presence with the therapist as a principal in the interaction.

The therapist assumes that whatever transpires between himself and the client will have immediate as well as latent effects in the interviews and that the content of earlier interviews might well be the experiential basis of the intensive interactions of later interviews. And so the therapist sometimes stores information and remains alert to the potential later reintroduction of the same material under more affective and anxiety-laden conditions. In this regard, the therapist assumes that as conflict generates and feelings build, the client's spontaneous associations to the emotional conditions of his extratherapeutic interactions will be increasingly related to, stimulated by, and an index of his perceptions of the emotional conditions in his relationship to the therapist and their interactions. Through those spontaneous associations, the therapist learns how the client dynamically links together the therapeutic hour with his current life outside of therapy and with his general life experiences.

The therapist listens for discrepancies between what the client anticipates, predicts, and perceives in relation to him, and what the therapist himself is experiencing in relation to the client. In those irrational reactions, the therapist knows there reside critical features of the conflict that must be encountered and that if encountered appropriately a significant hurdle in therapy will be overcome. The therapist also knows that those discrepancies between his feelings and intentions and the expectations of the client mean that he has become a significant enough figure in the life of the client so that he can provide the client with an experience that is comparable in emotional valence to the original disabling experience. And, if properly approached, that moment in therapy can provide the client with the opportunity for substituting new learning for that which is disabling.

As the therapist searches around the interview for guides to his participation, he uses his own personal experiences in relation to the client. Insofar as the therapist is able to grasp the meaning of what he experiences in relation to the client, he has deepened his understanding of his client, for in accurately assessing his reactions he can infer some things about the stimulus value of his client. And he can then explore the client's motivations with him, what the client hopes to gain, and how his stimulation might work to reduce anxiety and preclude changing.

At times during therapy, the therapist might consider the client's reactions to him irrational with regard to his own feelings and intentions, but without careful examination of his own feelings he cannot abandon the hypothesis that the client might actually have picked up accurately some of the therapist's feelings and attitudes toward the client. Although the therapist might sense that the client's perceptiveness about those attitudes and feelings is exaggerated by the client's hypersensitivity or by some neurotic needs that are served by that sensitivity, the reality aspects of the reaction must be recognized and differentiated from the client's irrational reactions.

To understand his client and to participate meaningfully in the change process, then, the therapist must view his client's communication in terms of its interpersonal meaning with regard to himself and to what has transpired in their relationship in the immediate past and in the longer history of their interaction, with regard to what it reveals of the generic conflict, and with regard to its meaning in the client's present life situation. Unless the communication is viewed in the context of the therapeutic relationship as well as in relation to its overall meaning in the history of the client and in his relationships outside of therapy, the potential usefulness of that communication for therapeutic purposes will be limited.

THE SEARCHING PROCESS:
A BRIEF CASE EXCERPT

Before proceeding to an expansion of some of the specific ways in which the therapist looks around the interview for guidelines to his participation, it might be useful to study the way in which the generalized searching process works. Such a general baseline can provide a useful framework for understanding some of the specifics of the therapist's work to be discussed in the next chapter. A brief case excerpt might provide sufficient stimulus for applying some of the concepts described in the preceding section and for deriving some general principles which guide the therapist's search for the meaning of his client's conflicts.

During the first few moments of his initial interview with a young adult male client, the therapist listened to his client describe some of the frustrations that brought him to the therapist's office. The client seemed to have spent much of his life feeling frustrated and angry. On the one hand, the client wanted "to be someone who was respected and influential," but those wishes were countered by fears about acting on any of his fantasies.

At times the client felt very creative, but he always found an extensive set of reasons why his ideas were probably inadequate. At one time, the client was tempted to seek election for a student leadership role, but never carried out his desire. And the client proceeded to recite a list of reasons why he could not have carried out the responsibilities of office. He said he hesitated to make his opinions known or to have his impact felt. He feared that if he acted on what he felt, his convictions would alienate others. And, at any rate, he contended, he knew himself well enough to know that he would not be able to "stick to his guns" in the face of opposition.

The client felt that those who took leadership roles invited jealousy and that if he started asserting himself, "running the show," and "pushing his weight around," others would become jealous and in the process he would be badly "squelched." The client's anger at that point became evident but disappeared as rapidly. And then the client immediately commented that he found university life boring and resented his "student" status. He wanted to be established; yet the client felt that there was too much work involved and said that there was little likelihood that he would "amount to anything" anyway.

In his actual interaction with peers, the client said he stifled his own impulses to assert himself or "render" opinions. He felt that to maintain his friendships he needed to comply with the wishes of others even though his own convictions were to the contrary. He felt that his friends took advantage of him and his generosity, that they made him the butt of their jokes and had little regard for his feelings and opinions. He always ended up like a "doormat." Caught between his own wishes and fears, the client was often left feeling frustrated, angry, and helpless.

As the client talked, the therapist listened for the rise and fall of feelings as different facets of conflict were introduced. He noticed that the client's interest seemed to heighten as he talked of some of his own creative ideas; but he also noted that the client quickly flattened the affect and became rapidly and increasingly self-depreciating. At that point, the therapist wondered whether the client was disposed to reduce his own potency before giving others a chance to emasculate him. As a related question, the therapist wondered what occurred in his interactions with others that generated feelings of being rejected. How much were those feelings of rejection misperceptions based in the client's own internal fears about the consequences of having his real feelings known? And how much were they the actual consequence of setting up his relationships so that others would reject him or assist him in the emasculation process?

In that regard, the therapist wondered how deep the frustration, anger, and resentment ran that he glimpsed only briefly. And the therapist checked his own reactions to the client at those moments. He certainly felt the client's anger for a brief moment. But he had also gotten a first "feel" for the strength underlying the flattened, fearful exterior. For he experienced a fleeting glimpse of the client's constructive reactions and potency when the client's interest rose during his discussion of his creative urges and ideas.

The therapist also listened to the idiomatic expressions and graphic language that liberally intruded into the client's speech. Much of the language had a hostile ring to it; "sticking to his guns," "pushing his weight around," "rendering" opinions, "running the show," being "squelched," and ending up like a "doormat" had the flavor of someone who was set for battle and who feared reprisals.

The therapist listened for links that might provide underlying continuity and make the behavioral manifestations of conflict dynamically sensible. In his running commentary of his difficulties, the flow of the client's thoughts was revealing of some potential underlying dynamics. The progression of the client's associations as he described his conflicts not only supported the hypothesis that the client's fantasies of being influential were mixed with hostile components and fears of retaliation but suggested an additional hypothesis as well. From "running the show" and "pushing his weight around," the client spontaneously introduced thoughts about the jealousy of others who would tend to squelch him. Then the client immediately introduced the fact of his being bored with university life and concluded with the comment that he would not "amount to anything." In general, it seemed that the client tended to flatten his own affect, to emasculate himself in order to avoid being vulnerable to castration.

All of those thoughts and reactions were experienced by the therapist during those first moments. But they were simply hunches, fleeting glimpses, and a first brush with the person who was seeking his help. Whether and how his impressions would eventually emerge and affect their relationship, what observations and hunches would eventually be confirmed or rejected, how significant those impressions would be to the emotional life of the client, and how he could help the client, the therapist was uncertain of.

When the client finished recounting his problems, the therapist suggested that some of his conflicted feelings might have their sources in the past and that since he had heard little about the family, perhaps such an exploration might be useful. The therapist had no desire to allow the past to predominate the sessions, but the client had presented enough information about his current interactions so that the therapist thought that some associations to the past might prove useful.

First Things First: Dynamic Considerations Take Precedence

The therapist soon learned more about his client than any extensive discussion into the problematic encounters with parents, teachers, or siblings could have provided him. For the client's reaction to the therapist's suggestion was immediate. With a passion that was not previously evident in his rather uninspired recounting of his problems, the client contended that his family had nothing to do with his feelings, that he had come to see the therapist because he was having problems in his current relationships, that he wanted to settle those matters, and that they were the problems, not his family.

No sooner had the client encountered the therapist than he reversed his position by saying in a rather compliant way that he supposed that his family really had a great deal to do with the way he felt and that he just didn't like looking at their role in his feelings. Then he commented as an aside that he guessed that he was just frustrated with the thought of "how long it would take" to get the story told and asked the therapist rather docilely what he would like to know about his family.

If the therapist construes the client's initial resistance to exploring the past as *defensive* and accepts the client's compliance at its face value as suggesting a cooperative client rather than to view the *compliance as defensive*, then the therapist will have missed an opportunity to set the therapeutic processes into motion. For if the therapist operates on the hypothesis that the client resisted exploration for defensive reasons, then he might proceed to pursue the generic sources of conflict. And for dynamic reasons which will be suggested later, such an exploration under the existing conditions of the relationship will yield little that is immediately therapeutic and directly relevant. The material that emerges might be significant but its significance will be in its symbolic representation of the client's frustration with the therapist.

An alternative hypothesis, that the compliance is defensive, is a much more viable hypothesis and one that can yield some immediate therapeutic gains. The client's reaction to the therapist embodied significant features of the client's dynamics at work. Embedded in what the client had already revealed of himself behaviorally, verbally, and through his spontaneous associational process were clues to the meaning of what had been behaviorally just enacted by his client. The client's assertive, angry reaction and his immediate retraction was the behavioral enactment in the therapist's presence of what the client lived out in his life with his peers and authority figures.

For just a brief moment, the client had acted out, in the first few minutes of therapy, his strivings, his ways of coping with anxiety, and his frustrated feelings about being placed in a submissive role. Essentially, the client emasculated himself for his bold confrontation before the therapist had a chance to "cut him down" for being so aggressive. And, insofar as the therapist grasped the rapidly fleeting and ambivalent but assertive reaction and the immediate defensive counter to the anxiety that the angry outburst must have triggered, he is in a unique position to facilitate the therapeutic process. For he has experienced the conflict first hand with himself as a participant.

Placing Exploration of the Past in Perspective

How the therapist reacts to that initial encounter is critical. Any further exploration of the history of conflict at that point in therapy is secondary to other considerations. What has been behaviorally enacted in the therapist's presence takes precedence over any further information gathering for a number of reasons. In general, exploration of the past at that moment during therapy is dynamically unsound and works against several major therapeutic goals.

Perhaps the most significant reason why pursuing the past is dynamically unsound is that such a pursuit, under conditions of the client's complying with the therapist, reinforces the client's submissiveness and places him in an inappropriate dependent role. The dynamic consequence is to aggravate the submissive-dependent reaction, thus frustrating growth rather than facilitating it.

To digress for a brief moment it might be noted that, throughout the course of therapy, the therapist's participation is guided by an overriding principle about his participation. At all times the therapist's participation is motivated by the long-range goal of assisting the client to become increasingly independent of his need for his services. It is to that end that the therapist places all his personal and professional resources at the disposal of the client. It is to that end that he allows himself to become a highly significant person in the life of the client since only under those conditions will the client risk experiencing what has been traumatic and relearn ways of behaving that are more productive. And it is to that end that the therapist permits the client's dependence on him and identification with him insofar as that dependency and identification are the necessary and natural preludes to growth of the client. And in many cases the process of change is contingent on an intense relationship that is characterized by a period of emotional dependency as the client regresses in order to progress.

But that dependency is the healthy antecedent to growth. It is the natural state of relying on another for as much help as is needed to develop. Dependency becomes a problem in therapy when it is inappropriately nurtured at times when anxiety must be faced or at critical points where the client's emotional development is frustrated because the therapist needs the client to depend. At such times the therapist has reversed the roles for, in needing the client's dependency on him, he has become the dependent one.

Paradoxical as it might seem, throughout the course of therapy, the therapist works to reduce the client's need for him. If therapy is to be successful the client must become increasingly self-reliant, increasingly in less need of the therapist, increasingly motivated and able to search out the meaning of his own anxiety. The goal of therapy is to provide a solid emotional foundation on which to build. But the building is the creative work of the client and continues throughout life. If successful, the therapist will have provided the client with guidelines for how to search through his own processes for meaning so that he can continue to grow and expand the search beyond termination.

In this case, the therapist already knows from what the client has told him that he will react with resentment and anger—as anyone would—at being placed in a subordinate position. And that is precisely the position that the client would be placed in if the therapist proceeded to explore the past with a "compliant" client whose assertiveness was blocked by anxiety as this client's apparently is. The therapist would soon find, however, that the client, although outwardly compliant, is not so compliant underneath.

If a therapist exacerbates resentment and anger in a client whose submissive, dependent reactions are defenses against the dangers of being aggressive, he will find that such a client is generally quite clever at finding indirect ways of expressing that resentment. A client who has had to work underground for years to get his aggressiveness expressed without being caught at it can think of many clever ways of handling those who stifle his impulses. In this case, the potential for that indirect expression of aggression is already smoldering in the client's submissively phrased question to the therapist when he asked what it was the therapist wanted to know about his family.

In that question is a not too subtle shift in responsibility for therapy. And the therapist might discover in the not too distant future that he is exhausted from hard work while his client seems increasingly relaxed. The critical feature of that shift in responsibility is that a major goal of therapy—to facilitate the internalization of conflict as a first step and the only possible avenue to significant change—is thwarted.

The therapist might find that as they search for causes of the client's conflicted feelings little is found that is helpful. But passive resistance is only one avenue to frustrating a therapist. A more resourceful client who has had a particularly frustrating parent might take particular glee in thwarting the therapist by supplying him with mountains of meaningless data, all guaranteed to confuse and frustrate. And in the process, the therapist who nurtures submissive clients is apt to find them "acting out" all over the place, bringing in the news of their exploits, and literally driving the therapist "up the wall" attempting to control what he can't possibly control unless he catches the defiance and learns about the ways that he has nurtured it.

A third consideration is that if the therapist ignores the assertive side of the client's message, the therapist will be reenacting the counterpart of those who the client feels ignored his feelings, thoughts, and opinions. And the client— admittedly in an ambivalent, fleeting way—expressed the opinion that his family was not his most important concern of the moment. If the therapist pursues the generic sources of conflict because he has missed that message or chooses to ignore it, then he will become a participant in the problematic interactions. Essentially, he will be acting as though the client's feelings don't count in therapy any more than they do on the outside. And as such the therapist will symbolically represent those against whom the client rebels.

The client will inevitably identify the therapist with those who set the pattern in motion. And so long as the therapist is identified with those who ignore or discount his feelings, the client cannot dynamically afford to provide the therapist with anything that he perceives as useful. To supply the therapist with usable information when he isn't trustworthy or sensitive to the client's feelings essentially amounts to providing someone with the tools to complete the client's castration. No doubt the client will provide the therapist with content all right—but the nature of the content might be surprising to the therapist! The symbolic as well as manifest meaning of the content that a client provides at critical moments during therapy is one of the most interesting dimensions of therapy and will be expanded later.

For the several reasons cited, an immediate exploration into the past is likely to delay rather than facilitate the therapeutic processes. In all probability, that search will eventually become a critical feature of the change process. And, in the next chapter, the purposes, method, and therapeutic usefulness of studying the generic sources of conflict and linking those sources to their current manifestations will be discussed. But the point at this time has been that serious consideration must be given to issues about when, why, and how that exploration occurs.

The Internal Process in the Therapist: Responding at a Dynamic Level

Before proceeding to the way that the therapist chooses to respond, it would seem worth taking some time to follow the intervening internal process that a therapist might engage in as he attempts to reconstruct the dynamic interchange in his client which contributes to and perpetuates the manifest expression of conflict. ⁀Throughout therapy, the therapist constantly attempts to construct what is occurring in his client at that moment and as it relates to what has gone before. Only through such a continuous process of tentatively hypothesizing and constantly reassessing the meaning of conflict on the basis of deepening understanding can the therapist flow along with the client and facilitate his bringing into awareness those features of conflict which are submerged and perhaps nearing awareness.

Unless the therapist's reactions are based on some well-founded but flexible internal constructs against which he compares the client's conflicts, both he and his client might find themselves adrift as therapy deepens, engaged in a recycling of defensive maneuvers, or confusing genuine needs with neurotic satisfactions. Unless the therapist responds sensitively in terms of what he is stirring up in his client, therapy at best becomes a random process and at worst sets the client up for anxious moments that are devoid of any learning potential. The process of internally reviewing, studying, and hypothesizing becomes a problem in therapy only if it becomes an intellectual exercise for the therapist rather than a guide to responding in therapeutic ways, only if the hypotheses are rigidly maintained rather than as a means to organizing what is actually observed, and only if the therapist uses his hypothesizing defensively as a way of avoiding encountering the client at an emotional level or as a substitute for the client's experiencing.

That reconstruction of what is occurring in the client begins at the outset of therapy. Highly tentative as it is at the outset of therapy, those internal constructs provide the therapist with general guidelines to what his response might evoke at a dynamic level in his client. That internal process of the therapist is based largely on prior experience, is often not elaborate, and is not as considered or labored as the next illustrative paragraphs might imply. But for illustrative purposes let us proceed in slow motion through those rapid-fire connections that the therapist makes between the stimulation of the client and his response.

The therapist's response to the client will, of course, vary from therapist to therapist dependent upon how he formulates what has taken place. But, in general, if the therapist has observed the events that have occurred in his presence, has seen the parallel features of that enactment with regard to the client's reports of his current problematic interactions, and has noted the indirect confirmatory evidence for the behavioral cycle from the progression of his client's spontaneous associations, then the therapist is in a position to formulate a most tentative first hypothesis about the dynamic interplay of forces at work in the client which undergird and contribute to continuing conflict.

In its most compressed form, the behavioral cycle that the therapist observed from his client's reactions to him seemed to occur in the following sequence. The client asserted himself but in an angrily aggressive way that betrayed his frustration and resentment. Immediately, the client reacted against his own assertiveness by becoming compliant. The submissive behavioral reaction was then followed by verbalized feelings of frustration.

As a first rough estimate of what occurs dynamically in his client, the therapist might hypothesize that the client's aggressiveness triggers anxiety which sets counterforces into motion which are expressed behaviorally as submissiveness and compliance. Although the self-effacing reaction reduces anxiety, it also thwarts the aggressive strivings, leading to the client's experience of frustration and contributing to the heightening of angry, resentful feelings. Chances are that those feelings of anger and resentment then become incorporated into the client's next encounter, simply exacerbating the conflict since they tend to become linked to and overriding features of the client's assertions, thus clouding the genuine needs with predominantly hostile overtones.

When the therapist expands his observational base to include what he has learned of his client from the flow of his associations and from his reported interactions with others, the therapist can fill in some of the dynamic links in the behavioral cycle that he has observed. In addition, those supporting data provide the basis for additional speculations about what his client experiences, reacts to, defends against, and seeks to satisfy through his behavior.

At the most conscious level, the client feels frustrated and angry. He believes that what he thinks and feels is discounted. Nobody listens to him, he is taken advantage of, and he is the butt of jokes. If those feelings were separated, they might be found to represent both the client's frustrated reactions to his thwarted drives and his defensive maneuvers to avoid the experience and expression of those drives.

On the one hand, what the client seems to experience is the feeling that "I can't make an impact." That is the side of the client that wishes to be influential and that feels inhibited from doing, saying, thinking, or feeling in certain ways that are perceived as dangerous for emotional reasons that are not in the client's awareness. And that feeling at the level of the client's consciousness is the experience of genuine frustration.

Although that frustration is likely to have its roots in past interpersonal experiences which generated the anxiety that endangered the drives and drove them underground, the frustrated feelings are apparently experienced by the client only in relation to those in his immediate environment whom he perceives as inhibiting his expressiveness. It is that sense of being frustrated which tends to generate the feelings of anger and resentment that characterize the client's reactions to others. And it is that frustration which tends to breed the hostile fantasies which are evident from the client's symbolic language.

Those fantasies might be felt as a desire to get back at those whom the client sees as inhibiting him. But however they are experienced, such hostile, retaliatory fantasies serve to exacerbate the conflict by confounding the aggressive motivations with hostile components, thus aggravating the fears of retaliation and castration. The reasons are straightforward. In addition to the client's basic anxiety about being aggressive, the therapist has evidence that the client's frustration has worked to confound his natural tendencies to want to influence others through self-assertion. The client's motivation over time has become confounded with anger, resentment, and retaliatory components.

Such confounding of motivations is likely to have several effects on the client's behavior. The client's own hostile motives are likely to intensify his fears of retaliation. But more importantly, when interwoven with the client's natural strivings to be impactful, those mixed motivations are likely to confuse the client about what he really intends and feels whenever he is assertive. He is apt to equate his needs to assert himself with hostility, thus tightening his creative self-expression all the more.

And, in this case, there is considerable evidence from the client's graphic, idiomatic language, and from the way he girds himself in fantasy for battle that he experiences considerable threat from others. That threat leads to the second set of conscious feelings, the defensive reactions, which are embedded in the client's expression that "nobody takes me seriously." That conscious feeling is likely to be a rationalization for not risking being aggressive. By blaming others for his frustrated state, the client avoids facing his own anxieties. But that rationalization in itself is an insufficient defense to handle the intense threat the client must experience; it is essentially an auxiliary defense which shores up and reinforces the more basic defenses against the perceived dangers.

The basic means that the client uses to defend against fantasized retaliation are evident from his compliant reactions to his own aggressiveness, from his other self-effacing comments, and from supporting rationalizations about being unqualified to conduct himself as a leader. Behaviorally, those defenses are reinforced by still other self-emasculating interpersonal maneuvers. When the client says that he is the "butt of jokes" it suggests that he might arrange his relationships so that he is perceived as the joker, thus avoiding the possibility that anyone would take him seriously.

Some clients who are particularly vulnerable to the threat of castration set up their relationships in ways which encourage others to ignore them or to take what they say lightly. If a client is fearful of being aggressive, he might deliberately take the edge off of his own impact by clowning around. Through such behavior a client can deflect attention from himself as a serious threat to anyone about anything! And through such clowning around, a client can often achieve some partial expression of his anger without too much risk.

If the therapist were to integrate the various observational sources, he might reconstruct the conflict in the following way. There is a basic conflict about being aggressive; there is a secondary conflict that is generated by those frustrated motives which both complicates and perpetuates the basic conflict; and there is a multilevel defensive system which works to protect the client from the experience of anxiety. At this point the therapist knows little about the generating sources of the basic conflict. He knows of it only by inference from the intense threat that the client experiences about assertiveness and from the extreme self-emasculating measures and rationalizations that the client uses to protect himself from attack. Superimposed on that basic conflict is the secondary conflict which is generated by, interlocks with, and exacerbates the basic anxiety about castration. The behavioral cycle, consisting of frustration, anger, resentment, and retaliatory fantasies becomes interwoven with and undifferentiated from the client's basic strivings, thus confusing the client, heightening the castration fears, and further inhibiting the potential for self-expression.

Setting the Therapeutic Process into Motion

At the conscious level, then, the client wants his feelings and thoughts taken into account. That side of the client is the potent side that wishes to push through the blocking anxiety; it is the side that probably brought the client to the therapist. But the evidence from the client's defensive maneuvering at times when he becomes assertive suggests that at a deeper level the client fears being taken seriously and works to reduce his own potency because of the threat of castration. That delicate counterbalancing of the client's wishes against his fears is what keeps him in conflict and also works to maintain a low level of anxiety. Once that balance leaves dead center, then change is potential but the risks of a worsened emotional state are also potential. And that is why the therapist must respond with sensitivity to and awareness of what his response might evoke in his client.

Despite the many variations on the theme of how a therapist might set the therapeutic processes into motion, it might be worth following the thoughts and motivations of a therapist as he pursues one such course of action. It will be recalled that the client aggressively and angrily reacted to the therapist's suggestion that they examine his family's role in his conflicts. The client contended that his family's impact on his problems was secondary to his interests in therapy and that he wished to examine his current relationships. He then quickly retracted his statement that his family had no part in his problems, essentially contending that he had been defensive, and compliantly queried about what the therapist would like to know about his family. Considering the therapist's tentative hypothesis about the defensive character of that compliance, he might simply comment that "Well, perhaps the discussion about your family should wait; it sounded as though something else was more important to you. Perhaps you had other thoughts you wanted to pursue."

In responding as he did, the therapist hopes to accomplish several therapeutic gains. Of crucial importance in getting therapy underway is the need to recognize and counter the client's conscious experience that what he feels and thinks is not taken into account. Through his response the therapist attempts to begin the process of differentiating himself from being identified with those whom the client fights. Unless that differentiation begins immediately, there is little likelihood that therapy will ever deepen sufficiently so that the client will risk exploring some of the deeper, more generic sources of conflict.

Through his response, the therapist attempts to circumvent temporarily the client's anger and resentment that he experiences about those who frustrate his needs, and those needs are consciously experienced—despite the partially defensive character of that experience—as not being taken seriously. What the therapist attempts to avoid initially is becoming enmeshed in the secondary conflict—the frustration-anger-resentment-retaliation cycle.

Such an entanglement could be deadening. Since the secondary conflict could easily become a self-generating cycle, the basic conflict would go untouched and therapist and client might recycle through feelings of anger, resentment, and frustration for many sessions without apparent relief or progress. And with each recycling, the client's fears that the therapist might eventually retaliate for his anger would mount. Undoubtedly the client will become angry and resentful as therapy develops and as his basic strivings reach awareness and his anxiety mounts. But that eventual anger and resentment will be related to the primary conflict and as such will be a productive and a progressive feature of therapy.

Through his response, the therapist also hopes to communicate to the client at a conscious level that he does not value submissiveness in his clients. And at a deeper level, he hopes to convey the message that he does not fear the client's aggressiveness. Essentially, the therapist's response implies the question, "Where did you begin to feel that if you expressed yourself openly, you would get into trouble or be ignored?" But that question is not raised by the therapist, for it might be perceived as a demand to investigate an issue. For this client, such a question would undoubtedly be used defensively, serving only to activate the client's dependent-submissive defenses against the risks of taking the initiative. And in this case, the client's willingness to take the initiative and express what he feels and thinks is—idiomatically speaking—"half the battle."

That is why the therapist phrased his comment as he did. His comment that "perhaps you had other thoughts you wanted to pursue" is not an accidental arrangement of words. Nor is it gamesmanship to see if he can get his client talking. Rather, embedded in the comment is a purposeful first step toward helping the client to learn about his own internal processes, to gain insight into how they work, to learn to trust and value those processes whether thoughts, feelings, impulses, that have been devalued and mistrusted.

What the therapist hopes to avoid by encouraging his client to take the initiative and express what he feels is the defensive compliant reaction that most assuredly will be the generator for anger and resentment. What the therapist hopes to avoid is the client's inappropriate dependence to avoid the anxiety that is generated whenever the client initiates action. What the therapist is very willing to foster is the client's genuine need to find him reliable, to depend on him, and identify with him as necessary in order to face his anxiety and grow.

And, perhaps most importantly, the therapist's response communicates the therapist's feeling that the client's reaction is reasonable, thus setting into motion the process of assisting the client to separate his genuine self-assertive feelings from the hostile components superimposed by the secondary conflict. And that differentiation of the hostile, reactive components from the client's genuine needs for creative self-expression will probably eventually become an essential part of the client's therapy.

The Dynamic Effects of
the Therapist's Response

If the therapist is correct in his surmise that at a deeper level the client fears being understood because it activates castration anxiety, then the therapist's response will stir up two contradictory reactions in the client. On the one hand, the client will be attracted to the therapist because at some level he will recognize that the therapist has taken his feelings into account. He will perceive the therapist as understanding and will have a first glimpse of the therapist's perceptiveness and competence. The client's attraction for the therapist will generate the beginning feelings of reliance on him. The client will begin to depend on the therapist for help. He will experience the thought that "maybe he'll be able to help." And in that sense of attraction is the first step toward identifying with the therapist and being willing to learn from him.

But the therapist's response will also stir up anxiety because of the client's fears of what might happen if he became too assertive. The relationship is still young; the client doesn't know the therapist; trust is often long in coming, particularly if the client's past is replete with punishment. In his anxiety the client will experience some ambivalence about what is yet to come. And the client will have premonitions of greater anxiety in the offing. In addition, since his motivations are confused, poorly understood, and are partially based in hostile intent, the client is likely to fear having himself understood because if someone understood what he was feeling, the client's anxiety about being castrated *would no longer be a fantasy but it would be a real threat*!

And it might be noted as an aside that during therapy, those feelings of *real threat*, however fleetingly they are experienced, are the ones that activate ambivalence in a client about changing because they are at the generating source of intense anxiety. Yet it is only during those moments in therapy when the experience of real threat reaches fever pitch that the client's conflict is brought out into the open. Although the risks are greatest at those moments because the client is most vulnerable, the potential for significant change is at its height. It is at times during the experience of real threat, with all the irrationality and anxiety that accompanies those moments, that a significant therapeutic experience can occur as will be pointed out when an excerpt from a later interview with this same client is introduced.

Before proceeding to a later point in the therapy of this client, however, let us follow the therapist's thoughts about what the client's next immediate reaction to what has transpired thus far might mean. Interestingly enough, following the therapist's response that he was interested in what the client felt and thought and that the exploration of the past could wait, the client responded with heightened interest and spontaneously introduced some emotionally charged material about his interactions with his father!

When considered in the context of the events that had just transpired in the therapeutic relationship, the client's spontaneous introduction of material from his previous interactions with a parent is a complex communication, rich in meaning. Through an elaboration of some of those potential meanings, it might be possible to illustrate the unique processes that characterize the therapeutic relationship and guide a therapist's participation in the change process. In this section, an attempt will be made to clarify the complex meanings and therapeutic issues involved in such communications by following the therapist's thoughts as he attempts to understand the meaning of his client's communication and the import of that communication for his own participation. Using the case analysis as a springboard, an attempt will be made to abstract some general principles about what, how, and why the therapist listens as he does and what he reacts to as material is spontaneously introduced into therapy.

The Meaning of the Communication:
Its Manifest and Latent Content

As the client talked about his past interactions with his father, the therapist listened carefully to the manifest content of what was introduced. The therapist listened to what the client perceived as transpiring in those interactions, how he perceived his father's behavior, interpreted his motivations, and reacted to his own perceptions and interpretations of the situation. The therapist listened for what seemed to arouse anxiety in the interaction, how the client coped with the anxiety, and the means he used to reduce it.

And as he listened to the content, the therapist listened as well to the associated affect as evidenced during the client's discussion of his encounter with his father. He listened for apparent and muted affect. He was interested in the character and quality of the affect; in whether the content was devoid of affect, whether the affect seemed submerged, and whether the affect seemed appropriate when considered within the context of what was being portrayed. As the therapist listened to the content and noted the client's emotional reactions, he observed the client's nonverbal behavior. He observed his client's apparent comfort and discomfort during facets of the discussion. He noticed his client's gesticulations, particularly the freedom and inhibition of his movements as he talked about what had transpired.

As the therapist listened to the manifest content of what the client described and followed the flow of feelings, he listened as well for the latent content of what was being communicated to the father through that interaction. He considered the possibility that the interaction was a vehicle for the symbolic representation of his client's needs. And in that regard, he wondered what the client was attempting to communicate to his father through their interactions that could not be risked by direct expression but needed to be couched in symbolic language. In a more general way, the therapist listened for what the client seemed to be seeking through his interaction, what needs he was attempting to satisfy and how and whether those needs were met, diverted, or thwarted.

And the therapist listened with an ear to the outcome in the emotional life of his client. He wondered about the residual imprint of those interactions in his client's perceptions and predictions about what significant people want, do, expect, and reject. He listened for what the client still sought, wanted, hoped for, feared, failed to get, and still needed. From both sides of the picture—what was sought and what was given—the therapist attempted to approximate what the client was still searching for in regard to the significant people with whom he interacted and what he was attempting to satisfy through his interactions, particularly with regard to the significant male figures in his life.

As the therapist listened to the nature of that interaction he was guided by two overriding principles about the importance of that communication as a guideline to his participation in helping the client. In the first place, the therapist listened to the communication as a general expression of the client's needs. From the latent content, symbolic meanings, and accompanying affect that provided the emotional context of the client's discussion, the therapist had his first real insight into the client's still unfulfilled needs.

And those unfulfilled needs, damaged relationships, and unresolved conflicts are the dynamic links between the emotional life of the client's past and his future interactions with regard to what he needs from the therapist. Since those needs represent the still viable strivings of the client they are the stuff on which therapy will be built. That is one of the reasons why the therapist listens so carefully to the manifest content, and searches so carefully through the material for symbolic and latent meanings. For those unfulfilled needs provide the therapist with a preview of *what* must be reworked with him at a later point in therapy.

Although the manifest content dealt with the client's interaction with his father and that content is important in its own right as will be pointed out momentarily, a primary question with regard to getting the processes of therapy underway is what the communication conveys to the therapist about *what* needs were frustrated and are still seeking expression. By studying the interaction in its broadest emotional context, the therapist begins to sense what his client *is experiencing emotionally in the present* as it relates to his past interactions.

That is a crucial point! The therapist doesn't know what the client actually experienced at that earlier point in his life. At that moment, he doesn't know how much the client's recall is an accurate representation of his father's motivations or perhaps even of real events; he doesn't know how much the client's recall has been influenced by fantasy, by anger, by rejections, or has been elaborated and exaggerated by the client's wishes and fears. At that early point in therapy what the therapist discovers from listening to and observing his client as he talks *is what he is experiencing emotionally at that moment* during therapy when as an adult he looks back over his past!

But that is the essential first step in understanding his client. The therapist must first learn about what his client feels and wants. Only then is the task of learning about what contributed to those feelings and perceptions a relevant one; only then does the past fall into place, making the search for the meaning of conflict a more directed one. From what he communicates to the therapist through his description of that past interaction, the client informs the therapist about what he is still seeking to satisfy as an adult, what disappointments he still carries inside, what anticipations he holds about what will happen if he becomes involved again as he might have been as a child with his father. And from that understanding of what is still sought and needed, the therapist has a first guideline to what his later participation might be as that relationship intensifies!

In the first place, then, the therapist attempts to sense *what* the client needs. But the therapist listens carefully to the client's reported earlier interactions for other reasons as well. He listens to *how* and *why* the client's needs were frustrated. The therapist is vitally interested in the emotional conditions of that relationship since the therapist's experience will have taught him that those conditions are the raw material for the client's later transference reactions, irrational premises, and predictions about what the therapist will do and say if and when those needs begin to be felt and the anxiety provoking strivings threaten expression during therapy.

Whereas the unmet needs provide a link with the past, the manifest content, defensive maneuvering, and general character of those interactions provides the therapist with a guideline to *how* the client might later react to him when those needs emerge. From the content of those earlier interactions, from the way in which the client symbolizes his needs, from the way in which he defended in his interaction, the therapist is provided with guidelines to the *context in which those unfulfilled needs might be reintroduced into the therapeutic relationship.*

The therapist will have learned many times over that the way a client characterizes his father, the motivations he attributes to him, and the frustrations he associates to those significant encounters is the groundplan for his reactions to and anticipations with regard to the therapist. Whereas the content of earlier interactions might have been introduced initially largely devoid of affect, its later emergence is likely to be highly charged and with the therapist as a principal figure in the interaction. Through his early revelations, then, the client alerts the therapist to the emotional conditions that might characterize their later encounters.

The manifest content, then, of what the client reports of earlier interactions, the give and take of those interactions, the way in which anxiety was encountered and coped with, the character and qualify of affect, and the residual effects of that encounter in the client's perceptions of significant males provides the therapist with his anticipation of what he and the client might live through together interpersonally in order to meet the client's needs. The material introduced early in therapy then, when considered within the total emotional context of its presentation, provides the experiential backdrop for some one or another of the client's later encounters with the therapist.

Of course, the therapist realizes that not all of the content of what the client introduces of earlier interactions means that the client will replay those conflicts out in his presence. At times when a client enters therapy he is already living out his conflicts with those in his environment. But, here again, only if the therapist has grasped the significance of that reenactment as a manifestation of the emotional conditions which have been generated in earlier relationships is he in a position to help the client to work through the conflicts and provide him with appropriate support and insight during times of anxiety.

It is not intended at this point to discuss the many variations on the theme of how a client's generic conflicts and his current interactions, both within and outside the therapy hour, can be useful guides for the therapeutic work. The many complexities and subtleties of transference phenomena and irrational reactions as a client lives out his conflicts with whoever is convenient in his environment that he can manage to entrap into helping him to live out, rework, and resolve his conflicts is the subject matter of a later chapter. At this time it is simply proposed that the therapist, in getting the process of therapy underway, listens carefully to the content of what the client communicates for a number of reasons. Thus far, we have examined two of them. The manifest and latent content of that communication provides the therapist with guidelines to *what* the client needs and provides him with a preview of *how* the client might anticipate, project, and attempt to cope with the therapist as he attempts to meet those needs and resolve his conflicts.

The Meaning of the Communication: Introducing Motivational Factors

Thus far, the material that the client introduced has been considered from the point of view of what the client reveals of himself—his unmet needs, his modes of coping with stress, and his reactions to significant persons—through the manifest and latent content of the communication. Understanding the communication in those regards can provide a therapist with much useful information as has already been pointed out in the last section. But unless the therapist goes beyond the actual contentual matter and searches for what motivated the client to introduce the material that he did he has understood only a fragment of what is being communicated.

In a sense the content provides a carrier wave and serves as the conveyance for more subtle client motivations. And once we turn to issues of what motivated the introduction of that material into therapy—and at that moment of therapy—the meaning of the communication is immediately complicated, enlarged, and greatly enriched. A client's motivations for introducing material are subtle and complex and insofar as the therapist can grasp their significance, he greatly enriches his opportunities to understand who his client is, what he wants, and how he can be helped.

In this section, two motivational factors which seem particularly relevant to this case will be discussed. Although the two factors considered here are simply representative of other possible motivations, they will serve to point up the uniqueness of the communication process during therapy. First the potential *defensive functions* served by the client's introduction of material will be considered. And then, the *symbolic meaning* of the material as it relates to the client's experience in therapy and as a representation of his feelings about the therapist and the relationship will be discussed. In both of these representative samples of motivational factors, it will be noted that the content plays a role but the role served is mainly that of a carrier wave for the underlying motivations.

In the first place, as the therapist listened to what the client introduced, he was alerted to the possible defensive functions that the introduction of that material might be serving. In this case, the possibility that the client was defensively motivated is a reasonable hypothesis. It will be recalled that only moments before, the client had actively and aggressively resisted such an exploration into the past but then agreed rather compliantly that his family might be at the source of his conflicts and wóndered what the therapist might think was important to discuss. At that time, the therapist had construed the client's compliant reaction to his suggestion that they pursue the family influences as a defensive reaction to the anxiety that must have been triggered by the client's self-assertive behavior.

And so, when the client within moments of that interchange introduces the past, the therapist must question whether the client's behavior is an avoidant reaction to the anxiety that might be generated from consideration of other issues. And that hypothesis can be discounted only when the evidence to the contrary is carefully weighed. However, the hypothesis that the client is using the family discussion defensively simply because a moment before it was intended to serve that anxiety-reducing function is unwarranted without supporting evidence. To digress for a moment, the temporal dimension in therapy is a highly deceptive guide to a client's progress. At times during therapy, many sessions occur between what might appear to be almost minute steps in the emotional development of a client. And at other times, a brief temporal span might encompass tremendous growth spurts. And so, the therapist must be cautious about interpreting a compressed time span as a reliable measure of emotional change!

To assess the defensive value of the client's behavior, the therapist must look carefully at the way in which the content was introduced, he must note the accompanying effect, and he must place the material within the context of the emotional conditions of the relationship at that moment in time. And, in this case, had the therapist operated on the hypothesis that the client was behaving defensively, it would have been an unfortunate error for reasons that will become clear later. The context in which the client introduced the material argues against defensive motivations. The behavior of the client at that moment of therapy differed significantly from the client's previous compliant attitude. Whereas the past was a defensive maneuver before, its reintroduction followed a significant therapist reaction and therefore might have significantly different meaning. Behaviorally, the client's introduction of material was not done under the conditions of compliance and passivity that characterized his reactions before the therapist's invitation to be more expressive. The context in which the client introduced the material was under conditions of heightened interest, with spontaneity, and with initiative, and those conditions, as will be pointed out in a moment, are anxiety provoking conditions for this client and reveal—not that he is behaving defensively—but, on the contrary, that he is behaving potently!

A second motivational factor that the therapist considers as he listens to the client is what the introduction of that material might *symbolize with regard to the client's feelings about and reactions to the therapist* and to what has occurred in their relationship. In this case the therapist considered the possibility that his client was partially motivated by a wish to "gift him" through the introduction of the past. After all, the therapist had only a moment before suggested the relevance of the past. And then, immediately following the therapist's reaction that he was interested in what the client felt and thought, the client spontaneously introduced past material. In that regard, the content might represent a symbolic gift to the therapist. If so, then the client has provided the therapist with new avenues to understanding and helping him. For in considering that possibility, the therapist must recognize the client's responsiveness to him, and such responsiveness suggests an ease of identification, an eagerness to be accepted, and an underlying nurturance.

That aspect of the client's presentation also would reveal much to the therapist indirectly about the degree of anger and resentment that the client experiences. For if the therapist is correct in his surmise that the client wishes to affiliate and that his presentation of past material is partially motivated by those needs to identify, then the therapist might assume that the client's anger and resentment are not deeply embedded and that the processes of therapy are not likely to be bogged down for many sessions while trust develops.

In the discussion to this point, it has been suggested that the manifest and latent content of what is produced is important in its own right for what it reveals of the generic conflict, as an expression of the client's unmet needs, and as a guideline to the client's expectations about his therapist's reaction to his needs. In addition, it has been proposed that when the therapist takes into account the client's motivations for introducing what he does into therapy—at any particular moment in therapy—the therapist's opportunity to understand his client is enhanced.

Two such motivations—the potential defensive value of the introduction of material and its symbolic meaning as an expression of the client's positive reaction to the therapist—have been cited as representative of the many motivations that might underlie the client's introduction of material. It has not been intended to suggest that these motivations are exhaustive or mutually exclusive. On the contrary, the client's motivations are likely mixed and reflect different facets of his conflicts and his ambivalence about changing. Those motivations were selected because they seemed particularly relevant to the issues in this case.

The material that a client introduces into therapy is multidetermined, and the therapist must look beyond the manifest content of what is introduced if he is to realize fully the intent of the client and the therapeutic usefulness of the client's communication. The manifest content is just a fragment of what the client intends and of what the communication can reveal to the therapist about his client. The therapist must listen for latent and symbolic meanings as well as to the manifest meanings. The therapist must listen to what the client says for what it symbolically reveals of the therapeutic relationship, as well as to its face validity as an historical document. He must assume that the communication represents the product of accumulated affect and heightened feelings from his own interactions with his client as well as from the client's extratherapeutic reactions. And the communication provides the therapist with a predictive base for what the potential character of his future interactions with his client might be. The question that the therapist constantly asks himself when the client introduces anything into therapy is why the client is introducing what he is, why he does so at that moment, and what it means in terms of the therapeutic relationship as well as with regard to the generic conflict and the client's current life problems.

The Meaning of the Communication:
The Central Dynamic Issue

At this point, it is proposed to introduce still another and in this case the most crucial dimension of the client's communication. That dimension of the communication is based on considerations about the dynamic issues which are embedded in the fact that the client has spontaneously introduced material into therapy. From the point of view of our next considerations, the nature of the content of what was introduced is not at issue. What is critical from a dynamic point of view is the fact that the client, by spontaneously introducing material, has taken the initiative.

The many dimensions of the communication that have been considered thus far are useful guides to the therapist's understanding and eventual participation in the change process. But the facet of the communication that is most immediately relevant in determining the therapist's reaction to his client is based in whether he grasps the dynamic import of his client's initiative-taking behavior. From what the therapist knows of his client so far, taking the initiative, asserting himself, and being spontaneous are central features of conflict generating behavior in his client.

For this client, conflict and anxiety center around assertive, aggressive behavior. And so, when viewed from that perspective, the very fact that the client has taken responsibility to introduce relevant material alerts the therapist to the fact that something therapeutic has already occurred in their relationship! What has occurred might represent just one minute step along the way of significant change for the client. But no matter how feeble the effort, ambivalent the behavior, or subtle the cues, the client's behavior suggests that the relationship is developing appropriately since the client has taken some responsibility for the exploration.

If the therapist grasps the importance of that fact, he will be guided by several dynamic considerations about how to respond to his client. First of all, the therapist will be sensitive to the therapeutic importance that the client's initiative-taking behavior means. He will do nothing to retake the initiative, to flatten the client's spontaneity, or to reshoulder the responsibility the client is taking. The therapist would have erred, for example, if, in missing the dynamic issues involved, he had reacted to his client's introduction of material as though it were defensive. If he had construed the client's reactions as defensive, the therapist might have become much more diagnostic about what triggered the client's associations at that point, perhaps spending time in efforts to unearth the intervening links between the client's association and what had transpired in therapy.

Ironically, by becoming diagnostic the therapist would have behaviorally taken the reins from the client, undoing the therapeutic progress indicated by the client's initiative, and thus countering a major therapeutic goal. Secondly, if the therapist had done so because he doubted the client and thought the material was defensively introduced, he would have probably effected several additional unproductive results. Since his client is already confused about what is an honest emotional response, the therapist's doubting of the progressive features of the client's spontaneous reaction would most assuredly set the client back on his defensive haunches. Most clients are confused anyway about what they really intend because of their own mixed and poorly understood motivations. In this case, the client's feelings about his assertiveness are highly uncertain, mixed with anxiety, and confused with feelings of hostility. If the client had made an honest bid to reveal himself and the therapist through his own mistrust of the client began picking away at possible mixed motives, then he would likely reduce his client's spontaneity and increase his client's self-doubts.

Even more damaging, if the therapist had become preoccupied with whether the client was defensive, he would have behaviorally reenacted what others have done with the client. For, in doubting his client, questioning his motives, and suggesting that the material was defensively stimulated, he would have essentially flattened the affect, figuratively "squelching" the client. And being squelched and undersold are precisely the emotional experiences in the client that trigger anger and resentment.

Had the therapist acted on the assumption that the maneuver was defensive, he would have likely triggered the client's anger, thus aggravating the secondary conflict and setting into motion the frustration-anger-resentment cycle. And when triggered so early when the therapeutic relationship is young and is still a doubtful, highly tentative venture for the client, therapist and client are apt to spend considerable unproductive time, if the relationship continues at all, before the client again risks taking the initiative.

If the therapist, however, has hypothesized that his client's behavior is an assertive step forward and not a defensive maneuver, he will be able to confirm the accuracy of that hypothesis in short order. Paradoxical as it might seem, if the therapist is correct in his interpretation of his client's behavior, then an inevitable prediction following from that hypothesis is that his client *will become* defensive! Considering how the client reacts to his own assertiveness, the client is likely to run headlong into his own anxiety. To state that proposition in another way, if the therapist does nothing to squelch the client or to interfere with his initiative, then the client, because of his own dynamics as thus far revealed in the relationship, will soon behave in self-emasculating ways. Further he might attempt to involve the aid of the therapist in that emasculating process.

The therapist, therefore, must not only grasp the idea that the most immediately therapeutic thing for his client is in allowing his client to retain the initiative, but he must also grasp the fact that if he listens attentively, doesn't retake the leadership role, and supports the client's assertive behavior, the client's own anxiety about being assertive will work against him and in his anxiety he will attempt to get the therapist to place him in a dependent role!

The client, for example, might lash out at the therapist for not talking more or for not doing more. When such behavior occurs, the therapist must understand that the client is behaving as he is for defensive reasons. If the therapist doesn't catch the defensive character of the client's behavior; if he begins to feel guilty for not having taken a more active role, the therapist might easily get caught up in becoming diagnostic with the client, working harder and shouldering more responsibility, thus facilitating the client's self-emasculation.

If the therapist takes the initiative because he has missed the meaning of the client's defensive maneuvers, he will place the client in an inappropriate dependent role which the client might not initially object to because it has historically been a safer role for the client to be in. And the confirmation for the fact that the client has indeed been behaving defensively is readily available. For if the therapist takes over the leadership role, he will find that his client's anxiety fades rapidly, compliance reenters the picture, and additional unseemly side effects also make their appearance.

Once the therapist takes over the leadership role and the client has been returned to the safety of his dependent cove, once the client has been relieved of his responsibility for taking the initiative, then it is a fair prediction that the client will start complaining about his therapist. And, undoubtedly, the complaints will be the strident, whiny discontent of the child mixed with the genuine anger of the frustrated, oppressed adult. The client might reactivate with amazing resiliency his skill at rationalizing, and the therapist might find himself the brunt of his client's anger, resentment, and blame for having squelched him. Inadvertently, the therapist will find himself in the role of the significant others in the life of the client, embroiled in the frustration-anger-resentment cycle with limited progress and an imminent impasse.

As that secondary conflict cycle is set into motion, the therapist might find that he becomes frustrated and angry with his client for the role that he finds himself in. And when the therapist's anger is felt by the client, it will simply reinforce the client's fears about retaliation, thus reinforcing the secondary conflict and lessening the potential for any real therapeutic progress.

If, on the other hand, the therapist has grasped the dynamics of the interaction and understands the intensity of conflict that the client must experience for him to recoil so defensively, then he is in a position to respond in a more therapeutic way. And in this case, had the therapist simply commented that "I noticed you started becoming anxious a moment ago. It seemed associated with the fact that you were being spontaneous. Perhaps we are tracking something important here. What thoughts come to mind about that?" he would have effected several potential gains.

Through such a reaction, the therapist would have recognized, approached, and helped the client to label his anxiety. He would have communicated his perceptiveness of the client's distraught state, his willingness to help the client, and his concern about but not fear of what underlies the client's anxiety. More importantly, he would have supported the client's assertiveness and restored responsibility for the exploration to the client. Through his response, the therapist would have communicated his belief that the client has within himself the resources to cope with his problem. And, through his trust in the client, the therapist provides the client with the strength to begin to trust himself, to trust the therapist, and to risk exploring his feelings.

By inviting the client to reveal his thoughts, the therapist extricates himself from potential involvement in the secondary defensive struggles of the client. Through his response, the therapist does not attempt to reduce the client's anxiety. On the contrary, his behavior will in some ways make his client more anxious. What the therapist attempts to do is to reduce the diffuseness of his client's anxiety by providing the client with his observations about what the anxiety seems attached to so that it can be utilized productively. Through his response the therapist attempts to strengthen the relationship so that his client will risk more; yet he also knows that, as his client searches, he will continue to struggle against the therapist as well as to rely on him and that the relationship will be renegotiated many times before the client resolves his conflicts.

At the early moment in therapy described above, the client's assertiveness is couched in a great deal of ambivalence about being assertive. It is counter-balanced by greater anxiety about what it would mean to be assertive and the course of work necessary to resolve those conflicts might be extensive. If the client's fears are deeply entrenched ones, extensive excursions might be necessary into the client's family history. And it is equally likely that the client will traverse many anxious moments if he is to grapple more directly with those whom he encounters.

And as those wishes and fears about what the grappling is all about start reaching a point of counterbalancing each other, as the needs begin to struggle for satisfaction, as the generic conflict reaches consciousness, as accompanying feelings build, anxiety will mount. And as those feelings build, the client's feelings toward the therapist will become intense and, as happened in this case, the therapist might find himself the embodiment of some characteristics of the client's father that are projected onto him by his hypersensitive and anxious client rather than feelings he experiences in relation to the client.

But as was noted earlier and will be pointed out later, at those times during therapy when feelings have built to a point where they cloud the client's vision, when he behaves irrationally toward the therapist and expects reprisals, the emotional experiences in therapy will have reached comparability to those of the generic struggle and will open the avenue for significant relearning. And such a significant moment in the therapy of this client where the potential for change is good will be discussed next.

AN IRRATIONAL PREMISE AND
A MOMENT OF THERAPY

In this section, we will look rather carefully at a crucial session in the therapy of the client whom we have been following during the last few pages. This particular session is introduced because it represented a critical hurdle along the way. The interview was a pivotal one in the sense that during the session the client essentially reached a point of no return with regard to a central feature of his conflicts and defensive maneuvering. It became apparent during the session that the client reached a point in time where retreat to the submissive state and rationalizations that he found so comfortable early in therapy was no longer a viable alternative for him or an acceptable solution to the conflicts he experienced.

The client's feelings about and reactions to the therapist which characterized this session and provided the basis for the productive work ahead were building over a considerable period of time. The events, content, and interactions of those previous sessions provided the therapist with an experiential framework for conceptualizing what was happening to his client during the session in question, what his anxiety and behavior meant, and how he might react so as to facilitate the client's growth. And so, as we follow some of the therapist's thoughts as he worked with the client during the session, we shall digress at times to note some of the antecedents which paved the way for the crucial encounter as the therapist observed, interpreted, and utilized those understandings.

The client arrived a few minutes late for his appointment. Being late for an appointment was "out of character" for the client. His usual style was to be waiting outside the therapist's office for some time before his appointment. But on this occasion the therapist had just time to wonder what the client's lateness might mean when the client entered the waiting room, somewhat breathless and apparently agitated. When he entered the therapist's office, the client was anxious, he didn't remove his coat, and he looked as though he would skitter off at the slightest provocation.

Almost immediately, the client said that he needed to get something out into the open. He said that he had been feeling very irritable during the week and that he had been feeling angry and resentful toward the therapist in particular. And then the client immediately launched into a series of the thoughts and feelings that he had been having. With a great deal of feeling, the client said he felt he should be making more progress in therapy than he was. Essentially, he felt that the therapist had been holding him back. In addition, he somehow felt that the therapist didn't think he was man enough to look at deeper issues and feelings and that they were treating matters superficially.

First of all, the intensity of the client's feelings—his anxiety, irritability, resentment, and the projection of motives, feelings, and reactions that the therapist neither intended nor felt—alerted the therapist to the probability that the client's feelings had heightened to the point where the session was to be a significant one. And as the therapist listened to the client, he noted a number of interlocking layers to what the client was communicating.

Some Interlocking Dimensions
of the Client's Communication

In the first place, the major overtone in the client's communication was the feeling of being restrained. Those feelings of being restrained and frustrated were certainly significant features of the client's anger. And there was enough evidence from the client's history and his family relationships to confirm the fact that the client had encountered many restraints and frustrations in the past.

Over time during therapy, the client's history revealed that he was the product of a very controlling home. Apparently because of their own anxieties about impulse control, both parents colluded literally to beat the client's impulses out of him. The father in particular seemed to be an impulse-ridden man who oscillated between overcontrol and undercontrol. Often the father was angry and complaining, and his anger about whatever upset him at the moment was generally taken out at the expense of the client's freedom. The client was often restricted and punished for minor offenses, pranks, and normal childhood curiosities.

The father's behavior was a crucial factor in the client's development on several counts. There were many parallels between the client's eventual behavior and fears and what he observed happen to his father. And those observations apparently affected the client deeply. Apparently the father's angry, complaining, "picky" attitudes, and threatening behavior toward the client were the consequences of his own frustrations, and those frustrations were couched in anxieties about his own castration. The father communicated his fears to his son in many ways. In general, the verbal message was that being aggressive "gets you into trouble."

The other part of the message was behaviorally communicated to the client. For the client had seen his father live out those fears. The client's father had backed away from a responsible leadership role in an organization where he was employed. He had done so he said for reasons that sounded very similar to the list of excuses that the client gave during the first interview for his unwillingness to accept a leadership role on campus. The father had contended that leaders invite jealousy and resentment and that there are few rewards in the struggle. And those were precisely the client's rationalizations for his own withdrawal from the struggle. In many respects, the father seemed to be the model for the client's own ways of coping with his anxiety whenever he got himself into a position where competence was expected.

But such anxious, withdrawing behavior had apparently not always been characteristic of his father. At one time the father had been a very involved man but had pulled back for some reasons that were mysterious to the client. Earlier the father had taken a much more aggressive stance toward life. From what the client could piece together when his father would reminisce at times, he had been a respected leader in the community and was regarded as competent by his peer group. And the client himself remembered times when there was more joy in the home, when both parents were much involved, parties were held, and the circle of his parents' friends was large.

But by the time the client had reached his preadolescent period, things had changed; the father had withdrawn; and strife characterized the family relationships. The client remembered that it was after they moved to a smaller community and his father had taken a less visible job that his father's anger increased and punishment was meted out whenever the client attempted to strike out on his own.

As a preadolescent the client had never experienced comradeship, he was never able to "fool around," and he never developed any close relationships. During that period of his life, his parents kept close watch over his behavior and his father in particular seemed to become quite resentful whenever the client received invitations to spend a holiday away from home or had the opportunity to engage in some activity that the father apparently still missed himself.

Over time the therapist began to feel that the client's earlier development had been fairly sound and that the parents had coped rather well with the client's needs during the client's early childhood. Paradoxical as it might seem, the therapist thought it was rather fortunate for the client that the father's withdrawal was never a satisfactory resolution for his conflicts. So long as those conflicts were alive, the client was able to see both sides of his father's behavior. But being able to understand the behavior didn't provide the client with an outlet for his own feelings. In relation to his parents, the client had remained docile. The apparent anger and resentment that he must have experienced because of the early restraints of his parents were experienced as so much content devoid of affect.

From what the therapist had learned of the client's relationship to his family, the client had missed a great deal of the struggling, testing, and experimenting that must be traversed if healthy ego boundaries are to be established, masculinity is to be confirmed, and areas of competence are to be clarified. The therapist assumed that somewhere along the line his client would need to fill in those gaps in development, work through some of those impulses, and test out some of those feelings. And the therapist was equally sure that as therapy progressed and some of what was needed and missed began to be felt, the client would begin to experience the anger and resentment that he pushed out of awareness for the punishment, restraints, and criticalness of that period in his life. And it seemed from recent interviews that the client was beginning to experience rebellious feelings that might be close to the heart of those issues.

The undertones of those feelings of being restrained were making themselves felt in the previous session. In that session, the client had begun to feel that he was not involved enough in things. And his feelings about involvement ranged along several topics. In general, however, the client's feelings of wanting more involvement centered in his peer group. And the flavor of the client's feelings were those of a young adolescent. In many ways, the client viewed his peer group through the eyes of the preadolescent who wants to be accepted by the "gang." And those needs were an accurate reflection of where the client was emotionally.

The client's wishes to be involved with his peers and his irritation about being inhibited in those relationships had changed considerably since he entered therapy. At the outset of therapy, the client had viewed his peers as destructive. But, over time, as he and the therapist worked at what underlay his reactions, it became increasingly clear to the client that his peers were not the "ogres" that he had made them out to be.

In fact, the therapist had often "heard" the peer group subtly encouraging the client to take on more leadership responsibility. Apparently, they saw more competence in the client than he was able to credit himself with. And, as the therapist let the client in on what he had "heard," the client began to see how he attenuated those relationships for defensive purposes.

Earlier the client had rather effectively tuned out his own self-depreciating behaviors, and had effectively rationalized his own behavior by blaming others for not providing him with appropriate opportunities to prove himself. But as the source of the conflict in his own inner fears became increasingly undeniable, the client found it increasingly difficult to blame others.

And as his rationalizations decreased, the client began to feel what he had missed and his interest in involvement increased. And with those interests that had been cut off during his development revitalized, the rumblings of anger, resentment, and rebelliousness began to make their appearance. At the outset of the therapeutic session in question, the client's resentment for the restraints he felt was bubbling up. And, in his anxiety the client was irrationally directing his resentment at the therapist as though he were the inhibiting force.

But feeling angry and resentful about being restrained was but one facet of what the client was communicating. The client had also contended that he felt the therapist was fearful of his deeper feelings. The therapist thought that that dimension probably had several sides to it but for our immediate purposes the most crucial one was that the awakening of anger was frightening to the client and he projected that fear onto the therapist.

In a sense, at the outset of this session, the client's dynamic bind is out in the open. He feels frustrated and is beginning to feel resentful of that frustration. But the feelings of resentment themselves trigger greater anxiety because they are at the roots of heightened fears about castration. When those heightened fears about castration are coupled to the undeniable stirrings in the client of resentment and anger, then he is in a position of experiencing real threat of castration from the therapist. And that is a fairly good partial explanation for what has triggered the client's irrational reactions to the therapist. For he must be experiencing intense anxiety about what his anger will evoke and, in confronting the therapist, he is most vulnerable; he is in a delicate balance between progressive and regressive movement.

And so the second feature in the client's communication is that the feelings that are stirring in him are very anxiety provoking, and part of the anger that he is expressing toward the therapist is in part a reaction to his own anxiety about deeper fears of castration. It is critical that the therapist understand the intricate relationship between the experience of resentment and the threat of castration. If the client experiences anger toward the therapist, his fear must certainly be that his frustrated state might be exacerbated because the anger itself makes the fantasy about castration into a very *real threat*! And from that point of view, the therapist needs to be sensitive to the unconscious backlash that the client will experience unless his anger and resentment about restraints are dealt with sensitively by the therapist.

There is still a third aspect to the client's communication that is dynamically linked to other aspects. The third message in the client's reaction to the therapist undergirds the other two. It is at the heart of what will provide the client with the strength to go ahead and experience what is emerging. For the third message consists of the client's wish to become deeply involved with the therapist. If the client is to struggle with his anxiety about what is to emerge he must feel not only that the therapist is competent "to see" what is going on but he must believe also that the therapist will be reliable, interested, and will deal sensitively and in constructive ways with what he presents.

Those beliefs undergird the potential for therapeutic change in this case. The therapist must not only see the frustration; he must see the underlying anxiety about castration and the need for a strong relationship in order for those experiences to be integrated. And so the therapist must provide the client with the opportunity to depend on him for support as he experiences his anger, help him to direct his anger to its generating sources, and communicate to the client that his feelings and thoughts are not disturbing to the therapist.

The Therapist's Thoughts and Reactions

The therapist recognized that his relationship with his client had reached a critical point in its development. If the client's feelings of anger and resentment toward the therapist increased appreciably, the therapist realized that those negative feelings could become a problematic issue in therapy and increase the client's resistance to change. Yet, if a therapist becomes too preoccupied with his own anxiety about whether he can help a client to attach his feelings to their appropriate generating sources so as to reduce a client's negative reactions to himself, he will have missed the entire point.

For the opportunity for significant change resides in the intensity of those pent-up feelings. That is not to belittle the importance for the therapist to differentiate himself from those who restrained the client. And as will be pointed out momentarily, the therapist attempted to respond in such a way that those differences were highlighted. The point here is simply that if the therapist views the client's anger and resentment as a block to therapeutic movement, he might be blinded to the potential usefulness of those feelings as a working basis for effecting significant change.

A second point, and a rather crucial one, is that genuine differentiation from those who were disruptive forces in a client's development occurs in therapy as a natural by-product of the therapist's helping the client to expand his feelings. As we shall see, by working to understand his client's feelings, the therapist separates himself from others at a truly emotional level. Unfortunately, if the therapist becomes concerned with attempting to convince the client of his differences with words or contentions, he simply reinforces the client's suspicions that he is an anxious sort of fellow and is made of the same emotional stuff that the parents and others were who also reacted with anxiety to the client's angry feelings.

To state that premise another way, the client's irrational premise that the therapist wants to hold him back and that he fears his deeper feelings both complicate therapy and provide it with a vehicle for significant change. Since the client's emotional experiences are intense and since they are experienced in relation to the therapist, it not only means that the relationship is a highly significant one, but it means that the therapist is in a unique position to effect deep and lasting change if he can constructively utilize what has happened. And so what the therapist needs to do is to understand that the conflict is in the open and that he has the opportunity to break the pattern in the client's anticipations with regard to the behavior of significant others in his life.

At that moment in time when he expresses his anger and resentment, the client's anticipation must be that the therapist will react in ways that are identical to those of significant persons in his past. He must anticipate that reaction; he has grounds for no other expectation—and that is why he is so anxious about the confrontation. He must certainly believe that he will be "cut down to size" again as his father or others might have done for feeling and reacting as he has. The client's projections and irrationality reveal his anxiety and his internal emotional turmoil. And, as has been pointed out repeatedly earlier, those feelings set the stage for and are the necessary prelude to significant relearning. So, if the therapist can behave in ways which counter the inhibiting conditions of those earlier learnings, he can do much to help the client to break the restraints that his anxiety forces him to live within.

With that brief introduction to the therapist's thoughts as he listened to his client, let us follow his reactions to the client, noting the rationale for the therapist's behavior and some of the hypotheses that he formulated along the way about the meaning of the client's reactions. As we do so, we shall also suggest some alternative therapist reactions, hypothesizing about the probable effects of those alternatives on the developing relationship. And then, in retrospect, we shall briefly speculate about the meaning of some of the events of the session from other vantage points.

In responding to the client's feelings that the therapist was holding him back and feared exploring his deeper feelings with him, the therapist simply commented that "I imagine you have a lot of feelings about being restrained." Through that response the therapist hoped to effect several therapeutic gains. The therapist's response invites the client to expand the feelings he has about being restrained, it doesn't deflect the client's anger from the therapist but it does open up the possibility for a more general exploration of the client's feelings of restraint, and it begins a process of differentiating the therapist from the father at a behavioral level. Further, the therapist's response also behaviorally counters the client's projection that the therapist fears his deeper feelings; and most critically it touches on the anxiety which motivated that projection and communicates the therapist's trust that the client has the resources to tolerate the anxiety of that exploration. In the next few paragraphs, those dimensions of the therapist's communication will be expanded.

In the first place, the client's anger, although probably associated with the frustrating father, was directed at the therapist in a forthright way, and the therapist was particularly alert to the possibility that deflecting the anger back to its generic sources prematurely might simply flatten the affect. At that moment, the client was experiencing his feelings toward the therapist and not toward the father. And those reactions of the client must be dealt with at that experiential level first.

Of critical importance is the fact that through his response, the therapist leaves open the possibility that he himself might have unwittingly been behaving toward the client in ways that were perceived by the client as restraining. Although the more probable hypothesis is that the client's reactions are in fact transference feelings, the possibility must be considered that the client has felt some restraints during the therapeutic interaction itself. If so, those feelings will predominate the picture and unless they are appropriately aired, they preclude the client's looking beyond them to the generic sources of his anxiety. And the beneficial fact of the matter is that if those feelings do have some basis in the therapeutic relationship itself, then working them out there acts as a natural bridge to the awakening and reexperiencing of the earlier problematic interactions.

By holding open the possibility that the client's anger might have some basis in his own reactions to the client the therapist communicates to the client the fact that what the client says has an impact on him. And, most importantly, he communicates to the client the fact that he is interested in a continuing and deepening relationship with the client and in working out their differences together.

Still another important feature of the therapist's response is that the therapist's reaction is a behavioral contradiction to the client's anticipations. If the client's expectation is that the therapist will react with anger, admonitions, moralizing, or punishment for his angry, resentful, feelings, then a truly startling and anxiety-provoking reaction must occur in the client if the therapist responds in ways that are the polar opposites of those expectations. And in that process of reacting in a therapeutic way, the therapist's behaviorally separates himself from the father in the emotional experience of his client.

Through his response, the therapist *demonstrates* that he doesn't wish to restrain the client. If the therapist were to comment, for example, that "I don't wish to restrain you"; "I don't feel that way about you"; "Perhaps what you feel has more to do with your father"; he would be contending something that is not within the experiential framework of the client. Those responses would all seem to suffer from the same malady. They are verbalizations and are likely to be perceived by the client as attempts at intellectual cotrol. At best, they tend to flatten the affect before it is fully experienced and expressed.

Significant persons in the client's past have acted to frustrate him and the client has no grounds for trusting the therapist's or any other significant person's words. The therapist doesn't differentiate himself from those in the client's past by stating it in so many terms; he differentiates himself by actually living out the differences. When, however, the therapist invites the client to expand his feelings, when he helps him to associate, and when he leaves open the question of his own behavior with the client, then he is creating emotional conditions which counter that earlier learning. Essentially, the therapist's separation from the restraining forces of the past is effected as a by-product of his behaving differently.

Through his response, the therapist also hopes to counter the client's contention that the therapist was afraid to explore his feelings more deeply since the therapist invites the deeper exploration. But the therapist does so in a particular kind of way. He doesn't make the associations for the client. He simply opens up the potential for the exploration and makes himself available for supporting the client. And by inviting that deeper search, the therapist also communicates to the client his feeling that the client has the resources in himself to undertake the exploration. And in that complex of conditions the groundwork is laid both for therapeutic change and paradoxically for the heightening of the client's anxiety. For the responsibility falls back on his shoulders for accepting the invitation and searching more deeply.

The crucial point in the therapeutic session occurred following the therapist's response. Up to that point in therapy, the client had often expressed angry reactions, but they were invariably followed by self-depreciating comments which rendered the anger impotent. At this particular point in therapy, however, the self-depreciating follow-up was absent. The client apparently made the emotional decision to take some risks for he pursued his feelings. As the client began to talk more freely of his feelings about being restrained, he commented that one feeling in particular predominated as he approached the therapist's office that day. As he came down the street for the session, the client couldn't shake the feeling—as irrational as it seemed to him—that he would find the therapist outside looking for him to "get him in there to talk"!

At that point the therapist had several associations of his own. The client's concern that the therapist would attempt to "get him in there to talk" was an expectation that was associatively close to the way in which the client had rather dispassionately described in earlier sessions his father's efforts at attempting to control him by keeping him home and away from places where trouble might lurk, and standing between the client and his peers who might do "wild" things. And so the therapist made that brief interpretive link by commenting that "You mean you expected me to drag you in here and whip you into shape as your father might have done." Through that comment, the therapist attempted to touch on and counter the client's anticipations of castration for his feelings, thus reducing that anxiety sufficiently to allow the flow of feelings that were bottled up by that fear.

Apparently the therapist touched on a sensitive area, for some of the client's anger and resentment toward the undue restrictions of his father and the way in which he was inhibited as a youth began to come out. The client said that he remembered his father sometimes standing outside waiting for him when he was late, yelling at him to get home. Although the client had recounted similar scenes in earlier sessions, those pictures were apparently vivid and were reintroduced in a highly charged emotional manner. Along with those memories were intense feelings of anger and hatred for the father. The client was shaken by his own feelings. But the therapist allowed the client to experience what he was feeling without intruding into the client's feelings about that relationship. After, and only after, the feelings of resentment and anger seemed to have run their course did the therapist ask the client how the week had gone for him.

The client then related the fact that he had been trying out some things with friends during the week. He related an interesting evening or two that he had spent with some of his "buddies," incidentally, doing some of the things that his father would have objected to earlier. And as the client related some of the things he enjoyed doing during the week, a most interesting thing occurred. The client, almost in a conditioned way, began to depreciate the evenings that he had obviously enjoyed but caught himself at his own anxiety-reducing tricks, smiled, and commented in a rather self-amused way that he would have to live with his anxiety about having enjoyed himself! Since the session was about over, the therapist commented that he thought that the client had made good progress, it sounded as though the client was having fun, and he would see him next week.

By commenting that it was a good session, the therapist hoped both to increase the client's assertiveness and to reward the fact that he had expressed his feelings as he experienced them without pulling any punches. And by concluding the session with a comment that it sounded as though the client was having fun, the therapist hoped to free the client to become even more expressive and natural in his interactions with others. And again through that process the therapist also felt that he would diminish the potential that the client would continue to associate him with his father.

In succeeding sessions, the client talked more freely about some of the things that he was doing and enjoyed and although he vacillated at times, the client tended to become more assertive over time. As the client tried out new things, however, he found that he had missed some knowledge along the way because of his isolation from others. And he began to question. Those questions, however, were more reality-oriented questions. They were questions about things that the client had missed learning during his development. He wondered about girls and what made them tick. He wondered how they felt about sex. He wondered what made a person attractive to them. He wondered about his own sexuality.

In those regards, the therapist taught him some things that he had missed learning from his father. And at times, the client introduced fantasies that he had about sexual matters which he thought were abnormal. As the meanings of those fantasies were discussed, they opened new areas of conflict and exploration. But in the session described above the client had overcome a significant hurdle in his relationship to the therapist and as new areas of conflict were introduced by the client, they reflected greater internal strength, initiative, and a healthy curiosity about his own inner processes.

Some Final Comments
about the Interview

The interaction of the therapist and the client during that brief glimpse of process reflects several interesting features of therapy. The client's lateness for the session was essentially an "acting out" with the therapist of some facet of the client's conflict. In this case, the client's being late was a behavioral enactment with the therapist of a significant feature of his conflicted interactions with his father. What the client acted out in part was his resentment for his father's having inhibited and restrained him. Although the feelings of resentment had their source in his relationship to the father, the client experienced them toward the therapist and acted out the resentment toward him.

In a sense the therapist had been shaped by the client in terms of his own subjective experience into someone who would attempt as his father had done to restrain him—to get him back into line again. That brief controlled acting out served the client and the therapist both with a useful vehicle for change. For those events to occur the client must have been experiencing in the present some feelings which were similar in kind and in quality to the experiences that occurred in the conflict engendering interaction with his father. The comparability in emotional quality of those experiences in the client provided the therapist with the opportunity for effecting change since under those conditions significant new learnings could be substituted for what was poorly learned.

How a therapist might react would vary considerably depending upon how much the client was able to become aware of what he had reenacted with the therapist and how much he fantasized, associated, and could verbalize instead of simply "acting out." The therapist's reactions would depend, in other words, on how much the client was able to experience what underlay his feelings rather than to use the "acting out" of those feelings as a way of allaying deeper anxiety about castration or as a means of achieving some childlike gain from his resentful, angry feelings.

In this case, the client was just a few minutes late for the session. And he immediately revealed the feelings he was experiencing toward the therapist, particularly some of the resentment that he felt. In addition, the client himself sensed the irrationality of the feelings but felt them just the same. Those conditions were good prognostic signs and provided the therapist with his optimism that the session could be a productive one.

The client's behavior suggested that crucial feelings had surfaced, that the associative connections with the past were proximal, and that some minor interpretation might link up the present and past so as to release more fully the affect that was beginning to push into awareness. In addition, the client's willingness to introduce the conflict into the relationship without coercion suggested the importance that the client attached to working through the conflicts in order to sustain his relationship with the therapist. And lastly, the client's ability to verbalize the conflict and struggle with the accompanying feelings suggested that he was able to tolerate anxiety without "acting out" the transference elements more fully.

Had the client remained away for most of the session or missed the session entirely, the therapist's tact in approaching the client might have been very different based on several contingencies. Following the client's lateness, had he introduced his conflicted feelings, the same therapeutic gains could have been made and the therapeutic session might have followed the same sequence. On the other hand, had the client been late or missed a session and then become passively resistant the potential for change might have been delayed.

In that case, the therapist might have needed to involve himself in much more interpretive work to bring the pent-up feelings into the open. Passive resistance might also indicate that the client had closely associated the therapist with his father. And in that case, the process of differentiating himself from the father would have been a more extensive undertaking. In fact, if the client had become passively resistant, the therapist must consider whether the client's resistance, resentment, or whatever has been stimulated by therapist behavior that has reinforced negative associations and set resistance into motion.

Had the therapist, for example, become angry with the client or suspicious of his motives for arriving late for the session, his reaction might reflect an attitude toward the client that bears resemblance to the father's likely reaction to the client. Such an irrational move by the therapist would have most certainly inhibited change since he would have been playing out—admittedly with greater subtlety—the father's role of castrating the client and beating him into submission. But the effect would be the same. The client would close up, having had his concept of authority figures reinforced. And, in all probability, if he returned for more punishment, future sessions would find an increase in "acting out," making access to change more difficult and an intensification of feelings of resentment, eventuating in an unsatisfying termination.

Two moments during the session can be isolated as particularly crucial ones. The first significant event occurred when the client, despite his anxiety, pursued and expanded his feelings of anger and resentment without reverting to his usual defensive ways of depreciating what he had said and withdrawing to the safety of his former submissive state. Essentially, at that point in time, the client risked a great deal, for his fantasies about retaliation must have been intense.

The second critical moment took place when the client began to depreciate what he had accomplished during the week, caught himself at his own anxiety-reducing behavior, corrected himself, and was even able to be rather amused with what had happened. That event was particularly critical since it revealed that the client had gained some emotional insight into his own dynamic processes. And as often happens when a client has gained some genuine emotional insight into some self-defeating behavior, his own internal processes begin to work for his continued growth.

But the way in which those processes work for the client's benefit is not an unmixed blessing. Ironic as it may seem, those constructive processes also utilize anxiety to alert the person whenever his constructive growth is endangered. And so as any poor unsuspecting client who has ever traversed the process finds out, he is never free of his anxiety for it is as powerful a constructive force as it has been a disabling one.

That is a very interesting phenomenon. It seems at times of insight that a subtle shift in the valence of the client's anxiety occurs. It is as though the anxiety which signals danger to the person continues to do so. The difference is simply that the signal in the neurotic inhibits growth, whereas the signal in the normal is a guide to redirecting energy into constructive forces. And in this session anxiety changed hands and began to serve the growth process for the client increasingly experienced feelings of anxiety whenever he behaved in the self-depreciating ways that formerly had been the damper for his anxiety.

SUMMARY

In this chapter, an effort has been made to follow the thoughts and actions of the therapist as he searches for ways of understanding and helping his client. The emphasis in the chapter has been on providing an overview of that searching process. Case material has provided the basis for some general guidelines to why, how, and where the therapist looks for clues to the meaning of a client's conflicts and to the ways that the therapist uses his understanding to facilitate change.

In the chapter to follow, we shall continue to follow the therapist's thoughts and feelings as he attempts to deepen his understanding of his client and the nature of his conflicts. Whereas in this chapter an attempt was made to provide a general introduction to the way that the therapist works, the content of the next chapter will center around some specific ways in which the therapist searches for associations and behavioral parallels which link the client's behavioral patterns during the therapeutic session with the generating and sustaining sources of conflict as they are reflected in the client's past and current interpersonal relationships.

5

Further Guidelines to Participation: Listening for Links with the Past

To understand his client's conflicts and how he can participate constructively in helping to resolve those conflicts, the therapist must learn a great deal about the emotional life of his client. The general ways in which the therapist looks, listens, observes, and interacts to bring conflict into the open so as to understand and help effect change were introduced in the last chapter. In the present chapter several facets of that process of observing and participating will be elaborated further. Case material will again provide the basis for formulating and clarifying propositions about ways of participating meaningfully in the change process.

In this chapter, we will follow the way in which the therapist learns about the client's conflicts from a study of his relationships. We will note the way in which the therapist looks for underlying dynamic links, behavioral parallels, and recurrent affective themes that connect the client's current problematic interactions with the generating sources of conflict in the past. And we will note the way in which those dynamic links, when discovered by the therapist, provide him with clues to what and how conflict might be regenerated and reenacted in the present, both in the therapeutic session and in the client's other interactions.

The major portion of this chapter will consist of an elaboration of the way that the therapist searches for behavioral parallels and recurrent themes in the client's productions that dynamically link together the past, the present, and the therapeutic session. Toward the conclusion of the chapter, however, we will anticipate the content of the next chapter by introducing some material about how the therapist utilizes his understanding of the development of conflict in making predictions about how conflict might unfold during the course of therapy.

LISTENING FOR CONFLICT:
SOME INTRODUCTORY REMARKS

Over time during therapy, the therapist attempts to find out what transpires in the client's current relationships, what he seeks in those relationships, where anxiety intrudes, and how the client has learned to cover his tracks when anxiety occurs. The therapist notes the way in which the client sets up his relationships, whether they are sustained, whether they seem to recycle without relief, or whether they terminate in unsatisfying ways. And, as the therapist listens to those interactions and tries to trace the anxiety, he listens for associative links that connect those current interactions with the longer history of conflict.

Listening for Links between
the Present and the Past

All conflict, as has been pointed out before, in varying degrees, embodies elements of the past. Although conflict is reflected in current relationships, attitudes, and feelings that are troublesome, those conflicts are intricately wound with previous experiences and past interactions with parents, siblings, teachers, and other significant persons whose reactions, demands, and behavior acted as a generator for the conflicts that characterize the client's current interactions.

The therapist often finds that the client's conflicts embody fantasies that are attached to significant figures in the client's past. The therapist listens for the ways that the client might still be trying to satisfy a parent, attempting to complete old fantasies, or struggling to break through old anxiety barriers. Although the cast of characters might have changed from those in the client's developmental years—a parent, a teacher, or another significant person might have been replaced by a friend, a spouse, or a roommate—the therapist has learned to listen for the needs, the wishes, and the fears which underlie those interactions and not to be confused by superficial changes in setting or character.

Through a peer, a spouse, or some authority figure in the client's current environment, he might still be attempting to satisfy needs, resolve conflicts, master anxiety, or be released from old bonds. If the therapist listens carefully he can hear some clients struggle time and again to get something from a father or mother, but in ways that are inappropriate in the present. So long as the client continues to invest his energy in the unresolved conflicts of the past, that energy is not free for him to behave appropriately to the reality elements of his current relationships. In fact, the reality elements of the relationship are never perceived by the client. The client in his current interactions might still be bound up with ghosts of the past, with a parent long dead, but one, nevertheless, who is still his source of conflict. Even though the power that parent once wielded in a physical sense when the client was dependent and unable to fend for himself no longer exists, even though those physical bonds have long been severed, the client emotionally lives in that relationship and still tends to seek resolution to conflicts engendered there.

From listening to the client, the therapist senses the power of the early emotional experiences. And as the therapist works with the client, it becomes important for him to understand the emotional context in which conflict was engendered. To disengage the client, to break him free, that emotional context must be known to the therapist. The past history of the client's interpersonal relationships provides the therapist with a touchstone to the meaning of conflict. From that history, the therapist has a solid basis for understanding the meaning of the client's current conflicts.

In particular, if the therapist understands the past, he can make some predictions about what the client's interactions with him will be like. At times of stress, history is relived. And at those times the therapist's understanding provides him with the opportunity to touch accurately on the sources of anxiety, to make appropriate interpretations, and to help the client to break through the restraints his anxiety has erected. By knowing the emotional context in which conflict was engendered, the therapist is in a position both to modify those conditions through his own behavioral reactions to the client and to provide the client with emotional insight into the way in which those conflicts impinge on his current life situation.

The Present and the Past in
Perspective: Dynamic Considerations

Increasingly during therapy, the meaning of the client's behavior becomes clearer as the links between the present conflict and the past interactions emerge. But the therapist doesn't learn about the past and then proceed to do therapy any more than he fully understands his client and then proceeds to participate. There is a constantly deepening interactive process between present conflict and past interactions that develops over time during therapy. That process begins at the outset and continues throughout therapy as different facets of conflict emerge and as aspects of the client's present and past relationships bear on that conflict.

Sometimes from the client's present relationships the therapist has clues to what transpired in the client's earlier problematic relationships. At other times what happened in the earlier relationships provides the therapist with clues to what the client is attempting to evoke in his present relationships. And in either case, the work of the therapist is to attempt to bring the conflict into the open so that the client can see how he is reacting in his current relationships, what it means to him dynamically to react as he does, and how those reactions affect potential need satisfaction.

Unless explorations of the past are stimulated by considerations about how conflict is experienced by the client in his present relationships, those historical excursions might be limited to what they reveal indirectly of the client's general character traits and defenses. The historical gathers its force in facilitating change only as its contingencies on the client's current interactions are made clear to him. Although the client might be emotionally tied to the past, he is living his life in the present and the precipitating sources of anxiety which brought him into therapy are to be found in his current interactions.

The client, for example, who is having difficulties in his marriage might be experiencing such difficulties because of some attitudes that he still holds about the opposite sex based on his interactions with a parent. However, the process of breaking the client free from his anxiety does not begin with an historical excursion into his generalized past behavior or even into his behavior with the parent who was the source of his disturbed relationships.

The process of setting the client free begins with a consideration of what exactly is transpiring in his interaction with his spouse that stimulates anxiety. Only then does the historical excursion make sense. In that freely flowing movement between the anxiety of the day and the emotional context in which that anxiety was engendered, the client is provided with a meaningful therapeutic experience. For under those conditions the client is able to gain genuine emotional insight not only into the character of the generic struggle, but also into the way in which those dynamic forces are still at work in his marriage with his spouse. And from that insight, the groundplan is laid for change.

The linkage between those events is clarified and therapy unfolds if the therapist has consistently responded to the dynamic meaning of whatever the client introduces into therapy. When material is introduced into therapy, whether of present or past relationships or events, the therapist listens not only to the content of the communication but, more importantly, he wonders what dynamic functions the introduction of material serves and what experience in the client stimulated its introduction at that moment.

The introduction of a past interaction might mean that the client remembers because he has been freed of disabling anxiety and can remember. At other times, an earlier interaction might simply be reported as an informational item whose significance only becomes clear later when the client and therapist converge on conflict and its significance is revealed. Or the introduction of material, whether of the present or past relationships of the client, might be a defensive maneuver to avoid talking about an anxiety-provoking experience that occurred during the week or during a session.

With some clients, it soon becomes clear that they use the past defensively. Such a client focuses on the past during therapy because he fears the present. The past is a safe haven from the anxiety of the day. In progressive therapy there is a constant flow between the present and the past as conflicts are resolved and new and perhaps deeper conflicts emerge. In the process, the past is used productively by the client, insights are gained and applied in current situations. When the past is used defensively, the client might labor the past with little insight or provide such an overabundance of data that the therapist is lost in the morass of persons and events, all of whom are paraded past the therapist with little variation in emotion or evidence of their significance.

But if during the course of some sessions the therapist listens to the client's obsessional recounting of one past event after another, he sometimes hears an oversolicitous parent who has protected the client from life. And if he listens more carefully he hears the parent's anxiety being communicated to the client. In working with those clients the therapist might find that it takes a superhuman effort to dislodge the client from his preoccupation with the past. The client won't live in the present because *to experience himself as living in the present is too anxiety provoking.* Living in the present might mean that the client must take stands on issues, make decisions, and live out his life taking some risks along the way.

Whereas the past can be used defensively, so can the present. A second client might live only in the present, fearing looking at the past. During therapy he might discount the importance of the past. In fact, the client might react with anger if the therapist suggests the influence of a parent, contending that his parents have nothing to do with his day-to-day problems. Eventually, it might become clear during therapy that the client has renounced his parents; he has disowned his heritage.

For such events to occur, the past must have been traumatic. The client's resentment about his treatment in the past is so great that he wants nothing more to do with it. The unfortunate fact is that so long as the client cuts out the past, he has cut out a large part of his experience and must spend much energy in stepping around thoughts and feelings, blindfolded to much that is going on in him and around him. Until the client discovers what he is avoiding and why he is doing so, his current experiences are often unpredictable events known only to him by the experience of anxiety when he has made an inappropriate step forward.

But the point of this brief digression into dynamic considerations is neither to detail how clients defend against change nor to discuss the conflicts which might underlie those defenses. It is simply intended to point up the fact that the therapist must constantly assess the client's motivation in introducing whatever he does into the therapeutic relationship. And, for our purposes here, suffice it to say that an abundance of seemingly relevant material about past or present interactions might in fact be motivated to distract the therapist from getting to the. heart of the conflict. That fact does not detract from the therapeutic usefulness of the material for what it reveals of the client or of his ways of coping with anxiety. But it is only when and if the therapist goes beyond the content and listens for intent that the full import of the material is understood and its significance for the change process is revealed.

Listening for Repetitive Patterns of Interpersonal Behavior

As the therapist searches for links between the client's current conflicts and past interactions, he learns to listen for and observe the development of patterns of behavior as they recur in his client's interpersonal relationships. It is in noting the pattern and not the fragment of behavior that the therapist gets his finest clues to the character of conflict. And it is in noting the repetitiveness of the pattern that the therapist hears the client search for relief from his anxiety; and it is in that insatiable search for satisfaction that the client reveals who he is and what he wants.

The therapist learns to listen to the way in which those interpersonal themes echo back to the past, and his experience will have taught him to anticipate the day when they will reverberate in the therapeutic session itself. It is in observing the pattern of behavior develop during therapy, in hearing variations on the same theme often repeated and in many diverse relationships, in observing links that connect the present conflict with its generating sources in the past, and in observing the pattern eventually reenacted in his presence that the therapist learns most clearly how the client relates, what he wants, how he satisfies or fails to satisfy his needs, what he struggles to gain, and how he defends against anxiety.

In a client's current interactions, the therapist might find the client deeply involved in a continual recycling of behavior without apparent relief. And as the therapist notes those repetitive patterns of behavior, he sometimes sees some rather dramatic reenactments of conflict occurring in the daily life of his client. As the therapist learns more about the past as it relates to the client's current interactions, he begins to see that the client has reconstructed major experiences of his past in the present, that he is using his present relationships as a means to resolve past conflicts, for need satisfaction, or for fantasy fulfillment. Not only will he find a client repeating some minor facets of conflict in his interactions but when the behavior of some one or another client is subjected to scrutiny, it reveals that the client has set up and interacts in his relationships in ways which parallel major features of what were apparently the conflict-laden interactions of his developmental years. And the blueprint for those interactions often resides within the family.

As the behavioral parallels emerge, it becomes increasingly clear that the client is essentially reliving the past in the present. It becomes clear that the client's interactions in the present are simply ghostlike representatives of the client's still viable strivings as they relate to significant persons in his past, or that they represent the aftereffects of intense emotional experiences during the client's developmental years that left their mark and remained unresolved. It becomes clear that the client in increasingly frustrated ways and with increasing blatancy tries to rectify those earlier problematic relationships. And it becomes clear that the client remains unsatisfied. For often, if one relationship reconstructed for purposes of resolving conflicts collapses, the client immediately sets about constructing another relationship along similar lines.

At times, the parallels with the past are so dramatic, so undeniable, so blatant that the therapist wonders how the client can continue to recycle through one relationship after another as he does without insight. And yet, it seems that there is an inverse relationship between the blatancy with which the past is reproduced in the present and the client's insight into the meaning that a particular relationship holds for him. Often, such a client enters therapy because of his experience of frustration in his relationships for reasons that are unclear to him. For dynamic reasons, the client simply can't afford to see what is going on in his relationships. The predominant feelings that eventually are inevitably characterized in his relationships are alternating sensations of guilt, anxiety, conflict, and frustration.

To clarify the way in which a client might reconstruct the past in the present and repeatedly attempt to resolve conflict through a series of unhappy relationships, we turn to a case excerpt. As we follow the case, we will note how the unresolved conflicts of the past interpenetrate the client's relationships, affecting her perceptions, expectations, and interpretations of what occurs in those relationships. We will note how even during the initial stages of therapy those conflicts inevitably begin to find their way into therapy, influence the client's perceptions of and reactions to the therapist, and are reenacted there. As before, we will follow the therapist's thoughts and reactions as he works with the client, observing particularly the intricate interlocking of the client's current conflicts, her past experiences, and the client's experiences during the therapeutic session.

THE DANGERS AND INTRIGUES OF ENTANGLEMENTS: A PROLOGUE TO A CASE EXCERPT

Some clients approach a therapeutic interview with some rather clearcut ideas about how they would like the therapist to behave and they set about immediately to help the therapist to define his role. Their first words are expressions of concern about how the relationship is to be structured. Relationship is a poor word to use in this context because a relationship is precisely what the client contends he wants to avoid. Above all else, the client insists that the therapist maintain his professional status, warning him in various ways that he is not to become emotionally involved. It is important, the client contends, that the therapist remain objective. The client generally has no advise to offer the therapist about how he is to retain his objectivity, but there is an underlying fear that the therapist will become subjective and that therapy will rapidly deteriorate if he does so.

Such a client often has good reasons to feel as he does. Provided the client stays in therapy long enough to make his history known, that history often reveals a long series of confusing emotional entanglements with parents and others in which the client felt both emotionally bound and blinded to what was going on in those relationships. If the client's entanglements with parents have been very binding; if the behavior of the parents has been inconsistent— sometimes offering freedom but always with a price tag that rebinds the client;

if he finds that his relationships get sticky easily, that he can't extricate himself, and isn't offered a way out, then he will distrust and approach relationships with caution.

And that pattern is a critical factor in why the client wants the therapist to remain objective. In approaching the therapist for help, the client approaches the situation with what for him is very appropriate caution. When a person who has been repeatedly entangled turns to a therapist for help, his greatest conscious fear is that the therapeutic relationship, like previous ones, will simply become another entanglement, replicating what has happened in the past. The risks are great for the client; he fears that the therapist will become confused and emotionally involved, losing his perspective and thus his capacity to assist in releasing the client from his bondage.

If the therapist becomes distressed at having his tasks outlined or his role defined, he might respond in ways that are insensitive to what is churning in the client's insides and his response might lead to a premature rupture in what could have been a therapeutic relationship. If the therapist is insensitive to the client's fears about entanglements, he might push the client to be freer with his feelings, to become emotionally involved, to develop a relationship. He might say that unless the client can become involved with him, can see him not as a professional but as another human being, they might not be able to work together. When the therapist labors the fact that therapy is a relationship, that the therapist is human, and that they will need to get close if the client is to solve his problems, he is sure to drive the client from therapy.

If, on the other hand, the therapist simply allows the relationship to develop as the client finds him trustworthy; if he relaxes and considers the possibility that the client's history must have been replete with destructive relationships, he might be able to tolerate the distance that the client demands. If the therapist listens carefully to the initial words of the client, if he notices the caution, hears the pleas for objectivity and professional help, and doesn't assail the client for attempting to distance their encounters, then the client might remain long enough to reveal something of what he fears. And, as the therapist learns more about the client's previous and current interactions, as he becomes aware of the conflicts, problems, and strangleholds that have been exerted on the client, he will be able to see how the client has come to fear emotional involvement.

The therapist might find the client living out his emotions in confused ways without any grasp of what it is he is living out. During therapy the client might talk about wanting to deal with things rationally and at an intellectual level. Such a client abhors emotionalism because it is his emotional confusion that has gotten him into trouble in the first place. And when that emotional confusion is traced to its source, it is often found to have been stimulated by a subtly controlling parent who has bound the client in a confusing relationship.

Emotional entanglements that confuse and bind clients to a parent are as varied as the creative capacities of those who need to bind can design in order to hold the victim. In the extreme the client might find himself so entangled that he feels suffocated at every turn. Those entanglements are not always the work of mothers, although mothers seem to have a knack for thinking up particularly elaborate ways of binding their children which allow little freedom for movement. Although we can credit mothers with some rather marvelous achievements, fathers are apparently just as creative in binding their children when they put their minds to it, as many a confused son or daughter can attest.

Mothers sometimes bind their daughters to them by contending that they are very lonely people, thus activating indebtedness and guilt on the part of the daughter. Loneliness leads to heightened efforts at inducing indebtedness and guilt in the same way that the fear of entanglements in a client leads to distrust and to efforts to be rejected. A son is sometimes bound to his mother by the feeling that the mother needs to be rescued from the father. Although mothers seem to be rather adroit at entangling sons and daughters, fathers seem to have an aptitude for binding their daughters as will be pointed out momentarily in the case excerpt.

It seems that although the child is deeply involved in an entanglement with one of the parents, that is, that one of the parents is the primary source of entangling the child, the other parent plays a major supporting role in maintaining, deepening, and complicating the entanglement. It is as though one parent entangles the child and the other assures the other parent that he will participate in the trickery for his own gain in relation to the marriage partner. At first glance, one might not see the advantage to the mother to collude in and support the father's behavior if the father turns from her and favors his daughter, except that she might be glad to rid herself of the husband's attentions. But some of the gains for the mother emerge when the mother is observed to play on the guilt that has been generated in the daughter by the exclusiveness of her relationship to her father. Through guilt, the mother might bind the daughter to herself in a servile way, effectively having her neurotic loneliness tended to in the oversolicitous and overdetermined manner that only guilt can motivate.

Entangled relationships that bind a client back to a parent are always complex and are often mutually sustained collusions. The client's wish to be free of those entanglements is the healthy side of the client. It is the side that senses the destructiveness of those relationships, fears the entanglement, and seeks release. It is the side that recognizes that the fantasies generated in those relationships are limiting, anxiety provoking, and invariably frustrating. The side that wishes to be free is the side that seeks out the therapist and argues for objectivity.

But entangled relationships are intriguing as well. The intrigue of those relationships is a feature which stimulates the client to work in subtle ways to sustain those relationships and that rekindles them when those relationships are cooling. Interestingly enough, the client's preoccupation with distance and objectivity at the outset of therapy not only reveals his conscious fears that he will become entrapped in relationships that are destructive to his best interests, but that preoccupation reveals the client's susceptibility as well! The client's massive concern that the therapist retain his objectivity and maintain a professional stance are fairly good indices that the client's own unconscious wishes make him easy prey to becoming entangled in a web of confusing relationships. And, over time during therapy, not only do the histories of clients who demand distance reveal the dangers of entanglements but they eventually reveal the underlying pleasures, adventures, fantasies, and intrigue that such entanglements hold.

The client wants to be free and he fights the restraints imposed by those relationships, but he also wants to remain bound, to keep some fantasies alive. And it is that intricate blend of wishes and fears about entanglements which contributes to the client's continual efforts to recreate the emotional conditions of the past in the present. If the therapist listens carefully to the way in which certain themes permeate the client's current interpersonal relationships, he will note the client time and again constructing relationships that are patterned after those of the past. And if he listens to what transpires in those relationships, the therapist will see the wishes and fears about the entanglements with parents replayed vividly in those relationships. He will see both sides played out, the intrigue and the struggle to be liberated.

The Entangled Relationships of a Female Client

The client in this case was a young adult woman whose life had consisted of a series of entangled and broken relationships. The client entered therapy soon after she had broken a relationship with an eligible male who had become serious enough to focus his attentions on her exclusively. As the client felt herself becoming emotionally involved and as the prospect of marriage entered the picture, the client experienced intense anxiety, verging on a state of panic. Subsequently, the client broke the relationship for reasons that baffled both her and the interested man. Since variations on the theme of confusion, anxiety, and frustration characterized many of her relationships, the client became frightened that she would be unable to sustain a relationship and sought help to uncover the reasons for what she considered her irrational reactions.

The client began the session by saying that her relationships were a confused mess. She no longer knew what she wanted and didn't want. Often she seemed to become involved in relationships that got "all muddied up" and in which she felt as though she were in some kind of revolving door getting nowhere. But at other times when the man became interested and confronted her with the prospect of some permanent, exclusive relationship, the client would panic and terminate the relationship.

As the client started to talk of her confused relationships, she interrupted herself to say that she had come to see a therapist because she needed professional help and hoped to gain some perspective on her life. Somewhat embarrassed, the client said that she didn't want to tell the therapist his job, but she had heard that clients get involved and dependent on a therapist and that was exactly what she wanted to avoid. She wanted to learn to deal with matters rationally; she abhorred emotionalism. Whatever else she needed, the client said that she certainly didn't need another relationship! She was messed up enough as it was. The client waited a moment and since the therapist didn't say anything she asked him if he had heard her. He said that he had and suggested that perhaps if she told him something of what was going on in her relationships, he would see if he could help.

For the remainder of the session, the client talked in an almost uninterrupted fashion about her many frustrating and confusing relationships. The recent break-up with her boyfriend which precipitated her entrance into therapy represented one kind of relationship that was particularly anxiety-provoking to the client. The client said that her reactions in that relationship were thoroughly puzzling to her, and her anxiety mounted rapidly as she talked of what happened.

In retrospect, as she looked at it rationally, the client said that the relationship held promise of fulfilling what she felt she wanted—depth, security, and a commitment. Yet the client couldn't quiet the disquieting feeling that if she became emotionally involved, her emotions would limit her vision and make her vulnerable to being hurt. The client could find no rational grounds for her feelings and felt that they must be defensive; but despite her rational evaluation of the situation, the client couldn't surmount the fear that if she became emotionally involved, she would be blinded to what was going on in the relationship, and the client made clear that she was particularly contemptuous of naïve, emotional women.

For reasons she couldn't pin down, the client felt that men were an unreliable and uncommitted lot whose actions belie their words and promises. The client felt that if she allowed herself to need a man, sought his affection, made demands, or leaned on him for support, he would resent her and turn from her, leaving her needy, isolated, and lonely. In a general way, the client's fears seemed to be that she and the man would end up shackled together in a hollow relationship with no outlet for her feelings, cut off from other contacts, having lost her freedom but having gained nothing in its stead.

The client said that although she was confused about what she wanted in her relationships with men, the men in her life seemed to be equally confused about what they wanted from her. And then the client launched into a description of a number of relationships which seemed to drift along with both parties being bound together by some kind of vague attraction that kept the relationship recycling through a number of frustrating interactions with no apparent relief or future. According to the client, her initial expectations about the relationship never materialized. Initially, the client perceived the man as being strong yet sensitive and nurturant, qualities that she ideally felt a man ought to embody. But, invariably, as the relationship developed, the man often turned out to be ambivalent, conflicted, and passive, relying on the client as an outlet for his feelings and as a sounding board for his conflicts.

Of particular significance was the fact that despite the client's strident efforts to help the male resolve his conflicts, she was never able to find the appropriate key to unlock the conflicts. Her suggestions, advice, and reactions would lead nowhere. They never seemed to be particularly helpful or adequate and the client's general feelings often were that the situation was hopeless and that she was powerless to help. Yet she felt compelled to try and guilty if she didn't.

Although the client worked hard to shore up the male's ego and help him resolve his conflicts, the client came away from those relationships with little sense of what she meant to the man and what difference she made in his life. Despite her intense feelings about wanting validation of her sense of worth to the man, the client could not bring herself to ask for emotional support or responsivity and felt constricted about expressing what she felt. The client felt that she was in a bind. She wanted to know how the man felt about her; yet if she asked, she felt that she would have forced him into an awkward position, manipulated him, "put words in his mouth," thus never learning how he really felt about her.

The relationships would seem to recycle endlessly with the client arduously but frustratingly attempting to bring the man out of his shell, living with the unvalidated fantasy that the man was genuinely interested in her and valued her efforts on his behalf. And, after the relationship had run a fruitless, frustrating course and the client had given up on the man, he would show sufficient interest in and need for the client to rekindle the relationship, binding the client back into listening, soothing, and futile efforts at helping him to resolve his conflicts.

In still other relationships, the potential for the relationship's maturing into something substantial was offset by a crucial feature of the relationship. The male who attracted the client was already involved with another woman and the client completed a conflict-engendering triangle. In those relationships, the same unsatisfying pattern of futile efforts at helping a conflicted male, in nurturing, and in self-denial was evident with additional conflict stimulated by the client's feelings and reactions about the other woman. Often the client's predominant feelings toward the woman were characterized by contempt, anger, and a supercilious attitude, mixed with curiosity, sympathy, and rather strident efforts to understand what attraction held the man.

From the flow of the client's associations as she talked about one relationship after another it seemed that when the client became involved in a relationship that aroused anxiety because of the prospect of marriage and a commitment, the next relationship that she introduced seemed guaranteed not to go anyplace. It either involved a man, as noted above, who was already "spoken for" or it involved a male who seemed conflicted and who exhausted the client's repertoire in attempting to get clear with him about where she stood in relation to him.

At first the therapist thought that the sequence of associations reflected the client's defensive maneuvers. When she felt herself becoming involved, the client's self-doubts about being able to hold a man and have a satisfying relationship triggered anxiety and she retreated to the safety of a relationship with a passive male who was unable to make demands on her. The therapist thought that those relationships might represent a regressive feature, a flight from commitment for reasons of anxiety of the past.

But an interesting idea occurred to the therapist. Suppose, he thought, the pattern actually reflected a progressive healthy attempt by the client to solve whatever prevented her from maturing and meeting a male at an adult level. Perhaps, thought the therapist, the client is not so much retreating as she is attempting to recreate the problematic conditions which prevent growth so that she can mature. Instead of viewing those relationships as the client's efforts at completing old fantasies, it might be more useful to look at them for what they reveal of the client's efforts to rectify the past and gain release! That thought drastically changed the therapist's view of the client's relationships and opened the door for using what he learned in those relationships to see exactly what had "hung up" the client in the past.

The therapist's tentative internal hypothesis began to receive confirmation as he learned more about the client's family life. During the session, the client spontaneously introduced her relationship with her parents as being another source of conflict. The client was openly contemptuous of and angry at her mother. She saw her mother as a dependent, emotionally needy, and lonely person who was constantly searching for signs of affection from other members of the family. Although the client felt guilty and upset about the mother's condition, she felt that her mother had only herself to blame for her feelings of loneliness and isolation. The client wished that her mother had learned to fend for herself more and hadn't such narrow interests. The family was her mother's only outlet, and somewhat angrily the client pointed out that that was quite a burden on her father and herself.

At that point, the client immediately slid into a discussion of her relationship with her father. Apparently, the relationship between father and daughter had been both exclusive and excluding. Either because she was incapable of intruding into the relationship or because of some neurotic gains from being excluded, the mother did not actively interfere with the relationship. And as the client talked more of her relationship with her father, it could be seen that the relationship both intrigued and yet confused and conflicted the client.

On the one hand, the client's still active fantasies about her father were evident from her heightened interest, from her reminiscences of their earlier close relationship, and from the way she talked of his sensitivity to her feelings and mood swings. From what the client said, it seemed that her father sought out the client and invited her dependence. The invitation was conveyed through the father's perceptiveness of the client's changing moods; he seemed aware of very subtle behavioral cues to conflict and anxiety and his penetrating insights into what she was experiencing amazed and intrigued the client. But when the client, drawn to her father by the promise of help that is suggested by such sensitivity, accepted his invitation to depend and reveal herself, the father could offer no solutions to her conflicts. His ability to sense her mood changes, to pick up her anxiety, and note subtle indices of conflict seemed to start and stop with sensitivity. At such times the father attributed his inability to help to the fact that he and his daughter were very much alike. Although he could feel what she was experiencing, he would contend that he couldn't help her break free because he was conflicted in regard to the same matters.

And often, the conversation would then subtly shift to recenter in what the father was conflicted about, and the client would become the good listener. One area of conflict that repeatedly made its way into the conversation was the topic of the father's reactions to the mother. The client's father made no secret of his negative feelings about the mother's emotional demands. Over the years, as the mother looked for more support, the father became increasingly cold and distant, making his reactions clear to anyone who observed the interaction. But the client's understanding of her father's feelings toward her mother was not limited to what she inferred from her observations of her parents' interactions for her father communicated his feelings much more directly to her during his private talks with her.

During those intimate discussions, the father extolled the virtues of self-sufficiency and independence, often subtly alluding to problems in his relationship to the client's mother. The explicit theme of those talks was "be self-sufficient." But the undertone, the subtle message seemed to be, "Don't be like your mother." And as will be pointed out more fully later, the client is thrown into an unusual conflict situation when the message "be self-sufficient, ... not like your mother" is viewed in the emotional context of warmth and understanding in which it was given. For the two messages were clearly disjunctive. On the one hand the father invited the client to depend, to reveal her feelings, and he set the stage with his perceptiveness and sensitivity. But the counter message, which was as clearly enunciated and which the client saw her father live out daily, was his rejection of the very feelings he was trying to elicit.

Despite the conflict that her father's remarks must have engendered, the role of being her father's sounding board was apparently not alien to the client's interests and must have stirred up some interesting fantasies. For, as she talked of how her father relied on her for help, the therapist sensed the power she felt in being selected as her father's confidante. And from the breadth of topics that the client discussed with her father, it seemed that the father would use the client as his only emotional outlet for whatever troubled him.

But as the client talked on, her affect changed dramatically. The feelings of power could be seen to fade rapidly and in their stead emerged feelings of powerlessness. For the interesting and eventually frustrating thing was that when the client sought to help her father with his problems, she wasn't able to do so. Contrary to the father's ineptness in helping, the client would struggle with suggestions, advice, and whatever else she could muster up to try to break through his conflicts, but to no avail. The client even attempted tampering with the marriage by suggesting divorce. But a divorce wasn't forthcoming. And the client was left not only feeling powerless to help but guilty as well about the suggestions that she had made. And just when the client's frustration, sense of powerlessness, and guilt had reached the point where she became resentful and considered withdrawing, the father would become responsive to her feelings or make some gesture that he needed her. And the interaction would proceed through another cycle.

At the conclusion of the session, the client remarked that she probably had confused the therapist by rattling on as she had about all of her relationships. The client didn't see how anybody could make sense out of her incoherent presentation. She felt that if she had organized her thoughts better and could have kept from getting so emotional at times she would probably have done a better job. She also reminded the therapist that she was a defensive person and had probably hidden some of the really relevant facts about her relationships. The therapist commented that his feelings had been to the contrary. He felt they had made a start, that he had learned something of the client's conflicts, that she had provided him with material that he felt they could work on together, and that they could continue at the next session.

The Therapist's Thoughts about the Session

During the session the therapist listened carefully to what transpired in the client's current interactions. From how and what the client introduced as important, the therapist got an initial impression about what, where, and under what circumstances conflict was generated and how the client coped with her anxious moments. And as the therapist followed the spontaneous flow of the client's thoughts about one relationship after another he attempted to assess the emotional conditions in those relationships as an initial guide to what they revealed of where the client was developmentally.

The meaning of the client's anxious and pleasurable reactions to what was occurring in her current relationships became more understandable as links between the client's current feelings and her past interactions with her parents began to emerge during the session. Those links with the past are sometimes blatant, sometimes subtle, but always complex. At times the links are not too readily apparent if the client's reactions have undergone a series of defensive modifications to previous experiences. But if the therapist listens carefully with an ear to the recurrent emotional themes that transcend the specifics of a particular time, place, or relationship, he can often hear echoes of past conflicts replayed in the present.

Not only do a client's present reactions sometimes represent the residual feelings of past conflict-laden interactions, but at times those interactions are the unmodified behavioral reproduction of earlier problematic interactions. And so, we might expect to find some rather dramatic behavioral parallels between what the client repeatedly reenacts in the present in relation to the men in her life and what occurred in her relationship with her father during her developmental years. From his observations of that repetitive reenactment, the therapist increases his understanding of his client since those behavioral parallels are clear-cut indices of some of the still viable strivings of the client; they point to where well-worn fantasies are still active and they delineate unresolved conflict.

It is when the behavioral parallels emerge, when the recurrent emotional themes are noted, and when the generalized attitudes are understood as residues of the past that the therapist has some of his finest clues to what the client is still struggling to integrate and how and in what ways unresolved past conflicts motivate the client's behavior in the present. And it is from those observations about where conflict is still active that the therapist is provided with his first approximation to how conflict will be reenacted in his presence and with rough guidelines to what his participation in the change process will entail.

In the first part of this section, we will note the ways in which the client's past provides a blueprint for some of her interactions in the present. We will look at the way in which the client's fears, expectations, and interpretations of her current experiences were generated by and can be understood in terms of the learning that took place within the family. Following our discussion of the way in which the client's current interactions are linked with the past, we will alter our perspective and turn to a study of the way in which the client's conflicts are already finding their way into the therapeutic hour even during the initial session and how the stage is being set for the later reenactment of conflict in relation to the therapist.

Links with the Past: Family
Patterns That Set Conflict into Motion

Several features of what the client revealed of her past interactions with her parents seemed crucially linked to some of her present feelings and reactions. Although the client spent most of her time in discussing her relationship with her father, her cryptic allusions to her mother suggested, as is generally the case, that both parents played a role in the client's current conflicts. The client's conflicts would not have developed as they had unless the mother had played a significant supporting role in colluding with the father in binding the daughter.

But despite the mother's likely collusion, the father apparently played a dominant role in setting conflict into motion. The father's relationship to his daughter was an unusually complex and binding one. No one facet of the relationship was sufficient to explain the client's sense of panic when a commitment was in the offing or her unsatisfying repetitious interactions in other relationships. In order to understand the full impact of her relationship to her father on the generation of conflict, the interplay of a number of facets of the relationship must be understood in configuration.

In the first place, the way that the father used his own sensitivity to his daughter's feelings, mood swings, and moments of anxiety provided the emotional context for potential conflict. In themselves, the father's understanding, penetrating insights, and sensitivity to whatever the client was experiencing were indeterminate features of eventual conflict. They were laudable paternal characteristics since they invited closeness and held promise of meeting the client's needs. But when the client moved on the promise of help, accepted it at face value, and revealed her conflicted feelings to her father, instead of help and potential resolution, she found only impotence. After drawing the client out, the father's inability to help for whatever reasons was damaging. Essentially the father invited the client and then "cut her off at the pass"! The father's message "depend on me" was clearly given and then the father proved undependable. Although, as will be pointed out later, the client's feeling that men are an unreliable, untrustworthy lot and that their actions belie their words and promises was an outgrowth of many other related factors, her father's hollow promises probably contributed in some measure to those later feelings.

Had the father stopped with promising help and then disappointing the client, the relationship would probably not have developed as it did. Anger, resentment, and possible depression would be natural reactions to such a state of affairs. The person in need of help who has been offered some hope which is later withdrawn feels cheated and angry, and his sense of trust is shaken. In addition, since the client had abrogated her relationship with her mother in favor of one with her father, she was also likely to experience some depression about the loss of that potential source of help.

But, in this case, the client's reactions were conditioned by other facets of the relationship. And it was those contingencies that set the binding process into motion. In the first place, the father reversed the parental role. After drawing the client in to discuss her conflicts, the conversation subtly shifted to a discussion of how the father was also conflicted. Whereas the original message to the daughter was "depend on me," that message was subtly converted into its complementary—"I depend on you"—and such a role reversal generates conflict for several reasons.

There is something inevitably restraining about a parent's "needing" the child. In a healthy relationship, the parent might satisfy needs in relation to the child, but it is the character of the needs that makes the difference. The healthy parent's message is "I am concerned about your welfare." The binding parent says "I need you; I depend on you for emotional support." In the latter situation, the child's needs are sacrificed; they become secondary to the satisfaction of the needs of the parent.

Of equal significance in the generation of conflict is the inappropriate shouldering of responsibility that such parental behavior demands which outdistances the emotional maturity of the child. In the extreme, the child feels bound to help, guilty if he doesn't, and emotionally drained by the parental demands and pressures. And if the sense of guilt is intense enough, it even precludes access to the underlying anger and resentment that such a burden generates.

That emotional drain is experienced in yet another, more anxiety-provoking way. When a parent who is sought out for help justifies his inability to do so on the grounds that his own conflicts interfere, another feeling often begins to stir around in the child. The predominant feeling is one of fright about the parent's incapacitated state. Feelings of guilt, anger, frustration, or whatever might be coupled to the experience of fright. But fright is the overriding feeling that the child acts on. For the child, in his dependent state recognizes, and rightly so, that his own survival, growth, and vitality are tied in with and flow from the vitality of the parent.

To the end of stabilizing the situation, the child might begin expending energy in the direction of attempting to pump some vitality into the parent in the belief that, if the parent can be revitalized, the child will have gained in the process. And, in the case under discussion, bolstering up faltering egos was precisely how the client spent many of her waking hours, both with her father and later with some of the conflicted males with whom she interacted. Although the client's efforts on her father's behalf were spurred by other, more complex motivations as well, the fact remains that the client, in order to get anything in that and other relationships, invested a great deal which, incidentally, for reasons to be discussed in a moment, netted her very little in return.

On the one hand, then, the reversal of roles, the father's professed conflicts, and his dependence on the client were emotionally taxing and anxiety provoking. Such experiences would normally lead to efforts at release from the relationship; and to some extent the residue of those feelings probably contributed to the client's entrance into therapy. Release might be easy if pain were the only feature of a relationship. There are, however, major deterrents to emotional separation. In the first place, needs still remained unsatisfied. If needs are strong, the fantasy which takes precedence and keeps the relationship recycling is that satisfaction is just around the corner if only the right key can be found to set the relationship aright. The strength of such fantasies is a measure of the unmet needs. And in this case it will be recalled that whenever the client's father tended to the client's needs, no matter how fleetingly, the client was immediately reengaged in expending energy on his behalf.

That expenditure of energy brings us to the next point—the neurotic cycle. There is a more crucial dynamic which operates to rebind a person into what might on the surface appear to be a totally unsatisfying relationship. The fact is that the client does experience pleasure in the relationship. Although the basic needs remain unsatisfied, the client achieves some secondary gains from the relationship; and it is those secondary gains that set into motion a behavioral cycle that is relatively impervious to modification. The imperviousness to penetration and change is a measure of the intensity of the pleasure that the person experiences.

The entangling, binding process, therefore, is not a one-sided affair, and collusion occurs because the painful side of the relationship is countered by equally intense and pleasurable experiences for both child and parent. To understand both sides of the picture—the powerful fantasies, the neurotic gains, and the intrigue as well as the experience of anxiety and subsequent guilt generated in the relationship—it is necessary to turn to a careful study of what the client gained and lost from her relationship to her father, what kept the client bound, and how she colluded in sustaining the relationship. And once the nature of the collusion is clarified, its effects in the client's later perceptions, feelings, and repetitive unsatisfying interactions with conflicted, passive males becomes more understandable.

The Collusion: The Heart of the Conflict

The plot thickens rapidly and the conflict-engendering nature of the interaction becomes clearer when the father's message to the daughter is spelled out in greater detail. It will be recalled that the content of the conversations when they recentered on the father's conflicts often consisted of complaints about the mother, her emotionalism, overreactivity, lack of self-sufficiency, and demands. Those conversations took place in the context of a warm, receptive interaction, quite the contrary to the father's relationship with the mother, which was generally characterized by coldness and disdain.

When the content of that communication is coupled to the emotional context in which it was delivered, the groundplan is laid for an unusual conflict situation. There are two interrelated messages embedded in that communication. If it could be formulated in words, the essence of the first part of the father's message to the daughter would be something like "I depend on you as an outlet for my feelings *because I can't depend on your mother.*"

A father-daughter relationship founded on such a premise is intrinsically collusive; it breeds disaffiliation from the mother and is fertile ground for the generation of powerful fantasies in relation to the father. And, as will be pointed out, those two factors—the disaffiliation and the fantasies—work against each other to heighten conflict and generate intense anxiety. As the daughter colludes with the father in attempting to liberate him from the offending mother as the client did in this case, she widens the communication gap between herself and her mother and in addition her subterfuge stimulates guilt.

As that gap widens, the client loses her model; and as the client reported, she felt that she could not learn from her mother and devalued any contribution the mother might make. Those attributions were probably based in part on accurate observations of some of the mother's actual inappropriate behavior. But to a large extent, those feelings were likely stimulated by the client's fantasies about her father, by what the client learned the father valued and found reprehensible in the mother, and by the client's own rationalizations to offset the experience of guilt about her motivations.

But there is another side to the client's feelings about her mother. The client was contemptuous of the mother; she felt the mother was naïve and blinded by her emotions. Those reactions probably reflected the client's genuine anger toward her mother for not interfering in that relationship between daughter and father. Whereas the client's "bitchiness" was a defense against guilt about her collusion with the father, her genuine anger was a healthy reaction based on the wish that the mother had more "backbone" and would interfere to liberate the daughter from her entanglement with the father. For, despite the intrigue of that relationship and the pleasure she achieved, the selfsame fantasies that were stimulated by the client's position of power had to be a source of intense anxiety as well.

With the mother out of the picture, the relationship with the father was guaranteed to stalemate. That is, all children have fantasies, sexual and aggressive, about one or the other parent. And insofar as the relationship between the parents is in good order, the child can have his fantasies, test them out, and learn something of his feelings and the reactions that he elicits from significant people. But when the interaction between the parents has cooled as it had in this case, then those fantasies become anxiety-provoking experiences because the reality of the situation is such that the child has no guarantee that those fantasies might not materialize. What might be an interesting fantasy to toy around with becomes quite a different matter if the potential for its being converted into action occurs.

But what must have been an even more crucial source of confusion and anxiety in this case was the father's reactions to the client's collusion. The client, it will be recalled, began suggesting, advising, and even hinting about the potential dissolution of the marriage in her efforts to help her father resolve his conflicts. But nothing worked. The marriage remained intact and the advice went unheeded. The consequence in the client would be dramatic. Whereas the father's turning to the client and away from the mother would generate fantasies of power, the client's fruitless labors would lead to the experience of powerlessness.

As an aside it might be noted that the client's efforts were destined to be frustrating. What the child who tries to help a parent by intruding into the relationship between the parents cannot possibly realize is that the parents "need" the relationship as it is. Tampering with the relationship, contrary to the expectation of the child does not lead to change or even to rewards for being "helpful." What it activates is anxiety in the parent, and the child, contrary to expectations, might be dismayed to find that he is punished for his efforts.

The second part of the father's message provides additional perspective on the binding nature of the relationship and its effects in the client's eventual anxiety about emotional entanglements. As stated earlier, the content of the father's message to the daughter often involved his complaints about the mother. The predominant complaint, reiterated on many occasions, was that the mother was too emotional, too demanding, and too dependent. As he discussed the mother, the father often extolled the virtues of self-sufficiency. The explicit content of that part of the message was "be self-sufficient" and implicit in that message was the deeper, more conflict-laden message, "Don't be like your mother!"

The way in which that message tends to create an intolerable bind in the client's relationship to her mother has already been discussed. But the message carried other, and equally destructive consequences in the client's emotional life.

If the message "be self-sufficient ... don't be like your mother" is compared with the father's sensitivity to the client's feelings, his penetrating insights into her conflicts and his repeated invitations to the daughter to reveal herself to him, then one can begin to sense the client's confusion and resistance to involvements.

One can only conjecture at the confusion the client experienced when the father's disjunctive messages are considered together. On the one hand, the father arranged the props to invite a close, warm, dependent relationship. Yet when the client moved on the invitation, the father rejected the client's bid for help not only by suggesting that he was unable to do so because of his own conflicts but in equally clear behavioral language the father made known that he rejected emotionally dependent women.

It is no small wonder that intense anxiety was stirred up whenever the client felt herself becoming emotionally involved. For if the client heard both messages, she must have felt the trap, and a most destructive trap at that! For to accept the invitation to become emotionally close and reveal her feelings to her father was to set herself up as vulnerable to being rejected on the very grounds that led to the father's rejection of the mother. That is, if the client moved to the open arms of her father, expressed her conflicts, and leaned on him for help, she would essentially be behaving as her mother did and *would set the process into motion for her own rejection*.

Feelings in the Present:
Residue of the Past

In the last few pages, some of the therapist's speculations about the conflict engendering nature of the client's family interactions have been discussed. Despite the highly tentative nature of those thoughts, impressions, and hypotheses about how the trouble started, their introduction at this time has provided something of a general overview of the way that the therapist listens to the past as a guide to the meaning of present conflict. In that discussion, either directly or by implication, the way in which the client's past affected her present behavior was noted. But it might be worth revisiting a few examples in order to point up the power of those early interactions on the client's current anxiety, feelings, and reactions.

For example, the sense of panic the client experienced when her relationships intensified and she felt herself becoming emotionally involved is more understandable in light of her observations and personal experiences in relation to her parents. Several interlocking features of those interactions seem appropriate to consider in this regard. The client's feelings were probably stimulated by what she observed transpiring between her parents, by what she personally experienced in relation to her parents, and most critically as a consequence of the collusion that eventually characterized her relationship with her father.

In the first place, the client's observations of her parent's interactions must have had a significant effect on her. The client observed her mother's affectional needs going unmet. In many ways, the client learned of the disdain that the father felt for the mother and she saw its devastating effects in the relationship. She saw and heard the father reject. And the more that he rejected, the more desperate and blatant became the mother's demands. Progressively worsening with time, hostility, then apathy, isolation, and loneliness seemed to be the marks of the parents' deteriorating relationship. Those behaviors were paraded back and forth in front of the client during her developmental years and most certainly must have affected the client's eventual fears about the isolating consequences of becoming emotionally involved.

The client saw her mother and father shackled together in a hollow relationship—and that was precisely one of her fears about what would occur in her own relationship with men. Whereas the client's observations provided one basis for her fears in that regard, those fears were grounded in other, more significant experiential learnings of her developmental years. Not only was the client an observer of the parental scene, she was a central participating figure in those interactions. In her collusion with the father, the client not only set the stage for the induction of guilt about her role in the mother's distraught, compromised state, but in addition that collusion probably set into motion fears of retaliation.

Those fears, although not experienced directly in relation to the mother, must have been experienced in terms of the feeling that she would someday get her "just deserts." Considering her observations and her own successful collusion with her father, what guarantee did the client have that her own commitments would fare any better. When the client's father turned to her from the mother, the father was a living example of the untrustworthiness of men, their unreliability, and their lack of commitment. Since the client and her father lived out that untrustworthiness together, it is no small wonder that the client wanted to remain rational and feared losing her perspective when she became emotionally involved.

Above all else, the client feared her own credulousness. The client felt that she would be blinded by her own emotions to what was transpiring in her relationships. Those fears were not mere fantasies of what might be; they were the reality-oriented consequences of what had been. The client's mother had been essentially blinded by her own emotions and needs to what was transpiring in the relationship between the father and daughter. The collusion with the father, therefore, not only induced guilt, but it acted as a powerful determinant of the client's eventual distrust of men.

But there was an even more crucial determinant of the client's pessimistic outlook about the future course of her relationships that the collusion alone was insufficient to explain. Had the father turned to the daughter and then remained consistently warm and receptive, the collusive aspects of the relationship would have created problems, but the client's anxiety would not have taken the turn it did. The client's "irrational" feelings that men sport with a woman, that their actions belie their words, and that a woman ends up needy and lonely seem associated most closely—not with the collusion—but rather they reflect the consequences of the father's reactions to the client's responsivity to him.

When the father reacted to the client in essentially the same manner as he had to the mother after stimulating her responsivity, he set into motion what was perhaps the single most crucial factor in the development of her later reactions. The crucial learning that took place was that the client was like her mother. Despite her conscious disidentification with her, at a deeper level the client became thoroughly identified with the neurotic side of the mother.

Whereas the collusion itself was living proof of the untrustworthiness of men, the client's actual experience in the collusive relationship not only reinforced her feelings of distrust, but they served to forge an identification with the mother which acted as a powerful predictor of the client's own future, unhappy relationships. When the client felt the internal pressure to become emotionally close to men, her anxiety intensified. She would try to choke off her needs, felt she couldn't trust a man, and resisted her urges to lean—needs that were alien to her better judgement. Essentially the client feared that she—like her mother—would end up "high and dry," lonely, and isolated. She felt what she sensed her mother felt—despair about her interpersonal impact. And that is at the heart of what was symbiotic in that relationship. The reality of her mother's unhappiness became the predictive basis for what "would be" the client's unhappiness!

Reflections of Conflict
during the Therapeutic Session

Thus far, we have introduced some ways that the therapist tries to understand his client—by synthesizing what he learns of his client's present conflicts, the historical development of those conflicts, and general theoretical material about the developmental processes. But we have yet to consider other dimensions of that synthetic process. To the manifestations and generating sources of conflict as they are revealed by what the client reports of his life outside of therapy and of his developmental past must be added the reflections of conflict as they are manifest by the client's general behavior during the therapeutic session, and in particular by his reactions to the therapist.

Once consideration is given to how conflict is manifested in the therapeutic session, then a most crucial dimension is introduced—the experiential basis of the therapist's understanding. The client's behavior within the session not only strengthens at an experiential level some of the therapist's hunches about the nature of conflict, but it provides the therapist with guidelines to how the relationship might develop, to how conflict might generate during therapy, and to what the therapist's participation in the change process might eventually entail.

Even during an initial session as therapy gets underway, there is an immediate and constantly complicating interaction between therapist and client. Although the client's behavior during the session is stimulated in good measure by his own internal constructions based on past experience, his reactions are constantly interwoven with and increasingly affected by the therapist's responsivity to him. At this time, however, the rapidly complicating interactive nature of the developing relationship and its effects on therapy will not be the principal focus of study. The primary focus of this section will be on what the client's behavior during the session reveals of his conflicts and how the client's behavior, expectations, and reactions to the therapist not only reflect conflict-laden areas but point to the probable nature of the developing relationship and course of therapy.

From what the client reveals of himself, from the way he construes his conflicts, from the spontaneous flow of associations, from his nonverbal behavior and symbolic language, the therapist learns of his client and can make some tentative guesses about the nature of his problems. But it is only when the client's presentation of himself *is viewed in terms of its meaning within the interpersonal context of a therapeutic relationship that the therapist gets insight*—not just into the nature of conflict—but *into the nature of the therapeutic venture*. It is when the therapist listens to what the client expects of him, how he reacts to him, what he projects, and how he interprets the therapist's reactions that the therapist begins to understand what the course of therapy will be like, how the relationship will develop, how conflict will find its way into therapy and be expressed there, and what his probable role in the change process will be.

And so, in this section, as we look at the behavior of the client during the session, we will note how feelings based on past problematic interactions are already generating in relation to the therapist and how the stage for the potential reenactment of conflict is being set. As we follow the client's reactions during the session, we will flash back to his history in order to assess the probable latent effects of the client's behavior as they might affect the eventual course of therapy. And we will speculate rather freely about the potential therapeutic effects of differing therapist reactions to the client.

As the therapist thought about the client's behavior during the session, he was immediately struck by the massive amount of information that the client introduced about her many confusing relationships. The introduction of any material into therapy is determined by many and often conflicting motives. And when the quantity of material that the client produced during the initial session is viewed in the context of the client's history of conflict, several hypotheses are suggested about the client's possible mixed motives in presenting herself as she did.

On the one hand, the therapist considered the possibility that the client's behavior might be defensively motivated. At the most conscious level, the client's incessant rambling on about one relationship after another could be construed as an effort to control the session. Through her uninterrupted talk, the client might have been attempting to keep the therapist from intruding and focusing on those aspects of what she was saying that were anxiety-provoking, thus keeping her feelings in check. And the client, of course, made enough comments about "distance" and "rationality" to support such an hypothesis.

Although such a general hypothesis has merit to it, it is generic in nature and as such provides the therapist with little insight of a differential nature into the meaning of this client's behavior. A related but more salient hypothesis is suggested when the extensiveness of the client's productions are considered in light of the content of those productions. In that regard, the therapist hypothesized that the client's anxiety about emotional closeness could have motivated her to attempt to "fill up" the session in order to stave off any emotionally charged interaction with the therapist.

Considering this client's history of conflict, the emotional conditions inherent in a therapeutic relationship would be especially anxiety-provoking. First of all, the therapist, by training and disposition, is a perceptive and feeling-oriented person. Second, the therapeutic venture carries an implicit "invitation" to the client to reveal herself. Both of those conditions of the therapeutic relationship are associatively close to the preconditions that characterized the client's conflict generating interactions with her father.

It will be recalled that the client's father was a sensitive person who invited self-disclosure. And when the client accepted that invitation and revealed herself, she found herself bound in a relationship which was destructive to her better interests. The client had no experiential grounds on which to assume that the therapist would use her disclosures any more constructively than her father had. Considering the unproductive use to which the client's father had put his "penetrating insights," to provide the therapist with the opportunity to intrude with insights of his own would be tantamount to setting herself up for another letdown.

Although the client's anxiety about the risks of another emotional involvement and another disillusionment might provide a partial explanation for the way the client presented herself, a second and somewhat complementary hypothesis also suggests itself. By overwhelming a therapist with data, an adroit client can manage to keep her ongoing relationships intact—not only to avoid the anxiety of change—but because the relationships are intrinsically pleasurable! And, as the therapist thought about how easily the client became entangled in seemingly interminable relationships, he assumed that those relationships attracted as well as repelled the client.

As was stated earlier, the client's involvement with her father was many faceted—some basic needs went ungratified but that loss was compensated by neurotic gains which tend toward perpetuating the status quo. The fantasies of being more powerful than the mother and having the "inside track" with the father are pleasurable experiences, and such unresolved experiences are powerful determinants of later behavior; they tend to be reawakened easily; and they stimulate efforts at recreating those emotional conditions whenever the opportunity arises so that the fantasies can be acted out again and again.

It would be reasonable to hypothesize, then, that the client would resist the penetration of those fantasies. And a confused therapist is as effective a way as any to forestall the perforation of such satisfying fantasies. By confusing the therapist, the client not only retains the fantasies but she nets an added bonus as well. If the therapist is rendered ineffective, the client resets the stage for an equally neurotic entanglement with the therapist himself. Once the therapist becomes confused, doubtful of himself, passive, and feels unable to help, his behavior recapitulates the reactions of other significant men in the client's life and sets the wheels into motion for the transfer of feelings and the reenactment of those problematic interactions during therapy.

That is not to imply that the development of the relationship along those lines is good or bad. At this time, it is simply noted that if the therapist reacts in a confused, passive manner, some consequences are inevitable that he will eventually need to deal with if the client is to change. As an aside, it might be noted that if the therapist eventually "catches on" to how his behavior has stimulated the regeneration of the client's feelings and reactions to him, he is in an unusually good position to help the client achieve more far-reaching therapeutic gains than might otherwise be possible!

There are, however, some serious difficulties that are likely to develop if the client readily confuses the therapist and stimulates anxiety in him about how to cope with the massive amount of data that the client has introduced. To consider the consequences of the therapist's anxiety about helping, a third hypothesis must be proposed about what the client intended by all the information that she provided. So far, it has been proposed that the client's anxiety about emotional closeness and her resistance to change might have contributed in part to her way of presenting herself. The next hypothesis is that the client intends to confuse the therapist to confirm her contention that men are an unreliable, untrustworthy, and unhelpful lot. This hypothesis suggests that the client gains satisfaction from retaliating against men for the hurt and disappointment they have rendered.

In considering this hypothesis, the therapist drew on what he learned of the client's disillusionment about men as it was generated in relation to her father. The father invited and then rejected. Such behavior tends to trigger frustration, anger, resentment, and retaliatory feelings. As noted earlier, when the client is confronted with a therapist who is sensitive and inviting as her father was, she is apt to associate the preconditions with their consequences. In other words, those parallel emotional conditions in the family and in therapy suggest that the client is likely to expect that if she reveals herself, she will be "cut off" as her father had done. Not only does that expectation set into motion anxiety about emotional closeness, but it is also likely to set off the accompanying angry, retaliatory feelings that she must have experienced in the earlier parallel situation.

By confusing the therapist, the client frustrates him—an experience that she has often felt. And one can only imagine the satisfaction that the client might gain from observing a man frustrated for a change. Second, if the therapist becomes confused and communicates his confusion *as helplessness* to the client, his behavior must touch the client's ears as an echo of her father's words, "I hear your problem, but I can't help you."

Such a message would create contradictory reactions in the client. On the one hand, the message has safety in it since it precludes the expansion of the underlying anxiety about becoming emotionally close; it recapitulates the family picture thus validating the client's feelings about the unhelpfulness of significant men in her life; and it justifies the recycling of unprogressive angry, resentful reactions to the therapist. But the same message must also stimulate intense anxiety. For if the therapist's effectiveness has been negated, the client recognizes at some level that her chances of gaining release from her bondage have been lost.

Thus far, we have considered some possible defensive motives which might have contributed to the client's presenting herself as she did. It has not been intended to suggest that those motives are mutually exclusive or that they are even separable in time. In addition, a client's defensive maneuvering is often intricately interwoven with the progressive, integrative, and constructive motives of the client. As any therapist can attest, from moment to moment during therapy one can observe the delicate balancing of defense and productive exploration. Not only does the therapist note a rapid shift in motive but embedded in any verbalization—although the defensive or progressive feature might predominate—are the seeds of its opposite. And that brings us to the next hypothesis about what the client intended.

The client's reasons for entering therapy, although mixed, were motivated by a conscious wish to change. That side—the constructive, healthy side—of the client suggests another and a most intriguing hypothesis regarding the presentation of data. By presenting the therapist with a massive amount of data about her many different and confusing relationships, through her rapid speech, and through the way she skipped back and forth from one entanglement to another, the client *conveyed behaviorally the confusion that characterized her life more dramatically than she could have in any other way*. Through her presentation, the client revealed her susceptibility to involvement, her need for perspective, and her wish to be released. If at the end of the session the therapist felt confused by the morass of data, by the many entangled relationships in which the client was immersed, then *the therapist was feeling what the client was living out*. And the client has done a very good job of presenting her case to the therapist.

But the most compelling hypothesis about the meaning of the client's presentation of herself during the session remains to be formulated. According to the next hypothesis to be considered, it is proposed that *through her extensive productions the client was in effect "acting out" in relation to the therapist a central feature of her conflicts with men.* Viewed from this perspective, it is proposed that even during the initial session the client was already deeply involved with the therapist and was beginning to live out some of her wishes and fears in relation to him. To consider the full impact of this proposition on the developing relationship and the change process, several relevant features of the interview need to be briefly reviewed.

The Unfolding of Conflict During Therapy

Perhaps the first rough guidelines to the way in which the client's conflict-laden interactions were finding their way into therapy and being experienced in relation to the therapist might be inferred from the way in which the first and last few moments of the session were dynamically linked together. In the first few moments of the session, the client's preoccupation with rationality, with avoiding entanglements, and with dependency revealed the client's susceptibility in those regards. The client revealed her vulnerability to becoming emotionally involved by her adamant stand against it.

The client's preoccupation with rationality and distance not only suggests that she was defending against involvements but her obsessional concerns revealed the weakness of the defenses and the strength of the underlying drives. Through her behavior, the client revealed that she was still harboring feelings that had not yet been resolved, that she still needed and sought something, that despite her fears the drive to become emotionally close was strong. And so long as those needs were viable, the therapist knew that in her own time and way and on her own terms the client would close the emotional distance.

Second, through her preoccupation with remaining rational and uninvolved, the client not only clued the therapist to the strength of the needs but from the way that she equated emotional closeness, involvement, and entanglements, the client revealed something of the character of the disabling interactions. And, during the course of the session, from what the client described of her many confusing relationships, and from the way in which many of her relationships recycled in frustrating ways without relief, she confirmed the fact that she had good grounds to defend against another emotional involvement.

Third, in her anxiety about maintaining distance, the client revealed that not only was she easy prey to becoming enmeshed in emotional entanglements, but also that her rather strident efforts to assist the therapist in defining his role suggested the neurotic character of those interactions. In clarifying the therapist's role, the client made clear that her fears of involvement were mixed with fantasies that she was powerful enough to entangle the therapist and cloud his vision. Alternately, the client's suspiciousness of the motivations of others alerted the therapist to the possibility that significant others in the client's life had played out the reciprocal role by entangling the client in relationships that were destructive to her better interests.

But for purposes of the present discussion, the interesting development in terms of the therapeutic relationship was that despite the client's often repeated "self-reminders" to remain rational and uninvolved, the client was already involved by the end of the session. During the session, the client "gave" the therapist a great deal. She revealed many sides of herself, provided much useful material, and, except for a few comments intended to facilitate the client's freewheeling productions, the therapist provided the client with little in return.

Yet at the end of the session, despite the amount and richness of material that she produced, the client wondered whether she had provided the therapist with enough information, feared it might be irrelevant, and wondered whether she had been defensive and too emotional. When the client's concluding remarks are viewed within the context of the client's history of conflict in relation to men, a significant behavioral parallel is evident in the two sets of interactions. Historically, in relation to her father and men generally, the client would work hard, provide a lot, and yet come away feeling that what she gave was insufficient, irrelevant, or insignificant. Those selfsame emotional conditions characterized the client's reactions to the therapist. She worked hard for him, wondered whether she had "dented" him, felt that she had been too emotional—a characteristic her father abhorred—and finally felt that her efforts were probably insufficient and irrelevant.

Dynamically speaking, through her reactions to the therapist and her expectations with regard to his feelings about her—based not on the therapist's actual feelings and reactions but on her internal constructions of what those feelings *must be* in light of her past experiences—the client linked together the therapeutic hour with her past and present experiences with men and set the stage for productive therapeutic work. Through her irrational reactions, the client not only pointed up the central features of her conflicts but in experiencing those feelings in direct relation to the therapist, she brought the therapist into the conflict arena and provided him with a solid experiential basis for helping her to counter those disabling feelings.

Once the therapist grasps the dynamic parallel between the client's reactions to himself and her behavior with others, the therapeutic task begins to take shape. In the next few paragraphs, let's briefly follow the way that the therapist might conceptualize the first steps in setting therapy into motion, what he might anticipate as roadblocks along the way, and what facets of conflict he might expect to emerge as anxiety is triggered by his participation in the change process.

As the therapist thought about the process of therapy with his client, he felt that if therapy was to be productive it was of crucial importance that he begin immediately to counter the client's feelings of powerlessness in her interpersonal relationships. Variations on the theme of powerlessness interpenetrated many of the client's relationships, the theme was repeatedly introduced in different contexts during the session, and it was a variant of that theme of being without the resources to affect others that was expressed in relation to the therapist at the conclusion of the session.

Those feelings had a significant history to them as has been pointed out elsewhere. It is not intended here to review the development of those feelings except to note that in her relationships the client was often left feeling empty and frustrated; she never learned what she had to give or what was appropriate to give because what she offered was never acceptable. And, eventually, the client began to believe that she had nothing to give, that she lacked influence, and that she, like her mother, would end up isolated and lonely.

When the feelings that what she had to give was insufficient, irrelevant, and insignificant were experienced directly in relation to the therapist, the client provided the therapist with the opportunity to affect and eventually alter her perception of her impact on others. And the therapist set into motion the process of modifying those perceptions when he countered the client's closing remarks with the comment that he felt that *she had provided him with material that they could work on together*.

The therapist's cryptic comment at the conclusion of the session that they had made a start was intended to communicate several things simultaneously to the client. Among other things, the therapist wanted the client to know that he viewed therapy as a joint venture. Second, the therapist felt that the client needed to know that she was understandable. But the most crucial message that the therapist wanted to convey was his feeling that *the client had provided useful material*, that he valued her contributions, and that he felt they were appropriate.

The last point is particularly crucial in this case. The client usually left her relationships feeling empty which is a variant of the intensely disabling feeling that one lacks the inner resources to cope with and modify one's life situation as needed. Through his response the therapist hoped to pave the way for helping the client to learn of her inner resources and how to use them effectively. In this as in other cases, that process of helping the client to build on her own internal resources begins in the initial session and is expanded throughout therapy.

And, as the therapist thought about future sessions, he felt that the therapeutic task was certainly not to derogate the father or even to try to force insight into how the father's reactions had affected her. Such insight would come in its own time. At the outset of therapy, the therapeutic task in part was to use what the therapist understood had gone wrong in that relationship as a guide to what the client still sought and needed. The task was to allow the client to have an impact on him, another significant person in her life. And the task was to help the client to learn what she had to give and how to give appropriately.

In that regard, the therapeutic task is most assuredly not one of fabricating situations or scampering around trying to create opportunities for the client to feel useful. Such a manipulation of the relationship would be experienced as manufactured and degrading by the client. But if the client offers useful material on which to work as she did during the initial session, or if she makes good associations at times of anxiety, then the therapist, unlike the father, searches for ways of using constructively what the client has offered. And, as therapy progresses, each time an association pays off the client will experience a strengthening of her own inner resources and she will risk searching deeper within herself.

But the therapist can anticipate that the course of therapy will not be smooth. The client's problems suggest an extensive history of anxiety-provoking experiences and a complex pattern of protecting herself from that anxiety. The only route to change is through that anxiety barrier, and the client will most certainly resist that painful journey. The therapist might as well prepare himself for the fact that his client will have learned some interesting ways of avoiding anxiety, that she will resist having her favorite fantasies perforated, and that she will combat the therapist if her usual ways of achieving satisfaction are tampered with.

And, as therapy progresses, the therapist ought not to be surprised to find that as he touches on and reckons with one facet of the client's conflicted feelings, their polar opposite or the complement of those feelings might characterize the following therapeutic session. Although such behavior might simply reflect oscillation between the two sides of the same conflict, it often reflects a progressive movement toward deeper anxiety and convergence on the core of conflict.

And so, in this case, if the therapist has successfully communicated his willingness to join with the client in her efforts to resolve her conflict, he ought not to be surprised if he activates anxiety and resistance. Ironical as it might seem, once the client senses that the therapist is interested in helping her and that she "makes a difference" to him—the very feelings that the client was struggling so desperately to realize in her relationships with the men in her life—her productivity in sessions might drop off markedly.

The reasons are straight forward. At the close of the initial session, the client acted out one side of her wishes and fears—the wish to relate and the fear that she lacked interpersonal impact. But when the therapist "comes through" and makes himself available to help, another side of those fears becomes a reality. Once the therapist reacts constructively to what the client has provided, the fears of becoming emotionally entangled and dependent surface. As an aside, it should be noted that those fears are not unmixed. Intermingling with the client's fears about an entanglement, there are probably a good share of rather interesting fantasies about the intrigue that such an entanglement holds which will also surface and compete with the threat of becoming involved. But we will delay discussion of that side of the client's reactions for a moment.

Considering the client's history, the probability of her "pulling back" is high once she senses that she is "involved" with a receptive and perceptive person who is offering to help. The reasons have been set down earlier in this chapter. Those characteristics are associatively close—much too close—to the emotional conditions which characterized the client's relationship to her father, and anxiety about being bound in another potentially destructive relationship and fears about what a commitment means will take their toll.

In addition, relying on a man for help is a particularly anxiety-provoking thought for the client. The client had learned from her father that men don't like needy, dependent women. And the client's mother was a living example of what happens if a woman reveals her needs—she is left "high and dry." The father's message, "Don't be like your mother" must have reverberated through the client's unconscious whenever the client felt herself drawn to someone to seek emotional support. As noted earlier, the significant lesson that the client overlearned from her father was that to depend is to set into motion the processes for one's own rejection. One crucial outcome of those encounters is that dependency remains a highly undifferentiated concept, walled around by intense anxiety which precludes the acceptance, expansion, understanding, and modification of any feelings which are felt by the client as "being dependent."

Whether the client panics at the thought of a commitment as she did in other relationships and seeks ways of terminating therapy will depend in part on what the therapist communicates to the client at those crucial moments. Verbal reassurances that he wants to help will either stir up more conflict about being dependent or at best fall on deaf ears since the client has already expressed her belief many times over that men's actions belie their words and promises. If the therapist, in other words, crowds the client for a commitment, if he becomes invested in changing her, or if he experiences concern about whether he can help, he will in all likelihood communicate that he is in significant ways like the father, thus simply exacerbating anxiety and possibly losing the client.

At such a critical moment in therapy when a client falters and considers finding a way out of the relationship, the therapist's simple recognition of those feelings is often sufficient to reactivate the relationship since it communicates two things simultaneously: that the therapist understands and that he is not trying to bind the client. However, in this case, considering the client's experience with perceptive males who never followed their sensitivity with constructive help, the therapist might actually "go the next step" and suggest to the client that if she freely associated to those feelings, the two of them might uncover the reasons for her anxiety.

Although the therapist might guess that an emotional parallel exists between the client's feelings of the moment and her earlier experiences with regard to commitments, an interpretation to that effect might not be very useful for several reasons. Most importantly, such an interpretation would be premature since the therapist does not know his client well enough yet to support the validity of such a hunch. Second, considering the client's shaky feelings about her own resources to cope with her situation, an interpretation at that early point in therapy might have the negative effect of taking the initiative away from the client. Third, if the therapist makes insightful interpretations of the client's own poorly understood emotional life, he adds to the client's conflicts about being dependent because the overall effect in the client might be to experience herself as a child in the company of a knowing adult.

So far, it has been proposed that the therapist's offer to help and his constructive reactions to what the client has presented contradict her expectations and might attract the client. But the therapist's interest and willingness to help is a mixed blessing for the client. Although the client might sense some satisfaction in being understood and in having what she provides valued, those selfsame emotional conditions set into motion anxiety about the risks of another involvement, feelings of panic about a commitment, and concern about the dangers of depending. And that concern might be acted out by resistance, an appreciable decrease in productivity, and thoughts about terminating.

But that is one side of the client's reactions; it is the side that fears and resists. That side, the fearful side, is held in delicate balance with the side that is attracted to the therapist and the prospect of help. And it is when we turn to considering the dimensions of that attraction that we open the way for making some significant predictions about the future course of therapy. The therapist can predict with some certainty that the attraction the client feels toward him is mixed with rich fantasies associated with the intrigue that characterized the client's entanglements with her father, that those fantasies although dormant are easily stimulated, and that the client's behavior toward him will eventually take on the flavor of whatever those fantasies embody.

The point is that once the therapist counters the client's feeling that she is powerless, the "flip side" manifests itself and in her attraction she might begin to reexperience some of the pleasurable sensations of "power," accompanying fantasies, and associated needs that she tried to nourish and satisfy in relation to her father. And those fantasies, feelings, and unmet needs will make their appearance in various and rather interesting ways.

The evidence for the likelihood of such a reenactment is compelling. From what the client revealed of her many relationships, the theme that pervaded many of them was that the client was easy prey to becoming enmeshed in relationships that were similar along significant dimensions to her relationship with her father. And so the therapist might assume that through her current relationships the client is still actively attempting to complete some fantasies that are inappropriate in the present and that have been transferred from and rightfully belong in the relationship with the father. And, so long as those fantasies remain active and the needs underlying them remain unresolved, the conflict will eventually find its way into therapy and be reenacted there. And, as noted earlier, during the initial session the client was already beginning to relate to the therapist in the manner that she related to men in other important relationships.

But to discuss the complexities of the fantasies that are reactivated during therapy and the way in which dormant needs and feelings still encapsulated and directed in fantasy toward a father or other significant persons are regenerated and emerge during therapy and provide the groundplan for significant change, we need to broaden the base of our discussion considerably. For, when we turn to a consideration of how feelings generated in one relationship are inappropriately transferred to another relationship, how the conditions in the second relationship are perceived and shaped to fit the conditions in the generic conflict-engendering relationship, and how the person attempts to use the second relationship to rework old conflicts, to satisfy needs, and to rectify the past in the present, we introduce a most significant dimension for understanding clients and the change process that deserves careful and extensive consideration. For that reason, the next chapter will be reserved for a discussion of this and related matters pertaining to the way in which conflict is regenerated during therapy.

6

The Generation and
Unfolding of Conflict
during Therapy

During the course of this chapter, we will note some manifestations of the reawakening of conflict during therapy, focusing in particular on the way that the client's hypersensitivity to environmental cues alerts the therapist to their convergence on conflict-laden material. As feelings, experiences, wishes, fears, and frustrations are stirred up during therapy, we will note the way in which the client's perceptual processes, his interpretations of his experiences, and his spontaneous associations become increasingly clear reflectors of his inner struggles, thereby providing the basis for the therapist's deepening understanding and guiding his participation in the change process.

As we proceed through the chapter, we will note the way in which the intensification of conflict affects the client's interpersonal relationships. As conflict generates, the therapist is particularly attuned to what the client perceives and to how he interprets what is transpiring in relation to those with whom he interacts. And when the client reports his stressful interactions with others, we will follow the therapist as he attempts to uncover the underlying and unifying themes which link together the client's discrete perceptions and point to the dynamics of conflict.

Often if the therapist listens for such recurrent themes he can hear his client tuned to certain emotional conditions, highly reactive to these conditions and preocuupied with internal prophesies about the motivations of others. If the therapist searches through the client's behavioral reactions at times when the client's inner struggles have intensified and are readily projected, he can sometimes detect a preformed pattern that the client places over his behavior with others and in terms of which his current experiences are interpreted. And that preformed pattern shaped from past experiences connects the present with

153

the past and makes the irrationality of the client's present reactions understandable, necessary, and predictable.

During the course of the chapter, we will focus our attention on the way in which the residual effects of previous problematic interactions continue to interpenetrate, affect, and take their toll of energy in a client's reactions to his present life situation. As conflict intensifies, we will note that a client might begin to feel and act toward those in his current environment in ways that outdistance their stimulus value, pointing to the fact that the basic conflict is being reexperienced and reenacted in the present. In a particular case, we might observe a client repeatedly reconstructing and living out the past in the present, cloaking those whom he encounters in his daily life with the attitudes, feelings, and reactions that were central features of the conflict engendering interactions of his childhood.

Once we turn to a consideration of how the client transfers feelings onto those in his current environment and then proceeds to react to the representatives he has created out of his own conflicts as though they were significant past persons, we have introduced a most significant dimension of the dynamics of change. And so we will digress during the chapter to discuss rather fully some of the complexities, subtleties, and varying degrees with which the conflicts of the past are recreated and reenacted in the present.

During the course of this chapter, we will consider the complexities of transference phenomena from several vantage points. We will pay particular attention to the clues to the transference nature of certain relationships, the stimulus for the client's irrational reactions, the dynamic functions they serve, and the therapeutic usefulness of transference reactions. As we discuss the usefulness of such reactions, we will note in particular the way in which the client's intense transference reactions in specific relationships provide the therapist with unique information about the dimensions and changing character of conflict.

From following the course of those relationships, in hearing the introduction of new relationships that are constructed along similar lines, from noting how those relationships change, intensify, and terminate, the therapist is provided with unique understanding of the client's changing emotional state. From the client's reactions in relationships which seem interpenetrated with elements of the past, the therapist learns what the client seeks, how he attempts to satisfy his needs, and why he remains frustrated. From listening for the changing nature of those needs as reflected in those relationships, from noting what needs become paramount and which ones fade from prominence, the therapist has an ongoing index of the client's progress in therapy.

But of most importance for the therapeutic venture, we will note the ways in which the client's reactions in his ongoing relationships provide an index to the client's feelings about the therapist. As we progress through the chapter, we will follow the effects of the heightening of conflict in the therapeutic relationship. In particular we will note the way in which the client's irrational behavior toward the therapist complicates the therapeutic process but also provides the experiential basis for significant change.

As noted in other contexts throughout this book, it is when the client brings the conflict into therapy and involves the therapist as one of the members of the conflict-laden situation that the therapist has the opportunity as never before to help the client to break through that anxiety. At those moments the client has put together the present, the past, and the therapeutic hour. And when the client has brought the struggle into therapy, if the therapist allows the client to use him to work through that conflict, then the therapist simultaneously reduces the potential for the client's continuing to act out his conflicts with others and he at once intensifies their own relationship.

At those moments, the base of the therapist's understanding is considerably broadened. The therapist's own experience, feelings, and reactions become a part of the change equation. When the client reacts to the therapist out of his own inner struggles, he provides the therapist with the opportunity to check his own feelings against what the client projects, interprets, and the ways in which the client construes his experience. And from that discrepancy between what the therapist intends and what the client attributes to him the therapist is in a position to provide the client with a significant emotional experience. At those moments of intense interaction, the client's irrational reactions become increasingly complex communications which link together the present with the past, highlight conflict, and provide the basis for a truly significant therapeutic experience.

During the course of the chapter, we will again follow the therapist's thoughts and reactions, noting where and how he looks for clues to the generating sources of conflict. We will note the way in which he uses his own feelings as a guide to understanding his client, and most importantly, the way in which he uses himself to help the client resolve those conflicts. In the material that is presented, an effort will be made to reintroduce and integrate the many avenues to understanding that have been described in the first section of this book as those understandings bear on the therapeutic work and naturally unfold during the course of an ongoing therapeutic relationship. That integration will be attempted through brief case excerpts which will again provide the generating base for hypotheses about the dynamics of therapeutic interactions that facilitate or inhibit change.

THE GENERATION OF CONFLICT DURING THERAPY: SOME GENERAL CONSIDERATIONS

In the introductory material of this book, it was proposed that, as conflict intensifies because of the therapeutic work, the client will react to the anxiety he experiences in many ways, dependent upon the nature of the conflict, the strength of the needs pressing for gratification, and the intensity of the fears which act to counter and thwart satisfaction. Anxiety, it has been proposed previously, can open and further the therapeutic work—unless this anxiety becomes diffuse or so intense that the client redirects his energy from using it as a vehicle for his inner search and focuses on the anxiety itself. Later, in a different context, it was proposed that anxiety can facilitate or inhibit therapy dependent upon a number of conditions, including the gradient of anxiety experienced. In both contexts, it was suggested that one of the major therapeutic tasks is to help the client to tame his anxiety, to learn of its usefulness as a guide to his inner processes, and thereby to turn it to productive use in searching out the sources of conflict.

Anxiety heightens the client's sensitivity to events, to the characteristics of persons, to features of his relationships, and to the emotional conditions of his interactions that cross the time barrier and link present conflict with the generic, anxiety-provoking interactions of the past. As needs press for gratification and anxiety is aroused, it is as though the client's entire being becomes sensitized to the nuances of behavior in others and to the events in his emotional life which touch in even the most subtle ways upon the conditions which surrounded and provided the emotional context of the generic conflict.

In a general way it is true that everyone, clients included, perceive events in terms of their needs. They observe and interpret events in terms of the backlog of experiences by which they organize, provide meaning to, anticipate, and react to the behavior of others. But there is almost a qualitative difference in the way in which the client's perceptual processes, his interpretations of his experience, and his associations become finely tuned and highly selective instruments at times of heightened anxiety when conflict is regenerated in therapy.

That hypersensitivity to the events, conditions, and interactions that stimulate conflict is an index of the client's vulnerability, but it is an equally clear index of the client's motivation to change and to satisfy thwarted needs, else the client would close the issue without bringing his observations and interpretations of those experiences into therapy. The client's hypersensitivity indicates proximity to the critical features of conflict, it heralds potential change, and it suggests the intensity of the therapeutic relationship. The client's anxieties "set his perceptual processes on end" and what the client notices, selects, and responds to, what he is most sensitive about, and what he exaggerates and minimizes between and during sessions at times of stress provide the therapist with increasingly clear directional guides to the dynamics of conflict.

In this section, through a brief case excerpt, we will follow a client's anxiety as conflict intensifies, noting the effects of that anxiety in the client's reactions to the therapist and more generally in her extratherapeutic relationships. We will note the way that the client's observations, interpretations of her experiences, and her spontaneous flow of thoughts, feelings, and reactions to those experiences at times of stress interlock and become increasingly clear reflectors of the predominant feelings and experiences that are emerging and creating conflict.

In particular we will suggest the usefulness of those reactions in opening the way for productive therapeutic work. For it is from that configuration of observations, interpretations, and associations that the client provides the therapist with clues to the underlying and unifying dynamic threads that link together discrete perceptions, make sensible what the client is presenting, and point to central dynamic issues.

Although a principal purpose of the case excerpt will be to highlight the client's reactions at a crucial moment in therapy when the conflicts of her past are experienced in the present and are felt in relation to the therapist and others in her current life situation, the case presentation will serve other purposes as well. The way in which the client's perceptions of her ongoing relationships and her reactions to the therapist are shaped by and interpenetrated by elements of the past will provide a preview of the next section in this chapter when the transference character of relationships is taken up more extensively.

In addition, although the excerpts of the case are brief, many of the considerations about the differentiating characteristics of therapy and the processes unique to it that have been introduced earlier in this book will be reintroduced as they bear on and are illustrated by the work of the therapist. To that end, we will spend considerable time in following the therapist's feelings, thoughts, reactions, and associations as carefully as we follow those of the client, noting what the therapist reacts to, and how and why he reacts as he does. And as we do so, we will attempt to capture the dynamics of the interaction, especially noting its rapidly complicating character and the way in which the therapist's and client's reactions affect each other and mutually influence process.

Several Crucial Moments in the Therapy of an Unresponsive Client

For purposes of our present discussion, it is not proposed to go into many of the details of what transpired in sessions with this client between the beginning of therapy and some crucial moments of a later session. However, in order to provide a backdrop for understanding the dynamic issues of that crucial session, that interview must be viewed within the context of the dynamics of conflict as reflected in the content and interactions of preceding sessions. So we will first turn to a consideration of several features of those earlier interviews which provided the therapist with some preliminary insight into his client and made the client's eventual reactions understandable and predictable.

Some Early Impressions and Understandings: A Prologue

A few introductory comments ought to be made about the client's way of presenting herself for therapy since the client's entree stimulated reactions in the therapist and set therapy on a course of action that played almost immediately into a central feature of the client's dynamics. The client was a young adult woman in her early twenties who entered therapy because of a sense of dissatisfaction and frustration that seemed to interpenetrate all aspects of her life. She found life boring, felt apathetic, and said that she was disinterested in her course work at the university and was seriously contemplating withdrawing; but those thoughts were countered by equally strong feelings of being "boxed in," of having no special skills, and a general sense of being unprepared for life on her own. The client said that she felt as though she were "vegetating" and wanted some help in trying to get into the mainstream of living. Although she resisted the idea of seeking help, the client felt that she didn't have the "tools" to correct her situation alone and concluded by saying that she was at a complete loss about who she was or where she was going.

During the first few moments of their contact, the therapist observed his client carefully. He listened and looked for consistencies and contradictions between what was verbally expressed and what is so often as clearly communicated nonverbally through such modes of communication as dress, posture, and voice. The therapist noted, for example, that the client was rather drably dressed, but that the drabness was broken with some slight splash of color. Considering other facets of the way she presented herself, the color seemed almost out of character. As she talked the client sat well back in her chair, hidden by her coat and hair, as though attempting to shield herself and remain out of range of the therapist. And as she discussed her problems, the client's voice was in harmony with the content of her verbalizations, coming across in a dull monotone with few inflections.

Early in the interview, the therapist had his first insight into his client's dynamics from a sequence that was acted out between the client and himself. As the session progressed, the client ventured little other than to respond to what was asked of her. In her reactions to the therapist, the client was generally docile, presented her problems cryptically, and then remained silent as though awaiting directions, instructions, or advice from the therapist. The message underlying the client's words, reinforced by her dress and manner, seemed to be "do something about me and my state."

The interesting thing that initially got the therapist into trouble and yet proved very useful in the eventual therapy of the client was that the therapist felt an inner pressure, almost a sense of urgency to do precisely that—to ask questions, to become diognostic—to do something to alleviate the client's distraught state with as little pain to the client as possible. And, before long the therapist caught himself randomly asking questions about some specifics of the client's life in an effort to unlock her affect. But the therapist's questions led nowhere.

When the therapist, for example, suggested that the client talk more generally about the events that she felt contributed to her general feelings of apathy and the circumstances in her life that motivated her to seek therapy, the client contended that she didn't know exactly what was being asked for, that the question left her at a loss about what was wanted. From the client's responses, the therapist began to feel that he was asking the wrong questions, that they were unhelpful, or that he had missed the point completely. Yet the client had a knack for informing the therapist that he was on the wrong track in such an ingratiating way that the therapist found himself redoubling his efforts and feeling guilty about having missed the point.

And at the moment in therapy when the therapist took note of his own frustration, he began to sense what he had acted out with his client. Through her helplessness, the client invited advice and an early solution to her conficts. The client, in essence, set the therapist up as an authority, as someone who "should be able to" lessen her discomfort. When the therapist moved on the internal pressure he felt to help through an active, searching, and authoritative manner, he had inadvertently accepted and acted out the authority role that had been proffered. In doing so, the therapist unwittingly cast the client into the submissive role—a role that offered safety to the client and simultaneously justified and provided a vehicle for the indirect expression of her resentment. And from the safety of her reinforced shelter, the client was then able to poke away at the therapist's "authority" without much danger of the attack's being returned.

From that sequence, the therapist learned with some discomfort to himself about one of the dynamic functions that the client's docile, helpless exterior served. Apparently the client, for reasons that would only emerge later, had learned to use passivity itself as a vehicle for the indirect expression of resentful, angry feelings that could not be expressed more openly. In addition, the client set the relationship into motion in such a way that she invited others to respond *so that she could* frustrate—a rather elaborate but effective safety valve for otherwise bottled up feelings.

When the therapist grasped the impact of what had been enacted, he was able to relax and let his own creative processes work for him. From what had transpired so soon in the relationship, the therapist wondered how invested the client was in castrating men or perhaps anyone in authority. He wondered what the risks were to the client and how willing she might be to explore the underlying sources of conflict. He wondered how much the client's passive hostile ways of expressing otherwise pent-up feelings had become a self-perpetuating cycle which would overshadow her motivation to explore and risk giving up that partial gratification.

In essence, the therapist wondered how much the client needed to snipe away at him and how willing she was to relate, explore, and tolerate the anxiety of revisiting the experiences which provided the emotional context for the underlying conflict. But the therapist's awareness of what had occurred was sufficient to release him from the diagnostic role he had shouldered and the sense of guilt he experienced "to do something" which were limiting his creativity in the relationship. And, interestingly enough, when the therapist relaxed, the client worked harder.

The therapist's questions were partially answered by his client's ensuing reactions. Immediately following the sequence cited above, the client stated that she "supposed the therapist would want to know" something of her family relationships. The client hesitated for a moment and then, almost as though reaching some emotional decision, provided some material about her family that, considering what had just transpired in therapy, was important for several reasons.

Before proceeding to a discussion of the actual content of the client's productions, it might be worth digressing to review some of the dimensions that the therapist takes into account if he is to understand what the client is communicating at those moments following an intense interaction. In a general way, the therapist listens to the manner in which the client introduces whatever he does independent of the content; he listens to the content itself; and he listens for what the material reveals of the client's associations to the transactions of the therapeutic relationship itself.

Independent of the content of the productions, the manner in which the client approaches material reveals much to the therapist about the client's defenses, motivation to change, and ambivalences about the relationship. Second, the actual content of what is introduced is vitally important in its own right for what it reveals of the client's history of conflict. But perhaps of most importance is the fact that the client associated to some previous interactions at a crucial moment when an intense interaction had occurred in therapy. In that regard, the therapist assumed that the client's associations to that material were determined in part by what had transpired in the relationship in the immediately preceding few moments. The therapist must attend, therefore, not only to what content reveals of past interactions, but he must attend with equal care to what the fact of its introduction at that moment reveals of the client's feelings, thoughts, and reactions to his relationship with the therapist.

In this particular case, the client's manner of introducing the material was noteworthy. The client introduced the topic by stating that "she supposed the therapist would want to know" about her family, thus reinstating the therapist as the authority and reshouldering him with responsibility for the direction of the interview. The client hesitated, as though caught in the swirl of her own ambivalence about whether to relate and work or to revert to some partial satisfaction from again setting up the therapist for another fling at his competence.

But the critical determinant of the direction of therapy occurred when the client apparently decided to provide the therapist with what turned out to be very revealing information about her past interactions. Had the client simply waited for the therapist to respond to her manner of introducing the material, one might assume that she had considerable investment in fighting; but of her own accord she went on to reveal herself, thus suggesting that she wanted to rectify and further the relationship.

A second critical determinant of the direction of therapy was in the hands of the therapist. Had he been simmering with frustration at what had just transpired, he might have anticipated another set-up and reacted with anger, assuming that he and the client were going to "go another round." Had the therapist, in other words, not grasped his own part in what transpired, had his frustration not cooled and been replaced with understanding, he might have prematurely judged the client and cut off potential movement by pointing out to the client that she was setting him up for another knock-down. Again, considering the client's ambivalence, such a reaction would most assuredly have eventuated in a continuing battle with little productive work.

The content of what the client revealed of her past was important in its own right. It contributed to the therapist's understanding of the client's past, pointed to areas of conflict, and provided the therapist with guidelines to what the client had missed, feared, and wanted. In her family, the father had been "boss"; he was unapproachable and never wrong; he ruled the roost. The first glimmer of affect—anger intermixed with sardonic humor—occurred as the client discussed her parents. Within the same sentence, the client talked of her father's "ruling the roost" with a flash of anger and then with a note of sarcasm referred to her mother as running around "clucking" like an old hen.

The client's father apparently liked women docile. He was able to make everyone in the family feel inadequate by the way in which he could always do the job better, no matter what it was. Nothing was sacred; he even invaded the kitchen, the mother's domain, would "stick his nose in," take over, and finish what others had started. And the unbelievably disabling fact of the matter was that he could often do things better, leaving the client, her mother, and anyone else who happened on the scene stripped of any feelings of self-esteem.

Apparently the client happened on a very happy and rather clever way of getting back at the father by messing up everything so badly that the father was completely frustrated at trying to teach her anything. In the main, the client set it up so that the father would have to take over, leaving him overworked and frustrated. And as she mentioned those incidents, the client could be seen to be entertaining herself with the fantasies that those memories reawakened. And the client admitted that the whole family waited with bated breath for the day her father would fall "flat on his face."

And, as the client related those incidents, the therapist was internally amused at the way in which the client had enacted that entire sequence with him as the "goat" a few minutes earlier. In retrospect, he found himself working hard, taking over, and the client had simply stood off at a distance and poked away at his competence, leaving him frustrated and the client much the less for wear. But the fact that the client revealed those incidents close on the heels of their occurrence in therapy suggested that the gains from such a performance were insufficient to compensate for her having to remain in such a submissive, "boxed in" state with passive resistance as her only creative outlet and expression for her frustration and resentment.

The interesting fact was that the client associated to the material following its reenactment in therapy. The therapist wasn't sure how conscious the client was of the parallel between what had transpired in therapy and her earlier reported interactions with her father. But through its introduction, the client had essentially warned the therapist about how she reacted to all-knowing authorities, told him what to avoid, and touched on what she needed. And it was the therapist's own insight into the fact that the client had made an effort, however consciously was not the issue, to rectify the situation and get help that provided the therapist with his optimism that his client wanted help and would provide him with the help to help her along the way.

At that point, the therapist made no assumptions that therapy with his client would be easy. In her associations to past relationships, the client had simply pointed out that she was a highly reactive person and had some considerable investment in "getting back at" those whom she found frustrating. But the basic conflict and the therapeutic work would likely center around issues about what it meant emotionally to the client to give up the submissive, docile, and apathetic ways that characterized her life and relationships.

The therapist assumed that there was much safety in submissiveness. In the first place, the person who has been beaten into submission has a great deal of learning to do about himself and his resources. More importantly, there are often considerable risks involved in moving out of that role, depending upon a whole complex of factors which have set anxiety barriers in the way. The therapist also assumed that the client's learned ways of coping with her frustration provided sufficient partial gratification for her resentful feelings to create a deterrent to changing and perhaps living with more anxiety. He also assumed that there was pleasure in being submissive, not only for what it avoided and the passively hostile profits it yielded but because the client probably entertained fantasies about being the "submissive" child for all that might mean in relation to her father.

As with many other wishes that people entertain about changing, the basic conflict is often deeply ingrained, the risks of changing are great, and a client's memories of what were crucial encounters sometimes act as screens for deeper anxiety that prevents a rapid change of pace and modification of well-worn behavioral patterns. Else this client would have readily taken on a more assertive garb. But as the therapist soon found out, the client's desire to explore more deeply the causes of her anxiety and her willingness to abandon the safety of being the submissive child who could strike out at those at the helm was hard in coming.

For, immediately following her introduction of past material, the client closed the issue. And other than for that brief glimmer of an inner fantasy life, the client's apathetic, humdrum life was again paraded past the therapist as a series of uneventful, unstimulating, unproductive, and nongoal directed activites. But the therapist felt that was "par for the course" and that his client had taken as much risk as she could during the initial session.

But before moving to a consideration of how other issues developed, it should be noted that the therapist's optimism about his client was based on other features of the session. Independent of the content of what the client introduced about her relationships in her home, the negative affect and bit of sardonic humor about her parents provided the therapist with his first sense of the client's inner fantasies. The client's graphic language and the metaphorical way in which she alluded to her parents provided the therapist with the sense that some interesting fantasies and strong feelings underlay the flattened, docile exterior. In a way, that brief exposure of the client's inner life—which was as immediately reconcealed—was also symbolically represented in the brief splash of color that intruded into the client's otherwise drab dress. And it was the therapist's sense of being able to get into touch with the underlying "color" that increased his optimism that he could help the client.

The Therapist Inadvertently
Reinforces the Conflict

As noted earlier, it is not proposed to study in detail the conflicts of this client as they slowly emerged during therapy. Rather, the emphasis in this section is on the dynamics of the therapeutic interactions which provided some partial predictive force for the events which transpired between client and therapist in a later crucial session. With that purpose in mind, some of the interactions of intervening sessions which provided the basis for those crucial encounters will be detailed with some care.

In succeeding sessions, some of the therapist's momentary intuitive flashes into his client's dynamics were confirmed as his client played out in slow motion her anxieties and ways of protecting herself. From those sessions, the therapist was able to understand and piece together something of his client's submerged needs and the way those needs were blocked by anxiety, contributing to frustration and anger. From the elaborate system the client had built to provide for the indirect expression of her anger, the therapist assumed that the anger must have met additional anxiety head-on, simply intensifying conflict.

In turn, the client's devious ways of expressing her anger were apparently both gratifying and taxing. The gratification seemed evident from the client's gains in "rattling" the therapist; the expenditure of energy seemed evident from the way that the client carefully covered her tracks with her ingratiating behavior. Once the client ingratiated herself in order to cover her anger, she immediately reset the conflict into motion again. In needing to ingratiate herself, the client "boxed herself in," preventing expressiveness and triggering frustration and anger, thus perpetuating the cycle. And the therapist saw the client recycle through variations of that general sequence repeatedly during sessions.

To illustrate one variation on the theme of that sequence, the therapist observed that the client would pull back and depreciate herself after having taken a progressive step forward, particularly if the therapist attempted to reinforce the assertive behavior. For example, at times the client would take the initiative, perhaps by making some insightful statement or associating to material in productive ways. Or the client might introduce some events in her current life in which she felt good about having expressed herself. If the therapist reacted favorably to such behavior, to a good association, an interesting fantasy, or some insightful self-reference by suggesting that the comment was insightful, interesting, or potentially productive, the client would immediately retreat to depreciating herself, noting that she was doing poorly in school, that she didn't have a thought in her head, and that she had no goals.

Following such behavior, the client would often conclude with remarks about "not feeling any better or getting anywhere" in therapy. And the therapist construed those remarks as the entree for setting him up "to do something." And, having been that route with the client in the initial session, the therapist was able at such moments to respond in ways which benefited the client, perhaps by making his observations about the intrusion of anxiety available to her or by suggesting that her reactions might mean that they were nearing some sore spots.

But the therapist eventually discovered with the wisdom that pain and hindsight provides that his client's aptitude for entrapping him into behaving as her father had and her repertoire for frustrating him were not limited to the few early lessons she had given him. Although the therapist was clear about the client's ways of coping with anxiety and he was able at times to help the client to focus on issues which precipitated anxiety, he was blinded to the fact that in other ways he was unknowingly colluding in reinforcing his client's submissiveness and thereby contributing to the recycling of conflict.

Despite his insights into his client's dynamics, the therapist colluded in the recycling of conflict in a rather interesting way. At times during sessions, the client would introduce some problems in her ongoing relationships with men, often complaining bitterly about how everything had to be done their way. As she described some specific instance, the therapist could see that the client, apparently fearful of expressing herself, would hand the baton to the man in such a way that the male companion would take over, much as the therapist had done in the initial session.

Essentially she behaved like a submissive child, inviting others to manage her, thus shifting responsibility for action to the other party and eliminating the risk to herself. And once the male companion began directing operations, the client's feelings of resentment for being subjugated would set her simmering. Upon reaching a "full boil" the client would begin dragging her feet in the relationship, never suggesting what might be done to make her happy but using her veto power as a deterrent to what the male companion proposed, thereby dampening his enthusiasm, interest, and sense of adequacy.

The therapist readily saw the pattern between those relationships and what had transpired in his own earlier encounter with his client. But what caught the therapist into playing back into the client's dynamics again was what she next did. After revealing the sequence, the client spontaneously associated to some past events in her interactions with her father in which he would take over. She recalled experiencing immediate relief when he did so; but she also felt frustrated. The danger was removed but so also were the pleasures of accomplishment. And the client clearly commented on how she felt angry and frustrated but also safe.

After she related the ongoing conflict and introduced a very relevant past interaction, the client sat and waited. It was as though she had provided the therapist with the "tools" to put the picture together for her. And that is what trapped the therapist, for he proceeded to do just that. The therapist made his insights known to the client, pointing out the parallels in her current and past relationships. The client didn't see it clearly. The therapist worked harder. The client was noninsightful. And the more noninsightful the client became, the more the therapist worked "to get her to see" what he had seen. And that feeling in the therapist was simply a variant of an old refrain.

Dynamically speaking, at the point where the therapist's insights motivated him to try to get the client to see what he saw, he reinforced her submissiveness! At that moment the client's anxiety abated for she had regained her position of submissiveness in the relationship. And after much work the client would simply "absorb" what the therapist said, but the insight was an intellectual one at best. And more than likely, the client's acquiescence was a variant of the client's ingratiating way of covering the hostility underlying her resistance. At any rate, the entire interaction was anxiety-free for the client, yielding no emotional gains, and leaving the therapist confused and frustrated.

As an aside, it might be worth commenting on the processes of therapy as revealed in the interaction just reported. What transpired between client and therapist provides an unusually good example of how the dynamics of conflict embedded in the content of a client's productions are sometimes simultaneously acted out in the relationship. In this case, that reenactment is what the therapist missed. He attended to the dynamics as revealed by content but failed to take into account the possibility that the client's manner of presenting the material was the embodiment of those dynamics in action with the therapist as participant.

Since this point is an important one in understanding process, it is worth elaborating. From the content of what the client introduced into therapy about her ongoing relationships the therapist gained some insight into the dynamics of conflict. And, from what his client revealed of her past interactions the therapist learned of some factors which affected her reactions, expectations, anxiety, and ways of coping with stress in her ongoing relationships. The expression of conflict as reported in those current and past interactions, therefore, provided the therapist with an understanding of the nature of conflict and insight into what his eventual participation in the change process might be.

But of greater importance for the processes of therapy is the fact that the content provides directional guides for the therapist's search into his own relationship with the client in an effort to determine when, where, how, and why those same dimensions of conflict find their way into therapy and are acted out. And in this case, the client and therapist were engaged in simultaneously acting out the very dynamic interchange that was being described. It was as though the client's productions were the cognitive carrier wave for the underlying dynamic interchange of the interaction.

Had the therapist attended equally to what he was experiencing in the interaction as the client was describing her extratherapeutic interactions, he might have sensed his client's anxiety at the point in the session where she provided him with the "tools" and waited. And instead of taking over at that point and thereby reducing the client's anxiety, he might have inquired into her thoughts without reference to or any sense of pressure to pursue, make sense of, or induce insight into the parallels with the past.

In retrospect, the therapist's behavior toward the client was inconsistent. In some ways, the relationship was developing in ways that tended to be therapeutic for the client; else she wouldn't have taken some of the risks that she did during those early sessions, no matter how gingerly or how hesitantly she did so. But, in other ways, the therapist would inadvertently reinforce his client's submissiveness, thus recapitulating the father's behavior, perpetuating conflict, and exacerbating the client's feelings of resentment and anger.

The comments that the therapist recapitulated the father's behavior and reinforced the client's conflict need to be spelled out in more detail. The therapist's motivation in working with the client was certainly different from that of the father. The client's father liked docile women and apparently acted to suppress affect with sufficient effectiveness so that the client had set up anxiety barriers around her feelings. Those defenses worked reasonably well, judging by her flattened, docile exterior. But the affect also sought outlet and apparently the client's defenses weren't working well or she wouldn't have risked therapy.

What the therapist got caught into reinforcing was the client's defensive maneuvering to ward off getting into contact with her affect. The client's submissiveness served as her interpersonal defense against affect. When the therapist acted in ways which activated her anxiety, the anxiety set off her defenses, and one very effective ploy was to engage the other person in "putting her down."

Although seemingly paradoxical, the client worked actively to "regain her position of submissiveness" in the relationship. It is, however, only a seeming paradox that one should work actively to achieve a role of submissiveness. The client needed to get the therapist into a position of authority for defensive reasons. She needed to see herself as subjugated, submissive, and docile. Otherwise her defenses would be perforated. When viewed in terms of its *intent,* the behavior is a beautiful defensive maneuver; had the client failed to reestablish the relationship in its proper order, she would have experienced intense anxiety.

A second seeming paradox then follows. If the client's defenses against affect are effective, a strong affective by-product—anger—is generated! And that is where the client's adaptive and creative powers came into play. For the client found a way of draining off the anger, not only without shifting the major dimensions of the relationship, but in such a way that she actually *reinforced her submissiveness.*

But for the crucial session to be considered next, the essential preliminary note here is that there was enough reality to the therapist's behavior to allow the client the potential for using it, magnifying it, and perceptually distorting the therapist's intent sufficiently so that she could outfit him more fully with the motivational garb of her father. And in the next session, as we shall see, the client began to attribute to the therapist motives that he had not intended but which served to spur therapy on a productive course.

A Crucial Interview:
The Client Drops Her Submissive Shield

At this time, we will briefly describe some of the highlights of a rather productive session, intruding into the description of what actually transpired repeatedly to acquaint the reader with some of the therapist's thoughts, feelings, and reactions that affected his interview behavior. In the course of the discussion, the potential effects of alternative courses of ·action will be introduced. Following this accounting of the events of the session, we shall return to it and comment additionally on some features of the case that provide insight into the dynamic processes undergirding therapeutic interactions.

The crucial moments to be reported occurred in an interview following a brief break in the weekly sessions of the client. In the preceding session, the therapist had informed the client that he would be unable to keep their next appointment because of some professional business that would take him away from the office. The client reacted in her usual docile, accepting way. She readily assented to his absence, understood, and agreed to see the therapist two weeks hence.

Upon the therapist's return, his client seemed more tense at the outset of the session. She greeted him, however, in her usual way, wondered how he had enjoyed himself, and made several other inquiries into his trip which smacked of the usual disinterested and uninvolved way in which some people can inquire into the lives of others for reasons of social grace rather than from any real interest in what has transpired.

The therapist said he had accomplished his business, had enjoyed himself, and then asked the client how things had been going for her. Immediately the client said that while in the waiting room—the therapist detected an emphasis and note of sarcasm—several thoughts occurred to her about some events that she had particularly noticed since they last met. In particular, the client had become quite irritated with a close girlfriend.

It seemed that the client's friend had a boyfriend who was taking advantage of her, who would stand her up on dates without warning, and who would generally expect her to be available when he had nothing else to do with his time. The client said that the more she thought about it, the angrier she got. And she was tempted on more than one occasion to tell her girlfriend to take a stand with the boyfriend and let him know what she thought of him and his behavior. But the client resisted doing so because she felt that such a reaction would simply alienate her friend and wouldn't affect the boyfriend anyway. With some affect, the client commented that men are self-centered, don't understand, and aren't easily affected.

Following her observations, the client's affect flattened rapidly. She then went on to say that she felt bored with school, that she was feeling depressed, and proceeded to repeat many of the things that she had reported in her initial interview. The client felt that she hadn't made any progress, that her university work wasn't going well, and she was contemplating leaving school.

Before proceeding to the therapist's response, a few of his initial observations are in order. The therapist noted his client's state of tension. She was more agitated than usual, and he felt that the session might be a productive one. He also felt that the client's allusion to being bored with school, feeling dissatisfied, and considering leaving "school" was likely a thin veneer for some feelings of boredom, dissatisfaction, and unrest with regard to therapy. The therapist assumed and the client eventually confirmed that she had been harboring feelings of terminating.

The interaction of several emotional conditions of the relationship would have generated such feelings at that moment in therapy. First of all, there was some reality to the client's feelings. She had made little progress in unraveling her conflicts and breaking free of her inhibitions. Second, the client's apathy and depressed affect followed close on the heels of her recounting of what had transpired during the therapist's absence. A central feature of the client's reactions to what she had observed was the pessimistic feeling that men don't understand and aren't easily affected. Since the client had no grounds to predict otherwise, the chances are that the client believed that the therapist, too, might be unresponsive to her heightening feelings as others had been.

But there was yet another and perhaps the most critical determinant of the client's thoughts of termination at that time. Although the client's reactions were consciously experienced as feelings of unrest, they were in all probability defensively oriented toward flight and had been activated by a resurgence of frightening feelings and the potential for some risky encounters with the therapist from which the client might have wished to escape.

Whereas the intensification of feelings would be frightening to his client, it provided the therapist with some optimism that the session could be a progressive one. Those indices of a potentially productive session were supported by other aspects of the client's presentation. In her initial reactions, the client provided the therapist with a number of intervening experiences which pointed to the nature of the feelings she was experiencing and also to her investment in the relationship. Had the client approached the session with apathy and depression, providing no links to her feelings except those the therapist might assume by the broadest of inferences, the therapist might have felt that the client was less amenable to working.

But that was far from the case. The client, in her introductory remarks, provided the therapist with help in knowing where she was emotionally. From what the client reported noticing between sessions, the therapist felt reasonably sure that the client's feelings, although experienced as angry reactions to how her friend was being treated by a man, were in fact thinly veiled emotional reactions to his having been away. And the client's comment that those thoughts intruded into consciousness while in the "waiting room" not only offered confirmation to the therapist's hunches that the feelings were deflected onto a safer target but suggested as well that the emotional gap might easily be bridged and the feelings redirected to and experienced in relation to their true target—the therapist.

Rather than to digress extensively at this time to consider the many subtleties about the dynamics of conflict and of therapeutic process that are embedded in the content of the preceding paragraph, expansion of those dimensions will be reserved until a later time. At this time, it might simply be noted in passing that the client's hypersensitivity to, perception of, and interpretation of particular events between sessions suggested that conflict was active. In addition, several important features related to the processes of therapy are reflected in the displacement of feelings, identification with the girlfriend, and the possible transference character of those relationships.

Since the therapist felt that the client's observations and angry reactions were generated by his absence, he reintroduced the topic. At first the client covered her feelings by efforts at justifying the therapist's absence. She knew he had other commitments. And then, in an effort to depersonalize her resentment, the client commented that she had no personal feelings "one way or the other" about the therapist; but she resented "therapy" because she had a tight schedule and had to hasten across campus to keep her appointments. And, finally, as a guilt inducing bonus, the client mentioned that she had forgotten about the therapist's being away and had shown up for her appointment only to be turned away by the receptionist.

Gathering strength along the way, the client's anger accelerated. And with the increase in tempo, there was a decline in censorship, resulting both in directness and projections. Dropping her guard, the client directly attacked the therapist for being able "to take off" whenever he wished. The client said that she felt as though she would never break out of her shell and that the therapist was providing little help along the way. Lacing her anger with guilt inducing reactions, the client said that at times she felt almost as though the therapist liked her docile, that he suppressed her feelings, and that she was actually afraid of speaking up for fear of being punished. Finally, the client likened the therapist to her father whom she contemptuously referred to as a virtual damper on her feelings.

By way of a brief digression, several comments might be made about the client's behavior and its effects in the relationship. First of all, to the dispassionate observer of the session, it might seem patently obvious that the client, in lashing out angrily at the therapist, is no longer the docile client she was a few moments earlier. But the therapist and the dispassionate observer are two very different people. The dispassionate observer doesn't sit in the therapist's chair; he doesn't participate in the change process; and he doesn't experience the many internal feelings—anxiety, guilt, anger, inadequacy—that occur in the person who has attempted to help and finds himself attacked, condemned, and likened to a contemptuous, suppressive father.

Although it is unlikely that the therapist would have missed the point that in condemning him for inhibiting her expressiveness, the client is being very expressive, his anxiety or guilt might intrude to tunnel his vision. If it does so, the therapist might respond to the client's words and miss the fact that those words are superimposed on a carrier wave of the very affect that the client contends she can not express. The interesting fact of the matter is that under conditions where the therapist attends to the underlying affect, the client's words—even as they are uttered—are past history. They are no longer applicable or valid.

Provided that the therapist allows and facilitates the expression of those feelings without dampening them out of guilt, deflecting them because of anxiety, or punishing them because they are unjustified, several immediate salutory effects occur in the relationship. In allowing the client to express her anger, the therapist has by that fact modified the emotional context in which the earlier significant learnings occurred. Not only is the client changed by that experience, but the entire interpersonal context which allowed and facilitated the expression of those feelings takes on a new meaning for the client.

The therapist errs if he believes that at that moment he must do more than allow the experience of those feelings in relation to himself. The fact that the client has experienced those feelings in relation to him and met reactions contrary to those that provided the emotional context of the generic struggle means that the experience *has already been* a therapeutic one. The client is no longer the same person and she no longer perceives the therapist like the father. In essence, the therapist has differentiated himself from the father *by his behavior*.

At such a time, the client might spontaneously make connections with the past, associate to earlier experiences, remember, and react to past events in which she was angered. And in this case, the client spontaneously recalled some instances from the past in which she was punished by her father for voicing her opinions. During that phase of the session, the therapist noted that the client's affect again increased in tempo with each memory. The client's anger became particularly heated as she remembered being warned that her anger "would get her into trouble someday!" But a major therapeutic task has been accomplished before the recall. The release of affect has provided the vehicle for the associations and further flow of feelings. Those connections, in other words, would not have occurred *had the affect remained attached in the client's experience to her relationship with the therapist*.

As noted earlier in this book, at the moment affect is released therapy has occurred and is about to occur. Under conditions of the changed emotional context of her relationship to the therapist, the client will experience momentary relief, hope, and tension. The client will begin to have access to other experiences; there is hope for retrieving those experiences and resolving attendant conflicts; but there is also a felt risk that the client will be flooded by those experiences once the dike has been ruptured.

And that point brings us to the longer-range effects of the client's experience on the course of the relationship. To introduce those longer-range effects, it is necessary to theorize for a moment about the generic conflict. The generic struggle was born out of a significant relationship, the interpersonal context of which was suppressive to the client's needs, affect, feelings, experiences, or whatever. Anger, a natural by-product of such suppression—in itself a strong affective experience—was also suppressed, leading to diversionary tactics for its relief. But such relief neither touches on the triggering experiences for the anger, nor does it permit access to the inner thwarted experiences. It is as though the anger walls around, precludes access to, and acts as a defense against the client's contact with those inner experiences, particularly with the deeper sense of deprivation that the client might otherwise learn about.

Once the anger which has walled in other experiences begins to break down, that sensation in the client is experienced as depression because the client *at some level begins to get in touch with the deprivation that has been insulated by anger*. And it is that beginning vague sense of feeling deprived which leads to reactions in the client that might be confusing to the therapist. After the experience of anger, the therapist might find that his client closes up, looks depressed and apathetic. Unless the therapist has caught the dynamic effect of his behavior in opening the client to the experience of those deeper deprived feelings, he might construe the client's subsequent depression as qualitatively similar to her earlier apathetic state and assume that therapy has been circular.

What the therapist must keep in mind is that the apathetic and depressed behavior of succeeding sessions is *qualitatively different* from the earlier experiences of his client. The later depressed and apathetic reactions are manifestations of very different dynamic issues. The earlier depressed feelings were manifestations of reflected anger. At that point in therapy, the client was still shielded from brushing against the disabling experiences of being deprived. As noted above, the later experience of depression is more likely associated with the client's sense of getting into contact with feelings of deprivation.

But depression because of the experience of being deprived is only one of a complex of stimuli which would account for any subsequent withdrawal of the client. During the session, the client briefly experienced anger in relation to a person who in the emotional life of the client had taken on some of the significance of a previous important figure. And that was therapeutic. But two contingencies must be taken into account. Although anger was briefly experienced and accepted—conditions which permit eventual self-acceptance and integration—that experience was a brief one and the client has a difficult road ahead in learning about, experimenting with, and integrating those feelings.

Of more importance for the client's eventual interview behavior will be the effects of the client's fears of retaliation for and possible guilt about her anger. Considering this client's background, she would most assuredly recoil from her own angry reactions in anticipation of being aggressed upon for her behavior. And the likelihood of that potential recoil is evident from the way the client attempted to cope with her rising feelings of anger. In attempting to cover her anger, convert it into guilt-inducing reactions, deflect it onto safer targets, and depersonalize the experience, the client revealed the intense threat associated with the experience of anger. And in future sessions, the client's fears that she will be assailed for her boldness will tune her sensors to the slightest nuances of anger, frustration, or punishment in the therapist's reactions to her. And at times, the therapist might even find the client creating instances to fit her fear as a means of mastering her anxiety or in efforts at self-imposed retribution for her behavior.

Whether those longer-range predictions were confirmed is outside the scope of the present discussion. To return briefly to the conclusion of the session, the client's immediate reactions were those of release, relief, gratitude, and a deepening of the relationship. As often happens when a client has touched on experiences that have been inhibiting and pent-up feelings have been expressed, the client's relief was evident, her affect shifted, and she began to talk of having missed the session because of the therapist's absence, commented that she looked forward to coming, and said that she felt some things had been going better for her.

Some Dimensions of Process Reflected
in the Interview: An Introduction

Several features of this interview are noteworthy for what they reveal of the way that conflict is regenerated and unfolds during the course of therapy. In this section, we will examine the interview from several points of view. After some general introductory remarks about the session, we will note how the therapist's conceptualization of his client and of the change process affects his interview behavior. As we follow the therapist's thoughts about his client, we will suggest alternative courses of action that the therapist might have pursued had he construed the meaning of his client's anger as reflecting different dynamic issues. And then, by way of bridging the material of this section with that of the remainder of the chapter, we will alter our perspective and consider how the intensification of conflict not only affects the client's interview behavior but how it affects as well her sensitivity to and perceptions and interpretations of events in her ongoing interpersonal relationships.

In retrospect, the flow of and changes in the client's affect during the session are of particular interest and can provide a useful general introduction to the material of this section. During the course of the session, there were significant changes in the object, intensity, and valence of the client's emotional reactions. The object of the client's felt experiences changed hands repeatedly and with each change there was an ebb and flow of feelings.

Feelings initially attached to and experienced in relation to an ongoing interpersonal relationship were transferred to and experienced in relation to the therapist. That experience opened the way for the recall of and experience of emotional reactions with regard to significant past events and persons. Following the flow of associations and feelings about her father, there was a change in the valence of the client's affect—from negative to positive—and the object of the positive feelings was again the therapist. Essentially, feelings flowed from an ongoing relationship through the therapist to the past and back again to the therapist, changing in intensity and valence along the way.

Embedded in the free-flowing movement of affect between the present and past are several interesting considerations about the process of therapy which might be clarified by tracing the movement in slow motion. The precipitating event that triggered the client's reactions is an important consideration in understanding the route that the client's feelings took. In this case, the precipitating event that "set the client off" was the therapist's absence. A complicating factor—and one which introduces a challenging dimension of process—was that the client's reactions, although stimulated by the therapist, were not experienced directly toward him.

Rather, the client noticed and reacted with anger to events in her ongoing relationships which paralleled at an emotional level the recent events of therapy. The client experienced her anger and resentment toward a girlfriend and a male companion. Essentially, the client perceived that relationship in terms of the feelings that were churning around in herself, identifying with the girlfriend's distraught state and displacing her feelings toward the therapist onto the male companion.

That external relationship was a real one, events occurred which the client could construe as she did, and the client's anger was felt toward those persons. The client construed the meaning of those events in terms of what was stirring around in herself. She identified with how the girlfriend *must have felt* in that situation and she reacted out of her own feelings about having that happen to herself based on her construction of the experience. But the generating source of anger, the stimulus for noticing, attending to, and sharpening the perceptual process along those emotional dimensions was found in the client's feelings about and reactions to the therapist.

That external relationship, in other words, was representative of the client's feelings in relation to the therapist. Those feelings were precipitated by and behaviorally grounded in the client's interaction with the therapist and the first step is to relocate those feelings in that relationship. So long as the client's anger remains attached to a relationship which symbolically represents her feelings toward the therapist, the client's anger will remain active and circular. In much the same way that the irrational components of the therapeutic relationship are transference reactions from the unresolved conflicts of the past, the ongoing relationship in this case is the inappropriate depository of displaced feelings.

Unless the anger is redirected back to its immediate generating source in the therapeutic relationship, the client will continue to remain angry toward those inappropriate objects and she will attempt to manipulate that external relationship in terms of those unresolved conflicts. In the meantime, the therapeutic relationship itself will stalemate, with anger recycling without relief. Once the therapist successfully redirects those feelings toward himself in relation to the client, then several things happen simultaneously. The therapeutic session becomes the center for intense emotional reactions and the client's perceptions of those persons in her environment, freed of the displaced feelings, are modified. That is what is meant when it is said that when the conflict is brought into therapy "acting out" diminishes. Essentially, the external relationship is stripped of its transference components and can be seen for what it is.

As an aside, a proviso must be added to the foregoing comments which will be expanded at a later time. If the client's perceptions of and reactions to events in that ongoing external relationship are based mainly in the fact of its convenience as a fleeting representative of the client's feelings toward the therapist, then the ephemeral character of that deflection will soon be apparent. For as the conflict recenters in the client's relationship to the therapist, the client's reactions to the interactions in that external relationship will regain their reality orientation and the therapist might hear little about it during future sessions. If, however, deeper transference reactions characterize that relationship, then events in those encounters will continue to make an appearance at critical times during therapy. And, by way of anticipating a future discussion, the emotional dimensions of such transference relationships become useful guides to the therapist's understanding of the changing emotional life of his client.

But to return to our case under consideration, the first step in process is to redirect the client's feelings to their true target—the therapist. And that brings us to our second point. The client's feelings toward the therapist—much as those toward her friend—were magnified, distorted, and interpreted in terms of her own internal struggles. But the fact that those reactions were irrational with regard to the therapist's motives—although relevant to the therapist's eventual behavior—is immaterial to the client's feelings at that moment. The fact of the matter is that the client was angry with the therapist. A behaviorally grounded event in her relationship to the therapist was the immediate stimulus for those feelings and any efforts by the therapist to deflect those feelings to their generating source in the past without first attending to his client's feelings about him would have been fruitless.

The reasons seem straightforward. The crucial point is that the client *experiences those feelings in relation to the therapist for something that happened in their relationship.* She doesn't experience those feelings toward her father or the other men who acted to suppress her feelings. In the emotional life of the client, that event in the interaction is symbolically representative of the story of her life. At that moment, the therapist is the embodiment of all the significant persons in her past who have set conflict into motion.

For the client to react as she did, the therapeutic relationship has reached a significance comparable in emotional charge to the generic learning situation in which the conflict was engendered. How the therapist reacts at that moment is the critical determinant of whether the client will change. If the therapist facilitates the expression of those feelings toward himself without deflecting them, warding them off, or justifying his actions, then the therapist has permitted what others would not.

When the therapist behaves in ways that counter the client's expectations, he modifies the emotional context which fostered conflict, thus providing a therapeutic experience for the client, paving the way for relearning, and providing the basis for new learning. When the therapist reacts differently, he literally unburdens himself of some of the transference components of the client's reactions. Once he is unencumbered, the therapist becomes the guide for the deeper search into the meaning of those reactions.

It is the changed emotional context of the relationship which liberates the client, permits recall, facilitates associations, and allows the further flow of feelings. It is that renewed sense of freedom that stimulates positive feelings in a client. And that is why at the end of the session, the valence of the client's feelings changed and she expressed gratitude to the therapist. She had been helped. The client's expression was one of warmth for what the therapist allowed her to do. That reaction was based on some reaility factors in the relationship. And if the therapist construes that honest regard for his help as a transference reaction, he would diminish its importance in the client's feeling more human.

Before concluding these remarks, a few of the highlights of what has been proposed thus far about process might be reviewed from a somewhat different perspective. Since the events which precipitated the client's anger were behaviorally grounded in the therapeutic relationship, working out the client's feelings about the therapist takes precedence over and precludes any further movement in therapy until the working through of those feelings is an accomplished fact.

The interpersonal relationship becomes the hub of activity. On the one hand, the feelings that the client initially deflected outward from that relationship must be relocated in it. On the other hand, any efforts by the therapist to deflect the client's feelings to the generating sources in the past before they are attended to in relation to himself will simply create resistance.

The therapist could have erred in either of two directions, with each error creating a unique problem with regard to further progress. In the first place, had the therapist for reasons of his own anxiety, guilt, or whatever, missed the dynamic link between the precipitating events in his own relationship to the client and the client's reactions with regard to her friends, he could have spent much useless time in studying a relationship that for all practical purposes was simply a convenient symbolic representation of the client's feelings about himself. The consequences of such a course of action would have been manifold. There would have likely been an intensification of conflict in what might otherwise have been a benign ongoing relationship. The client's angry feelings toward her girlfriend would have recycled without relief. In short, the therapist's behavior would have probably stimulated additional inappropriate and destructive "acting out" of feelings in relation to those persons.

On the other hand, had the therapist erred by attempting to deflect the client's feelings to their generating source in the past without first allowing them to run their course in relation to himself, he would have colluded in an intellectual exercise at best. Considering this particular client's background, however, the more likely result of such a premature deflection would be the generation of resistance in the form of apathy and discontent. And, before long, the therapist would have found himself being "set up" as an authority, soon to be knocked off his pedestal, thus simply recapitulating what transpired in the initial session and setting therapy back on its haunches.

What the therapist who attempts to deflect feelings back to the past at crucial moments such as this one fails to recognize is that for the client he is the embodiment of certain significant characteristics of those past persons who are central to the conflict and therapy has reached a significance equivalent in power to the learning situation in which conflict was engendered. Under those conditions, new learning can be substituted for what was poorly learned. Within that emotional context, the therapist's behavior in allowing what others have not permitted *is the experience that is therapeutic* for the client. At that moment, the therapeutic relationship is a powerful relearning center. And, within the context of those modified learning conditions, the client is free to remember, to associate, and to release undischarged affect.

Finally, once the emotional context of the relationship is altered, release is experienced but anxiety sets in almost at once. Both client and therapist are soon struck by the realization that they have just scratched the surface. When any facet of the client's emotional life is upset, the entire internal organization is put into imbalance, leading to the client's efforts to resolve that imbalance.

Not only does the client have much learning to do with regard to the expression of her anger, but of more importance is the fact that buried under the client's anger are experiences, feelings, and impulses that the client might prefer to leave dormant. Those deeper experiences that have been walled around by anger might be relatively unmodified by time and maturation. As such their primitive character might be frightening to client and therapist both. As those experiences make their appearance, transference reactions of a different order are sure to appear. At those times, the strength of the therapist will have to withstand even greater testing. And at those times, the work of the therapist in participating so as to provide a constructive resolution will be most critical.

The Therapist's Conceptualization of His Client: Guidelines for Participation

A second vantage for considering the processes of therapy as reflected in this session is from the viewpoint of how the therapist's conceptualization of his client affected his interview behavior. In a general way, by continually working inductively and deductively, by comparing what emerges in sessions with his own theoretical constructs about disturbances in human growth, the therapist begins to get a sense of where his client is emotionally, where blockage occurs, and what is still needed. From his contacts, a therapist slowly gains insight into how his client learned to cope interpersonally so as to minimize anxiety, maintain equilibrium, and achieve some partial satisfaction of needs through indirect means.

And from that ongoing process, the therapist constantly formulates tentative hypotheses about the course of therapy. Those predictions are always held tentatively; they alert the therapist to eventualities, provide a basis for understanding what might otherwise be confusing and seem circular, and allow him to move to deeper levels with his client. His ongoing analysis, synthesis, and predictions function to deepen his understanding of his client and of their relationship. But that conceptualization will deepen and become increasingly specific only insofar as the therapist holds his hypotheses as open-ended guides to understanding and participation. Once those conceptualizations become rigidified, then his formulations might substitute for listening, learning, and revising. And at any point in therapy where hypotheses become prophesies, the therapist will attempt to fit the client to his formulations instead of using his constructs as a guide to making himself available to help the client to experience, understand, and integrate.

Although fragments of the therapist's conceptualization in this particular case are scattered throughout passages of the interviews reported earlier, it might be useful to summarize the therapist's speculations about his client's emotional development. At the most theoretical level, the therapist speculated that there was an inner core of feelings, wishes, impulses, and experiences that had been cut off from integration because the emotional context of significant past interpersonal relationships was intolerant of such experiences. As such, those unfulfilled needs remained encapsulated, untested, and unmodified by learning.

So long as those needs went ungratified, they would continue to seek expression. When needs are blocked by anxiety and continue to seek gratification, that blockage is felt as undifferentiated frustration. However, under the emotional conditions described above, anger, itself a strong affective by-product, must also be suppressed. Since anger is unacceptable, it is immediately converted into and felt only as anxiety. A second layer of anxiety, then, is generated which walls around and prevents the experience of reactive anger.

That reactive anger is both the outermost ring of unavailable affect and serves as a defense against the inner needs and emotions. In addition, since the client's needs are viable, frustration constantly regenerates anger and defenses must be instituted to ward off the experience of the unacceptable angry feelings. And, in this case, the client had learned to ingratiate herself when she felt practically anything, using docility and a flattened exterior defensively as a means of avoiding the experience of anxiety.

Over time, then, the client pulled a protective curtain around her feelings, using passivity and a flattened, affectless exterior as a way of avoiding anxiety. But a client such as this one would need to be constantly on guard because life is full of unexpected events that most assuredly would stir feelings and threaten exposure of underlying needs, thus heightening the sense of frustration. Such a tenuous situation would be intolerable unless the client found some alternate route for the expression of needs, frustration, and anger. And, in this case, that indirection was achieved by passively hostile behavior which drained off the anger without awareness of its experience. The passivity instituted as a defense against affect then doubled as an outlet for anger.

To suggest how passivity instituted to defend against affect might eventually double as an outlet for affect in the developing personality, let's generalize beyond this case to consider the circumstances that often occur in homes where a parent punishes the child who tries out his feelings, explores, investigates, and experiments. It seems that the parent who is as authoritarian as this client's father is often conflicted along the same dimensions that he punishes in his offspring. The offending parent might be conflicted about his own impulse life; so he suppresses in order to remain suppressed. He threatens because he is threatened. And if traced back to his own history, such a parent is himself often the offspring of suppressive, threatening parents. And so, in some respects, he is passing on and perpetuating the family heritage.

Such a conflicted parent, when he observes the product of his own doing might, operating out of guilt, try to rectify the wrong. Or, when he observes the docile, suppressed child he has helped to rear, he might see a reflection of his own conflicts. And such a mirroring of what he hates in himself is intolerable, leading to efforts to change the child. And those efforts are often directed toward trying to bring the child out of his passive shell.

Once the child recognizes the conflict in the parent, he can turn the tables on the parent and use the passivity as a means of frustrating the parent as he himself has been frustrated. Dynamically speaking, the child's emotional decision to hide behind his passivity and to use it hostilely is not the result of one-trial learning. In all probability, when the parent, from guilt or whatever, invited the child to be more expressive, the child at first might have taken the parent at his word. But what the child soon finds out is that when he becomes more assertive, he reactivates counter punitive behavior in the parent. In the process, the child has learned painfully; through his trust he has set himself up for another round of punishment.

It doesn't take many such lessons for the child to learn that it is useless to fight directly and to learn that he can get "more return for his dollar's worth" of energy by passive resistance. When the child has learned of the frustrating power of passive resistance, it becomes a powerful tool that he can wield without much danger to himself. And, in this case, once the client learned that she could drain her anger without risk to herself, then the passivity that was instituted as a defense against anxiety doubled as a convenient outlet for her anger.

Under conditions where anger is drained off indirectly through passive means, the person is set on a course that is one of the most difficult to break through in therapy. The client never experiences his anger; so he isn't violating any rules. He is being submissive as required by law, and when frustration builds it gets drained off with accompanying satisfaction. And that is a hard "hand" to beat!

There are additional lessons that such a client learns from the suppressive parent which reinforce his behavior patterns and counter progress. For example, when a parent, operating out of guilt, variously invites and then punishes, the child learns several damaging lessons that affect his own interactions with others. He learns first hand of the frustration and anguish of being set up for a letdown. And, the child eventually might make the rewarding discovery that by setting others up, he can create in others the same anguish he felt. Secondly, he learns how to play on and induce guilt in others to get what he wants or to avoid issues. Finally, the most damaging lesson is that the child learns of the dangers of trusting, of taking a significant person at his word. And that learning sets him on a path that makes reaching him difficult.

In early sessions with this particular client, the therapist met the full force of his client's repertoire for frustrating him. The client effectively set the therapist up for a number of frustrating letdowns. The client's guilt inducing maneuvers came into play when the client's anger was beginning to surge up. And the client's distrust was evident from the elaborate way she attempted to deflect, defend against, and induce guilt before finally risking the open expression of anger toward the therapist.

It was because the therapist conceived of his client's anger as the outermost layer of previously unavailable affect that he facilitated its expression during their session. The therapist felt that once that outer ring of reactive anger was perforated, the underlying needs which were screened from view by those feelings could emerge. Once the client is no longer simply reacting against someone, then several things happen simultaneously. The client becomes increasingly anxious because the internal search is about to begin. That search is threatening because the client's own resources are poorly understood, dangers are felt, and primitive feelings stir. At that point, the client's ambivalence about uncovering those feelings might be reawakened and her defenses reactivated.

Had the therapist construed his client's anger as reflecting different dynamic issues than those suggested above, he might have followed a different course of action. Anger serves many functions and whether its experience in the relationship is indicative of a progressive, circular, or deteriorating relationship depends on a number of considerations. In itself, the experience of anger, like any other feeling is a neutral condition. The therapist can't measure the success of his sessions by how angry his clients become. In fact, if the therapist attempts to facilitate the ventilation of angry feelings by a client who is anxious and sensitive to rejection, the consequences might be to drive the client out of therapy.

The expression of anger gathers its predictive force as a useful vehicle for facilitating change dependent on the dynamic purposes that its expression serves in terms of the overall personality picture. Angry feelings might be a cover for anxiety. As some clients become anxious and frightened, they tend to lash out at the therapist, feel hostile, and are generally irritable. Although the client's anxiety might actually hide deeper hostile feelings, the anger itself is often an index of intense anxiety that threatens the client's sense of well-being. If the therapist attends to the anger and misses the anxiety, he might use an otherwise fruitful session in hearing many variations on the theme of the client's anger. Unfortunately, such lack of insight on the part of the therapist simply convinces the client that he has much to be anxious about!

At other times, the profuse expression of angry feelings might be a ploy to divert the therapist from the real issue, to enlist the therapist's help in inappropriate collaborative efforts against a parent or spouse, or to avoid examining the client's role in the conflict situation. Such anger is often characterized by efforts at placing the blame on others; it might carry a "bitching" ring to it; or it might have a whiny, bratty feel.

The point is that the therapist's interview behavior is affected by how he construes the meaning of his client's reactions. For example, in this case had the therapist construed the meaning of the client's anger toward her girlfriend as a cover for· envy, he would have taken a much different tack during the session. Among other things, such a construction of events would have suggested a much more careful look at the dimensions of that external relationship since that relationship might have been a screen for the client's fantasies in relation to her parents. As such, the client's reactions might have indicated that unresolved childhood fantasies were being reawakened and would soon be acted out in therapy. And as will be pointed out later, uncovering the fantasies transferred to and experienced in that relationship rather than facilitating the expression of anger would be the primary therapeutic task.

The Client's Reactions: Indications
That Conflict is Active

Another perspective for considering the processes of therapy is from the viewpoint of how the intensification of conflict affected the client's behavior between and during sessions. In this section, we will speculate about the probable nature of the internal experience of heightened conflict in the client, commenting on its stimulus, and noting its behavioral effects in the client's relationship to the therapist and in her other interpersonal encounters. More generally, we will focus on how the intensification of conflict heightens sensitivity to subtleties of behavior and tunes a client's sensors to noting, interpreting, and reacting to persons, events, and situations in terms of the client's own internal strife.

By way of introduction, it has been proposed previously that some of the client's needs although blocked by anxiety were still active and pressing for gratification. It was that continual press of needs and blockage that the client experienced as frustration. It was that sense of being frustrated that brought the client into therapy. And it was that docile, flattened exterior and the secondary gains the passivity provided that made reaching the client difficult.

In early sessions, at those times when needs were felt, the client would cycle repeatedly through her usual defensive coping methods to ward off anxiety. But, judging by her behavior during the crucial session reported earlier, as the press of needs intensified, the client's submissive shield no longer adequately served its former function and the underlying anger started emerging. In essence, then, the sessions had been productive and the client and therapist were converging on needs which generated anxiety, heightened the client's sense of frustration, and triggered anger. And it was at some such point in the sessions that the therapist's absence acted to crystalize the client's feelings and set her off.

As an aside, two things ought to be made clear. First of all, it was because the therapist had been effective that the client was beginning to feel what was previously denied in awareness. Second, if the therapist's "absence" had not been the behavioral trigger to her reactions, something else would have done it. Perhaps the therapist might have been late for a session. Perhaps he might have missed some minor point and frustrated the client. The point is that conflict in the client had reached a fever pitch and heightened her sensitivity to any nuances of behavior which might have resonated with her internal strife and set off her reactivity.

For purposes of the present discussion, it is what the client observed and how she interpreted events in her daily life at a time when her feelings were running high that introduces a most interesting dimension to the way that anxiety and conflict affect the perceptual processes. At a time when she was feeling frustrated, the client "observed" frustrated women and frustrating men. Her hypersensitivity to the events in her ongoing relationships was a behavioral representation of her own inner feelings, strife, and anxieties projected outward into other relationships and viewed as on a passing screen. Although it is true that events occurred in that external relationship which the client could construe as she did, her sensitivity to and interpretation of the meaning of those events, her identification with the girlfriend's feelings, and her reactions to the man were internally motivated by and projections of her own frustrated needs.

It was not by accident that the client was hypersensitive to her girlfriend's being taken advantage of. The client's antenna was attuned to those events. The client's perceptions of events between sessions and her allusion to having such thoughts as she sat in the "waiting room" clearly pointed to her feelings about the therapist's having been away. Apparently the client had at some level felt anger toward the therapist for having let other matters take precedence over his work with her, but she hadn't experienced that directly. However, during the course of the intervening time, her perceptual processes—her observations and interpretations of what was going on in her life around her—became increasingly clear reflectors to what she was experiencing internally.

To generalize for a bit, a client's hypersensitivity clues a therapist to a number of interlocking dimensions of conflict which are worth elaborating. In the first place, the degree of a client's sensitivity is a direct measure of his anxiety and conflicted feelings. Events are magnified, distorted, interpreted, and reacted to in greater or lesser degree dependent upon the power of the internal experience of conflict.

Second, when a client's conflicts are activated during therapy, his anxiety works for the therapist. The client's reactions indicate a weakening or rupturing of the defensive structure and point to areas where underlying motivations are surfacing and can no longer be staved off. In his sensitivity the client sees his problem at every corner, and in his reports of those events he reveals crucial information about those conflicts and provides the therapist with help in understanding what he seeks and fears. Not only from what he is sensitive to, but from the way he behaves toward others in efforts to resolve the conflicts, the client provides the therapist with a charting of his inner processes.

It is as though the client's anxiety acts as a sensitizer, tunneling his vision and pinpointing with uncanny accuracy central features of his conflict. In his sensitivity, the client guides the therapist to the heart of the conflict. It must be obvious that such a state of affairs would not occur unless and until the client had made some internal emotional decision to trust the therapist and work toward a constructive resolution of conflict. Otherwise, he would not provide the therapist with the materials with which to help him or hurt him. And that is what makes those moments so crucial. Unless the therapist comes through at such times, the client will close the issue worse the wear for having trusted.

Whereas the degree of sensitivity is an index of the client's anxiety, the way in which the client construes those experiences clues the therapist to such matters as the nature of conflict, its proximity to awareness, the potential for internalization, and early resolution. Several examples might clarify some of those dimensions as reflected in the way different clients might react when conflict is active. In the case just cited, the client's conflict was near consciousness and the thinly disguised deflection of feelings from the therapeutic relationship was easily bridged. But even there, note should be taken of how the client reacted when conflict was generating. The client projected her own conflicts onto a girlfriend and then reacted to her own projections *as though her own conflicts motivated and were felt by the girlfriend and characterized her male relationships.*

At other times, as conflict generates, a client's sensitivity might take the form of anticipating serious reprimands or reprisals for some actions even though the behavior when considered on its own merits is insufficient to justify the fear. The client might suddenly be flooded with fears about being caught and severely punished for some recent insignificant misdeed in which the anticipated punishment far outweighs the infraction of some rule. Unconscious guilt might be the motivating force which sets that kind of sensitivity into motion. Such sensitivity might arise, for example, if the client is close on the heels of reawakening fantasies, experiencing feelings, or perhaps recalling some childhood behavior which would have been punished or would be punishable if discovered.

The client isn't aware of the motivating force for the guilt or anxiety. It remains unconscious. The client's preoccupation with slight infractions of rules is at once the wish for punishment to alleviate the guilt, the fear that he will be punished if he is discovered, and the more basic fear of discovering some painful things about himself or his motives that he would prefer to avoid learning about.

At times of heightened stress, the links between conflict and the stimulating events which trigger anxious reactions in a client are not always as readily apparent as those suggested thus far. When conflict is generating, the anxiety-provoking stimulus might be a symbolic representation of conflict. In a general way, the extent to which the conflict is experienced symbolically and conveyed primarily through symbolic language as well as the degree of transparency of those symbols are all indices of the unconscious character of conflict. The unacceptability of feelings, thoughts, or experiences and the anxiety they generate makes symbolic communication necessary. The portrayal of conflict in symbolic form suggests the amount of distance so to speak that the client must put between himself and the conscious experience of conflict.

To cite an example of the symbolic portrayal of conflict, it might be recalled that a brief excerpt of a case was included earlier in this book in which a woman was conflicted about her forthcoming marriage. It was suggested at that time that the client's fears about her own marriage were based in part in her observations of what had occurred in her parent's marriage. Her father's declining strength and her mother's increasing insecurity in that relationship provided a poor model for her own future happiness.

Of importance for our considerations here was the fact that the client, in her anxiety about the probable outcome of her own marriage, became highly observant of events that at first might seem to have little relevance to her conflict. In cleaning the basement during the week, the client observed a crack in the foundation and became extremely anxious for reasons that she could not understand. It was only with careful work during succeeding sessions that the symbolic value of that event in terms of her forthcoming marriage became clear. For, in the emotional life of the client, that cracking foundation was the *symbolic equivalent* of the decline in male potency that she had observed in her father, that she associated with her mother's insecurity, and that she feared in her own marriage.

Some Concluding Remarks about the Case

By way of concluding this section and introducing the material to be considered next, some final comments might be made. Thus far, using a brief case excerpt as a basis for generating principles, the processes of therapy have been viewed from several interlocking perspectives. One aspect of this discussion about the generation and unfolding of conflict during therapy deserves much more careful treatment and will be the subject matter of the next section. With regard to the particular case under consideration, it has been proposed that the client, stimulated by her own sense of frustration and anger, projected her own unresolved conflicts onto a girlfriend. And then, identifying with the girlfriend she had shaped out of her own concerns, the client reacted as though her own conflicts motivated and were felt by the girlfriend and characterized her male relationships.

Further, it was proposed that the client's projections into that relationship were a thinly disguised cover for and held the potential for extensive "acting out" of her feelings and reactions to the therapist. In essence, the client transferred those feelings from their generating base in the relationship and actually experienced them as though they were appropriate to the principals of the external relationship. Since the therapist had taken on a significance that made direct encounter dangerous, the girlfriend and her male companion provided a convenient and safer target.

It was next proposed that the client's reactions to events in that ongoing relationship were likely to be no more than fleeting representatives of her feelings toward the therapist. The therapist's guide to the ephemeral character of that transfer of feelings would be evident once the conflict was recentered in the therapeutic relationship. The potential for "acting out" in that external relationship would be reduced. Under conditions where the external relationship was stripped of the transference components, the therapist might hear little more about that relationship or the stresses in it.

On the other hand, it was suggested that if the relationship to the girlfriend embodied the potential for deeper transference feelings about unresolved past conflicts, the therapist might find the client repeatedly reintroducing that relationship as they moved to deeper levels of conflict. And, in passing, it was noted that the reintroduction of conflict in that relationship could then provide the therapist with an ongoing guide to his client's emotional life and to progress toward change.

Embedded in that discussion was a further proposition about the second layer of transferred feelings—those that are transferred to and inappropriate to the therapeutic relationship. In that regard, it was suggested that once conflict was recentered in therapy, the therapeutic relationship would become the center for an intense emotional experience for the client. And, interestingly enough, once the immediate stimulus for the client's feelings dissipated, then that relationship too would be stripped of its transference components, freeing the client to carry the conflict back to its generating sources in the past.

Those propositions were rather hastily sketched in the preceding sections, being somewhat limited by the specifics of the case under consideration. At this time, we shall broaden the base of operations considerably and generalize about such phenomena as they are reflected in, complicate, and provide the unique basis for a client's changing during therapy.

THE EVOLUTION OF CONFLICT DURING THERAPY: SOME FURTHER CONSIDERATIONS

During the course of therapy, there is an increasingly free-flowing movement of feelings back and forth between the present and past. As therapy progresses, it is as though what had been a membrane impermeable to the flow of feelings and connections between the past and present becomes increasingly permeable. As those feelings, impulses, anxiety, or emotional trauma are reexperienced in the present, they are experienced with an intensity comparable to their original emotional impact. And those conflicts, since they were born out of past interpersonal relationships, are not felt in the abstract. When they are reexperienced in the present, those conflicts are often felt with conviction in relation to the therapist or to someone in a client's interpersonal environment as though that person were the inhibiting, disabling, and anxiety-provoking past personage.

As the unresolved conflicts of the past are reawakened, the client interprets the present in terms of the past. It is inevitable that the client would do so since he has no alternative model against which to compare and predict. Not only does the client predict in terms of the past—in the cognitive sense of the word—but of greater importance for the processes of therapy is the fact that as conflict generates the client actually emotionally feels toward those with whom he interacts what he felt in the past.

As conflict generates, a client's perceptions of and reactions to persons and events in his daily life—whether of the therapist or those whom he encounters between sessions—might take some interesting emotional turns. The client might attribute motivations to the therapist, anticipate reactions from him, and feel in relation to him as though he was motivated by the same needs, would behave in kind, and would feel toward the client in ways that were identical to those past persons who set conflict into motion.

As conflict generates, the client does not limit his irrational reactions to the transactions of the therapeutic relationship. Persons in the client's immediate interpersonal environment might become the unwilling and unknowing participants in the reenactment of unresolved conflict. Events in those relationships might be distorted to fit the client's predictions; the client might attempt to manipulate those relationships to reduce anxiety, complete fantasies, or to meet needs which as vestiges of the past might be inappropriate to the reality dimensions of those relationships. In short, persons in the client's immediate environment might be placed in the company of the therapist and become the emotional equivalent of significant past persons, and the client might set about actively using those relationships to master his anxiety.

Not all of a client's irrational reactions to his extratherapeutic relationships are directly attributable to their generating sources in the past. To understand many of a client's reactions in his ongoing interpersonal relationships, one must turn to a careful examination of the immediate triggering sources of conflict— the therapeutic relationship itself! Conflict is generated in the client as a direct consequence of the therapeutic relationship. As such, that relationship intervenes between the generating sources of conflict in the past and the client's ongoing interactions.

For the client's feelings to reach a level of intensity where change is possible, the therapeutic relationship must have reached a degree of considerable significance. Once the therapist has become that important in the emotional life of the client, then the client's interpersonal encounters between sessions might in fact be reflections of his feelings about the therapist. The client might find some safer object in his environment with whom to act out what he feels in relation to the therapist in much the same way that the therapeutic relationship itself might be the depository for the reenactment of generic conflict.

In essence, the client's behavior between sessions, stimulated by his interactions with the therapist, takes on the semblance of a second order of transferred feelings. For that reason, it behooves the therapist to listen carefully to his client's reports of his interactions at times of stress not only for what they reveal of the generic conflict but as a running account of the client's experience of the therapist.

Some of the complexities of the way a client's feelings toward the therapist might affect the client's interpersonal relationships were introduced in the last section. If the flow of the client's feelings in the case presented at that time were traced along the course of therapy, it would be found to follow an interesting pattern. In general, the client's feelings generated by conflict arising out of past interactions were attributed to the therapist and felt by the client as though they motivated the therapist.

Since the direct experience of those feelings was unacceptable in relation to the therapist whose significance made him potentially hurtful, they were deflected outward and felt as though they belonged in an ongoing relationship. During the course of a particular session the client's feelings flowed back and forth from that external relationship through the therapist to the past and back to the therapist again, changing in intensity and valence and being stripped along the way of what was irrational to the therapeutic relationship and to the ongoing relationship.

In this section, following some general introductory remarks about the interpersonal expression of conflict, we will follow the various routes that different clients' feelings might take when conflict is active and the experiences of the past are felt in the present. Of special interest in this section will be an expansion of some of the various ways that conflict generated in the therapeutic relationship affects a client's ongoing interpersonal relationships. More generally, as we trace the flow of a particular client's feelings back and forth between the present and past, we. will attempt to exemplify some of the propositions advanced in the preceding section about how the experience of conflict links together the past, the therapeutic session, and extratherapeutic relationships.

The Client's Interpersonal Relationships: Shaped by Inner Conflict

In a general way, a client's perceptions, expectations, and reports of his behavior in his interactions with those in his immediate environment provide the therapist with one of many indices that he utilizes in his ongoing assessment of his client's changing emotional life and progress in therapy. But of significance for consideration here is the importance that the therapist attaches to a client's reports of his interactions at times when his feelings are running high. At those times, the therapist is often likely to hear echoes of past conflict interpenetrating those relationships.

He is apt to hear the present being shaped in terms of predictions from the past. He might hear the past being reconstructed in the present so that the client can live out what was attenuated, remodel what was poorly learned, or master his anxiety. In some cases, the client's craftsmanship might be intricate and extensive, and the client's present relationships might become the testing ground for what was permitted only in fantasy or had to be denied completely because of the disturbances of his developmental years.

If the therapist listens with an ear to the past as his client reports his interactions when anxiety is rampant, he can often see behavioral parallels, note certain repetitive interpersonal themes that are grounded in past conflict, or sense that the client's reactivity, outweighing the stimulus value of the other party, reflects feelings that have been transported intact from previous significant encounters. At times, the reenactment of conflict is so dramatically parallel to past interactions that the therapist might conclude erroneously that the client must certainly be aware of what is being acted out. But as noted earlier, the blatancy with which the past is reconstructed and reenacted in the present is often inversely related to emotional insight.

And as he listens the therapist must conclude that the reality dimensions of the client's ongoing relationships have been blurred and are experienced not for what they are but for what they represent in the client's unconscious. It is as though the client's unconscious holds the negative of previously photographed conflict-laden events that are projected into the actual ongoing interaction and efforts are made at correcting the print as though that would correct errors in the negative.

From a client's accounts of what he observes and reacts to in relationships that are interpenetrated with elements of the past, from the emotional conditions that the client perceives or tends to create in those relationships, from the course those releationships run—developing, changing, intensifying, and terminating—as the client progresses through therapy, the therapist gains unusual insight into the emotional character of conflict, is provided with a preview of how the conflict might be enacted in his presence, and is guided so as to participate in constructive ways. The crucial point is that the client's accounts provide the therapist with an index of his present day experience of the historical conflict. In reliving history, the client garbs experiences that might be devoid of affect with the critical emotional components of those experiences that create conflict *as they are currently felt.*

The foregoing paragraphs are not intended to imply by even the farthest stretch of the imagination that the therapist abets or sits by idly observing his client distort, reenact, or test out fantasies on those unfortunates who happen to reside in his immediate vicinity. On the contrary, the therapist works assiduously to avoid such reenactment and to recenter it in the therapeutic relationship, work it through there, and attach it to its generating sources when and if it occurs. But it is intended to suggest that such behavior is at times inevitable as the client's anxiety peaks when conflict is generating.

Sometimes it is only when conflict has reached proportions where it is experienced keenly in the present in relation to those in the client's immediate environment that the subleties and dimensions of conflict are brought into bold relief, that the therapist gains his best insights into the emotional life of his client, and the interpretive links with the past are most readily forged. Perhaps a brief example might demonstrate the way in which a client's feelings in an ongoing relationship, generated by her experiences in therapy, revealed crucial features of her emotional life and set the stage for emotional insights that were liberating.

Conflict is Active: Its
Interpersonal Effects in the Present

The client in this case had been reared in a home where the parents seemed to hold nothing in common. The client observed little that held them together; they seemed never to relate to each other, and for all the client could determine each parent held the other in disdain. The children, caught between the hostilities, swore emotional allegiance to one or the other parent and by that fact emotionally severed relations with the parent of the enemy camp.

The client at first tried to bridge the gap between the parents, failing in her efforts to accomplish anything of note except to elicit anger from both parents. Next, she attempted to divide her loyalties, subtly shifting allegiance back and forth, living with a great deal of stress and satisfying few needs in the process. Finally, in an effort to gain something, she pledged her loyalty to her mother and proceeded into adulthood with little contact with her father, losing in the process some of what she could have learned about herself as a woman from him.

As she grew up, the client felt the burden of her mother's needs. Her mother leaned on her, used her as an outlet for her emotions, and often expressed her sense of isolation and loneliness. And the client came to believe that she was her mother's lifeline, that unless she shored her mother up, her mother would lead a companionless life. And her mother proceeded to prove the client's hypothesis by becoming depressed and sick when the client was absent.

Sensing her loss and the burden she was carrying, the client specifically asked to see a male therapist. To compress events considerably, the client began to relate well to the therapist, felt immensely better about herself, and eventually became interested in a man who shared her feelings and she began to date regularly. But then the fireworks started. And it was the way that the client experienced her conflicts when she began to feel attracted and attractive that is important to our present considerations.

The client began to feel intensely guilty. And the guilt took an interesting turn for it was experienced as having let a girlfriend down whom she knew very well. The client had a longstanding relationship with a girlfriend with whom she had shared many things. The client felt that the girlfriend had no one but her, was lonely, and that her dating left the friend companionless. The client perceived her girlfriend as angry and resentful of her accomplishments and she felt drawn to nurture her at the expense of her own freedom. The client felt the girlfriend's isolation and pulling power so strongly that she even considered rejecting her suitor to spend more time with the girlfriend.

There are a number of interesting speculative questions about the dynamics of conflict and its interpersonal expression that are embedded in that brief accounting of the client's reactions. Of principal importance is the fact that the client's guilt feelings were consciously experienced in and attached to her relationship with someone in her immediate environment. The emotional conditions that the client read into that ongoing relationship, whether magnified or distorted is not the immediate issue, were strikingly similar to the emotional context of her earlier relationship to her mother. The client's actual interactions with her girlfriend, the experience of conflict in that relationship, and the way it was handled paralleled her earlier interactions with her mother. But the client didn't feel the guilt in relation to her mother; she felt it in terms of someone with whom she had been living out significant dimensions of the conflicts that characterized her developmental years.

When we turn to the question of how much the reality features of that relationship were distorted by the client's own inner conflicts, we open an interesting area of discussion. In all probability the behavior of the girlfriend was to some extent similar to the actual behavior of the client's mother. Whether the dynamics underlying the behavior were similar or whether the girlfriend was motivated by the same needs as the mother is of course a much different issue.

But it often happens that a client will seek out, locate, and form relationships with others who carry the seeds of the generic problem situation. And, in forming a relationship with that person, the client might proceed to live out some significant dimensions of those unresolved conflict laden interactions of the past.

There are many reasons why a client might set up relationships to parallel past interactions and often those relationships are multidetermined. Through such a reconstruction of a past problematic relationship, the client is in all probability gratifying some neurotic needs that were satisfied through interaction with the past personage. That is to say that the client's investment in reliving those experiences suggests that there is considerable gain for the client despite the losses, apparent suffering, and healthy desire to break the pattern.

If carefully scrutinized, the exacerbation of guilt when the client stopped attending to the girlfriend's needs might suggest additional motives for forming, maintaining, and fearing the dissolution of a relationship that is constructed along lines that parallel the past. Assume for a moment that the client's past solicitousness toward the mother screened out underlying hostility for having been burdened by her and for having been cut off from a relationship with her father. The client's motivation in reconstructing the past in the present and her nurturance of the girlfriend's needs might then have been motivated in part to reinforce the defense against knowing about her own underlying aggressive feelings toward the mother.

Dynamically associated with the underlying hostility toward the mother is the arousal of fantasies about the father. The therapist's warm response to her and his emotional support in her search—emotional conditions that she sought and missed from her father—might have stirred up fantasies toward the father which interlock with feelings of destructiveness toward the mother and set additional anxiety into motion. Under those conditions, if the current screen against those experiences breaks down, if the client no longer relates as she had with the girlfriend, if the oversolicitious defense is penetrated, the client might then get in touch with the underlying hostile motives.

In other words, the status quo of the current relationship must be maintained and its breakdown symbolically represents a breakdown in the mother-daughter relationship, provides access to hostile impulses toward the mother, and stirs up anxious fantasies about the relationship with the father. Such an interpretation might partially account for the sensations of guilt the client experienced and for her perceptions of her girlfriend's being angry with her, those perceptions being projections of her own hostile feelings or feared retaliation for her disaffiliative motivation.

Still other motives might partially account for the client's need to recreate a past relationship in the present. Through such a relationship, the client might also be seeking *to resolve the conflict* or master anxiety—and in this case to master the mother. It is that healthy wish to break the pattern that probably motivated the client to enter therapy. And it was the sense of incompleteness that might have stimulated the client to ask to see a male therapist. In itself, the client's wish to see a man carries some interesting possibilities about the workings of the unconscious. For example, perhaps the client at some level experienced the fantasy that if she could find a man strong enough to handle her mother or one who would be responsive to her mother's needs, she could be liberated from her responsibilities in relation to the mother.

Through the way his client relates, what he expects, and how he responds to those in his immediate environment at times of stress, the therapist gains much useful information about the nature of conflict. In this case, the introduction of conflict in relation to a girlfriend provided the therapist with useful clues to the nature of conflict and to its current experiential value in the life of his client. It was only after the client brought those conflicted feelings into therapy as they were experienced in the present that the therapist got his deepest sense of the emotional meaning of the conflicts that permeated his client's past interactions. The fact that those feelings of the past were active and experienced with such power in the present facilitates associations with the past and provides the opportunity for emotional insight into how those displaced and still active conflicts are affecting a client's current life situation.

Some Variants of the Interpersonal
Expression of Past Conflict in the Present

The degree to which a client's interpersonal relationships are interpenetrated by elements of the past and differences in the nature of the distortions that characterize the therapy of particular clients vary considerably dependent upon a number of considerations. In many cases, the client can be seen to be forming relationships with persons whose salient personality characteristics reflect in greater or lesser degree those of a disabling parent. In those cases, it is as though the client attempts to master the parent and the anxiety generated there by proxy. Anxiety generated in the parent-child relationship still actively inhibits the client's movements; so he sets about to effect release from the past by reliving it under more controlled conditions.

One male client attempted to master an overwhelming mother in an interesting way. The mother's relationship to the client during childhood was generally characterized by oscillating behavior; inviting warm behavior one minute often took a rapid-fire turn to aggressive, castrating behavior. When as a child the client reached out for the warmth, he met the hostility, followed by apologies and further invitations. After recycling through the anxiety-provoking sequence enough times to set the learning, the client responded to the inconsistencies by eventual withdrawal. The client entered therapy suspicious of the motives of women and equally skeptical of whether any man, the therapist included, could ever manage a woman of the emotional make-up of his mother.

The interesting thing the therapist noted was that eventually when the sessions centered on the client's conflicts with regard to his mother, he introduced the fact that he had been begun dating two girls. One girl was docile and sweet; the other aggressive, demanding, and cutting. Both seemed to be cut from very different emotional material and represented the two sides of the mother, very clearly differentiated.

It was as though the client tried to separate the elements of the conflict into two different women so that he could simplify the conflict, deal with the bipolar emotional conditions one at a time, thus bringing each emotional condition under ego mastery. It seemed to be an effort to manage the overpowering sense of anxiety in relation to women that the client experienced as a child when he tried to struggle with those rapidly oscillating emotional conditions in the same person and in someone as significant as the mother.

In the case just cited, the client attempted to master his conflict by separating the confusing emotional elements into two distinct persons so as to deal with them one at a time. In a second case, a female client was found to form dating relationships simultaneously with two males who were also very dissimilar, personality wise. On the surface it appeared that she too was trying to separate some confusing emotional elements of her past problematic inter-actions. But it soon became clear as she introduced historical material that the client's motives in forming those relationships were very different.

During early childhood, the client's relationship to her father had been warm and responsive; but, when the client reached puberty, for reasons the client only understood later in therapy, the father's behavior toward her changed dramatically, becoming cold and distant. During therapy, when the client talked of the two men to whom she was attracted, one could be seen to be cold, intellectual, and distant, much like the father-daughter relationship of her later developmental years. The other male was warm, responsive, and nurturant, much like the client's remembrances of her early childhood relationship with her father.

The very interesting thing that reveals the marvels of the unconscious was that the client was forever trying to get the two men to meet each other. In particular, she seemed interested in having some of the one man's warmth rub off on her more intellectual, distant companion. It was as though she held the unconscious fantasy that her father was still responsive to her and considerable emotional energy was invested in somehow trying to get the father to express those feelings toward her. But the conflict wasn't experienced in relation to the father. Rather the client was attempting to complete those childhood fantasies and bridge the emotional gaps of her earlier and later developmental years through her current relationships with the two men in her life who represented the critical emotional conditions of that developmental sequence.

Unfortunately, two male suitors don't always enjoy meeting and learning from their competition; so the client's efforts to bring them together were to no avail. But then the client apparently came upon a happy solution. The therapist's relationship to the client had been a warm, responsive one, much like the early father-daughter relationship. And during a session the client asked the therapist whether he would see one of her boyfriends who she felt was conflicted and needed help. The therapist didn't need to ask the client which boyfriend she wanted him to see!

The many variants of the way that past conflict affects present relationships can be seen from still another brief example. In this case, a client felt extremely uncomfortable that she had a boyfriend and her girlfriend did not. So she set about introducing the girlfriend to her own suitor and essentially tried to interest him in the girlfriend. One could speculate about what might motivate a client to behave in that fashion. At one end of a continuum, such behavior could simply reflect the client's declining interest in the male, the girlfriend's state providing a convenient way of ridding herself of him. In other cases, such behavior could be an index of some complex underlying conflicts.

However, as it turned out in this case, the client's parents were divorced and the client felt somewhat guilty about her role in the separation. Without going into the motivating force for the guilt in the family dynamics, the client at any rate perceived her mother as lonely, isolated, needy, and without the resources to manage her own affairs. Apparently the client felt at some level—whether from guilt, duty, or whatever—that, if she could get her mother patched up and remarried, she could have her own life. But those feelings based in conflict in the family were not experienced in the present as such. Instead the client's girlfriend profited from the residuals of the client's guilty relationship to her mother and was well provided for until the client began to grasp the way in which her present behavior was motivated by her own guilty feelings about her mother and eventually got to the source of the guilt in the family.

The Extensive Reenactment of Conflict: Some Special Considerations

In some cases, persons in a client's immediate environment serve a deeper transference value and resolving issues is much more difficult than those proposed thus far. Some clients enter therapy acting out their conflicts with a compulsion, constantly arranging their relationships to meet certain neurotic needs and to settle old scores. In those cases, the client might have traversed one relationship after another in noninsightful ways and in initial sessions as the therapist listens to the client's recounting of those relationships he might hear many variations on the same interpersonal theme interpenetrating one relationship after another. And the client's entrance into therapy might be the consequence of repeated frustrations, finding that those whom he has cloaked with certain characteristics manage to wriggle out of their preformed shapes and act contrary to the client's wishes.

The emotional energy invested in those relationships, their convenience, and the repetitive "acting out" of conflict without reflection counter the goals of therapy and make reaching a client engaged in the continual reenactment of past conflict difficult. At the slightest sign of anxiety, in order to avoid the feelings of rejection, insecurity, or inadequacy that the anxiety forewarns, such clients tend to set about immediately to regain their security and reduce the anxiety by whatever means are available and often in relation to those who happen to populate the scene at the time.

Although the recreation and acting out of past conflict in relation to someone in the client's current environment creates the problems indicated, the transactions in those relationships when compared to the history of a client's conflicts provide the therapist with much useful information about the nature of conflict as it is currently experienced. Of greater importance is the fact that the continual reenactment suggests that inner resolution has not been achieved, and since the selected person often does not know the right psychological answers in order to resolve the client's conflict, that conflict will eventually find its way into therapy and will involve the therapist as one of the principals in its reenactment.

In a general way, in any case where a client is living out the past in the present, however it is being enacted, the therapist can always expect that somewhere along the line he will be incorporated into the client's fantasies as one of the participants in that reenactment. The therapist can rest assured that the client will perceive those emotional conditions in the therapeutic relationship, create them as necessary, and react to his own creations. And when the struggle centers in the therapeutic relationship, if the therapist allows himself to be used to work through that conflict, then he simultaneously reduces the potential for the client's continuing to act out in his extratherapeutic relationships, intensifies their relationship, and lays the foundation for significant change.

Although it has been stated earlier in many different contexts, it is worth suggesting again that at those moments the client essentially has put together the present, the past, and the therapeutic hour. An emotional mergence that cuts across the time dimension has occurred. The conflicts of the past are again experienced in the present and felt in relation to the therapist with an intensity and conviction that is comparable to the generic experience. And it is that comparability in power that makes those experiences so therapeutically significant.

To illustrate a particularly intriguing way in which conflict is sometimes reenacted in the present and eventually finds its way into therapy, let's turn to the case where a client repeatedly attempts to reconstitute the family constellation in relation to those with whom he interacts in his current environment. If the therapist listens with an ear to the past as such a client recounts his various interactions, the therapist might make several sequentially important discoveries. First he might note that there is a major reconstruction of the past in the present with little revision except for changes in the cast of characters. But what is even more striking is the fact that, in cases where there is an extensive reenactment of conflict, many of the client's ongoing relationships might be triadic arrangements.

There are as many variations on the triadic theme as there are motives underlying it. But in general, the client will locate a man and woman in his current environment who are acquainted with each other, who might be engaged, or already married. The client might then become intensely involved with the couple, spending considerable time with each one or both and investing tremendous emotional energy in his relationship to them. On other occasions, a client might convert his dyadic relationships into triads by introducing one of his male or female friends to another acquaintance of the opposite sex.

Whatever the variation, the therapist can't help but be impressed with the ensuing interactions in those relationships once they are constituted. For if he listens carefully the therapist can note the blueprint for the emotional conditions underlying the repetitive themes of those interactions in the client's earlier relationship to his parents. The reenactment is so apparent at times that the therapist can conclude nothing other than that his client has reconstituted the family in the present and is proceeding to live out in relation to the selected pair who represent the parents something of what was missed at an earlier age, what was problematic, what was held in fantasy, or perhaps what was "acted out" in the family that still actively generates guilt, regret, or pleasurable reveries.

The client's reenactment of conflict in his daily life in relation to some couple selected to represent his parents provides the therapist with invaluable clues to the nature of conflict as it is presently experienced and also as a guide to its eventual reenactment in therapy with the therapist as one of the principals in the reenactment. From what the therapist hears in the client's interactions he prepares himself conceptually to understand what will eventually happen in his presence and is given a living preview of how and why the client will shape him as he does.

The therapist listens carefully, therefore, to what transpires in those triadic relationships that are constructed along the lines of past conflict-laden interactions. He listens to whether the client tries to manipulate one member of the couple against the other; whether he attempts to intrude for purposes of sharing something with them as a couple; whether he tries to identify with one or the other; whether he tries to compete or cooperate; whether he wants to learn from them or uses them as an outlet for anger and resentment.

The therapist listens to how his client perceives the relationship between the two persons, whether he experiences envy or expects jealous reactions from one or the other. He might hear the client attempting to relate as a child to the couple; he might hear the client trying to control the pair's hostile or sexual impulses toward each other or toward himself. The therapist might hear the client relating to the opposite sex member of the pair in ways that suggest the reliving of sexual fantasies about a parent. And the client might become repulsed if the selected person reacts by becoming sexually attracted to the client much as the child might entertain fantasies about a parent but be traumatized if the parent reacts in kind. And in those cases, the client's history might reveal a parent who became sexually involved with the child when the child was seeking affection or experimenting with his own sexual feelings.

In general, as the therapist listens, he internally questions whether the client is trying to live out his fantasies or is attempting to use the relationship constructively to learn and grow. And the therapist can fully expect that unless the client fortuitously happens to select a pair who are searching for a full grown son or daughter, those conflicts will remain active, needs will go unmet, and the conflict will be introduced into therapy with the therapist as a principal in the reenactment.

In a general way, the therapist eventually becomes a participant in any of a client's struggles, but in cases where the client has set up his relationships in ways that reconstruct the family in the present, the client will shape the therapeutic relationship in rather interesting ways. In those cases, the client might attempt to set up a triad in relation to the therapist by symbolically mating the therapist with someone who represents the opposite parent in the environment!

The way in which such conflict finds its way into therapy is of course varied, but one example might illustrate what is being proposed above. In this case, a female client who was seeing a male therapist had been arranging her relationships so that she was continually intruding into the relationship of two people who were already emotionally involved with each other. The client had a knack for finding a couple whose life seemed complete without the client's help. When she "zeroed" in on a suitable pair, the client would relate to both members in very different ways. She would become flirtatious with the male member of the couple and perceive the female member as envious of her and as threatened by the client's relationship to the male member. Generally, the client ended up rejected and frustrated because the pair would manage to do without the additional stress that her intrusiveness and needs added to what was often a relationship flourishing with conflict under its own steam.

For our purposes here, the interesting thing was the way in which conflict found its way into therapy. During a session following one of the client's many frustrating experiences in her interpersonal relationships, the client introduced some problems she was having in relation to one of her female teachers. In a number of succeeding sessions the client complained about the teacher, found fault with her lectures, felt she was incompetent, and apparently took some glee in raising questions in class which the client perceived as frustrating the teacher. Even more so, the client felt that she knew more than the teacher and that the teacher, aware of the client's superior abilities, was threatened, envious, and punishing.

It soon emerged during therapy that the client's feelings about the teacher and her past relationship to her mother had some rather significant parallels. She felt in the present toward the teacher in ways that were identical to what she experienced in relation to her mother. She felt that she was more of a woman than her mother, that her mother was unable to hold her father's attention, and that she could have done a better job in her mother's stead.

But a most critical feature of that past interaction which was being acted out in the present in relation to the male therapist was that *the client often complained to her father about the mother in much the same way that during therapeutic sessions she was complaining to the therapist about a woman in authority who had some measure of control over her!* The conflict was recentered in the therapeutic relationship and the client's behavior toward the therapist was a dynamic replay of central features of conflict. Essentially, the client was acting out the generic conflict situation in the therapist's presence with the therapist as one of the principals of the reenactment. And some poor, unsuspecting teacher—who probably wasn't quite sure what was happening to her—provided the client with the second principal in the modern-day version of the generic conflict situation.

As an aside, it might be noted that under conditions where the client has included the therapist as a part of her neurotic equation, he is in a particularly good position to help. Those conditions provide an experiential basis for relearning, thereby immensely broadening the base of the therapeutic operations and providing therapy with its uniqueness as a change process. But those conditions also suggest that the therapist's behavior becomes a crucial determinant of whether his client will change and grow or will reinforce her neurotic patterns.

For example, it is interesting to speculate about what would have happened had the therapist sided with the client, believed her complaints were justified, and encouraged the client. If, in the client's unconscious, the teacher and the therapist represented the replay of the generic struggle, such a therapist reaction would be equivalent to the father's denouncing the mother to the child and collaborating in weakening the mother's position in the home. And such behavior, when and if it happens in a family, not only generates some fantasies that live on for years into the adult life of a child, but it activates intense anxiety.

With the mother out of the picture, the female child must stifle the very fantasies about the father that are generated by his actions. The reason is that the father's action—colluding in the unseating of the mother—make his motives and self-control suspect. Since the mother's controls have been lifted, the child is then left with the onerous task—in fantasy at least—of acting as the father's controls, thereby seriously impairing learning about her own sexual feelings, leading to overcontrol of her own impulse life, and keeping infantile fantasies insulated and kicking. Translated to the therapeutic relationship, if the therapist inadvertently colludes in the client's unconscious fantasies by siding with the client and abetting the client's acting out in relation to the teacher, that dynamic replay will not only generate some interesting fantasies but intense anxiety as well and the client might flee therapy.

The point at this time is that the therapist must listen carefully to what transpires in his client's ongoing relationships, look for links with the past, and strive to see how the past is being replayed in the present. Through his interpersonal relationships a client might still be attempting to solve old problems, master anxiety, rectify the past, manipulate a parent's feelings, or complete fantasies. The client often selects persons in his environment who embody some characteristics that can be magnified or modified to fit the client's inner struggles and as such they become a useful guide to the therapist in understanding where his client is emotionally.

During the course of therapy, there is no such thing as a chance interaction any more than there is a random thought. The persons that the client introduces into therapy, in other words, can never be dismissed without careful exploration of their meaning in the life of the client. In a more general way, a client's running accounts of his relationships serve a most useful diagnostic function. From the way a client's relationships develop and intensify, from the way new relationships are formed and other relationships terminate—particularly those that are neurotically oriented—the therapist has an ongoing guide to his client's changing emotional life, to regressive and progressive features of that emotional life, and to the client's progress toward termination of therapy.

THE GENERATION AND UNFOLDING OF CONFLICT DURING THERAPY: AN EPILOGUE

As therapy proceeds, feelings that might have lain dormant for years sometimes begin to stir around again within a client. Sensations, impulses, and reactions that create anxiety might flare up with an intensity that frightens the client. Feelings that are poorly understood, vague, or felt to be outside the client's control might make an appearance.

As therapy proceeds, old conflicts that the client thought were resolved or that he felt had an insignificant effect on his current behavior might again characterize his feelings and reactions to others. In his interpersonal behavior, the client might become suddenly aware that he reacts and holds the same attitudes toward others that a parent held—and those attitudes might be ones that he despises and as a child vowed would never interpenetrate his own relationships with people.

As therapy proceeds, the client might again feel as he felt during childhood when he was dependent and had less control over his destiny. What were the reality dimensions of his childhood encounters—what he felt and how he acted to stave off anxiety in relation to a demanding, rejecting, controlling, or inhibiting parent—might reemerge as the irrational premises that characterize his adult relationships. In some relationships the client might feel overwhelmed or fearful of being rejected; he might experience guilt or undue anxiety in the presence of certain persons; or he might become irrationally fearful that others might take steps to interfere with his life, thwart his ambitions, or damage his career.

Although the client might have been living out his life in the shadow of such fears, those fears are likely to intensify as the client and therapist converge on the experiences that generated those reactions. As feelings and experiences that have been a source of anxiety in the past and have been walled off by anxiety and defenses against their recurrence are reawakened and push into awareness, as still viable needs and unresolved conflicts reemerge and seek expression and satisfaction, conflict is regenerated in the therapeutic relationship.

As the pressure for gratification and release of affect intensifies, so also does the danger. At such moments, the client will scramble around, variously attempting to satisfy the needs pressing for gratification and in efforts to avoid anxiety. At such moments the opportunity for integration and increased maturity is in critical balance with the potential for redefending and walling off the experiences at the cost of even greater expenditures of energy. And, at such moments when conflict is reawakened and intensifies, when the client's needs press for expression and are met by anxiety, the therapeutic session becomes the center for intense emotional interactions.

At times of stress, the client provides the therapist with a map of his inner life. Events which seem insignificant or unrelated might trigger intense reactions. The client will see his problem at every corner. At such times, the client will perceive, interpret, and associate in terms of the predominant inner experiences and feelings which are associated with the submerged conflict that is nearing awareness. In essence, the client projects his inner experiences in uncensored ways, thus providing the therapist with the opportunity for entering into his emotional life in ways that would not otherwise be possible.

As conflict intensifies during therapy, the client might become hyper-sensitive to the nuances of behavior in his current interpersonal relationships which resonate with conflict-laden experiences of the past. The client's perceptual process might become a highly-tuned sensor, searching out, locating, and reacting to persons whose behavior reflects, even in the most minute degree, the emotional conditions that characterized the conflict engendering interactions of his past. And, in his hypersensitivity, his reactivity, and his interpretation of the behavior of persons and events in his environment, whether of the therapist or those that he encounters between sessions, the client inadvertently alerts the therapist to the nature of his conflicts and guides him to their sources.

At times of stress, not only does the client's perceptual process become a highly tuned sensor that points to conflict, but the client's associational process as well guides the therapist. The client's associations become the rapid-fire connectors that spotlight the central dynamics of conflict and link the critical features of the therapeutic session with those of the client's current interactions and with the generic sources of conflict.

At times of stress, the client, in his anxiety, uncertainty, and anticipation of danger might malign the therapist for his efforts to help, or he might misconstrue his motives, sometimes aligning the therapist in fantasy with those who damaged him during his development. Or, more dramatically, as therapy progresses it might become clear that a client is still searching for closure to well-worn fantasies, attempting to satisfy still viable wishes that were experienced in relation to a parent, or avoiding irrational fears that at one time were a very real threat to survival.

And, in time, as those wishes, fears, and fantasies increase in intensity because of the nature of therapy, the therapist might find himself the object of undue affection or disdain, a source of conflict for the client, or the brunt of the client's anger. At such times, the client's reactions to, anticipations about, and behavior toward the therapist are carbon-copies of his reactions to those in his past, and the therapeutic session essentially has become the center for the reenactment of old conflicts.

It is at times of stress, when the client's censors are blunted and his conflicts are in the open that his social facade drops, and he reveals his feelings, thoughts, and motives in ways he would not otherwise do. It is at times of stress when the lines between the past and the present are blurred that the client, through his projections, irrational premises, and expectations makes himself known to the therapist.

And those revelations and irrational reactions hold the seeds for what is potentially therapeutic for the client. For if, despite his fears of alienation, rejection, and disapproval, the client expresses those feelings, reveals those fantasies, or confronts the therapist, those experiences can be an emotional turning point in the life of the client. Those reactions under stress hold the potential for replacing fantasy with reality, for the acceptance and modification of feelings, for the internalization of conflict, and for increased emotional maturity.

The build up to those crucial moments when the client's conflicts are in the open is often extensive. Conflict generates and evolves over considerable time during therapy. The actual moments of intense interaction are brief. Although those moments are brief, their outcome is far-reaching, for at those points the client is most vulnerable, the potential for emotional insight is greatest, and significant change is possible.

Whether the full potential for change can be realized at such times is contingent on whether the therapist reacts appropriately to what is occurring in his presence. At crucial moments of intense interaction, the turning point in the client's emotional life can be achieved only if the therapist understands what is needed and is emotionally able to allow his client to express his feelings, whatever their valence or intensity, to reenact conflict in his presence, and to challenge his motives.

At those moments the potential for change is good if the therapist can use his own feelings and understanding to the client's advantage to help him to live through those experiences, to break through the anxiety barrier, and to integrate the experience at an emotional and insightful level. Otherwise those crucial moments in therapy might be lost.

Whether the therapist can help the client at such moments, then, is dependent in part on his understanding of the way in which conflict is generated, develops, and is experienced and expressed over time during therapy. How that understanding arises, interlocks with, and deepens because of and in relation to the therapist's participation in the emotional life of his client has been the subject matter of this book.

Because the therapist understands, he can participate meaningfully in the change process. And because he participates, the therapist experiences and deepens his understanding. Because the therapist participates, the client experiences and understands. And because he understands, the client's own resources are strengthened and he risks deeper participation.

That constantly deepening interactive process begins at the outset of therapy and continues through to termination. With each constructive interaction, the relationship deepens. As the relationship deepens, the client risks a more searching look at himself. Throughout therapy there is an ever expanding, deepening, spiraling into the personality and into the sources of conflict. With each thrust into the personality, there is regression, but there is also progression. There is anxiety, experiencing, remembering, emotional insight, and integration. With each thrust and cycling through to integration, the client's resources are strengthened. And with an ever increasing sense of his own strength, the client's need for the therapist's assistance diminishes. And a mutually agreed upon moment of termination occurs when both client and therapist recognize the client's inner strength to meet and manage the stresses of life.

Selected Readings

Alexander, F. *The scope of psychoanalysis 1921-1961.* New York: Basic Books, 1961.

—— & French, T. M. *Psychoanalytic therapy.* New York: Ronald Press, 1946.

Arlow, J. A. & Brenner, C. *Psychoanalytic concepts and the structural theory.* New York: International Universities Press, 1964.

Berne, E. *Transactional analysis in psychotherapy.* New York: Grove Press, 1961.

Blaine, G. B. & McArthur, C. C. *Emotional problems of the student.* New York: Appleton-Century-Crofts, 1961.

Bonime, W. *The clinical use of dreams.* New York: Basic Books, 1962.

Bordin, E.S. *Psychological counseling.* New York: Appleton-Century-Crofts, 1955.

Bullard, D. M. (ed.) *Psychoanalysis and psychotherapy: selected papers of Frieda Fromm-Reichmann.* Chicago: University of Chicago Press, 1959.

Coles, R. *Erik H. Erikson: The growth of his work.* Boston: Little, Brown, 1970.

Combs, A. W. & Snygg, D. *Individual behavior.* Rev. ed. New York: Harper, 1959.

Crowder, J. E. Relationship between therapist and client interpersonal behaviors and psychotherapy outcome. *Journal of Counseling Psychology*, 1972, 19, 68-75.

Dollard, J. & Miller, N. E. *Personality and psychotherapy.* New York: McGraw-Hill, 1950.

Erikson, E. H. *Childhood and society,* (2nd ed.) New York: Norton, 1963.

——. *Identity: youth and crisis.* New York: Norton, 1968.

——.(ed.) *The challenge of youth.* Garden City, New York: Doubleday, 1965.

Fenichel, O. *The psychoanalytic theory of neurosis.* New York: Norton, 1945.

Fromm,E. *Escape from freedom.* New York: Rinehart, 1941.

——. *Man for himself.* New York: Rinehart, 1947.

—— *The forgotten language.* New York: Rinehart, 1951.

Fromm-Reichmann, F. *Principles of intensive psychotherapy.* Chicago: University of Chicago Press, 1950.

Greenson, R. R. *The technique and practice of psychoanalysis.* Vol. 1 New York: International Universities Press, 1967.

Hartmann, H. *Ego psychology and the problem of adaptation.* New York: International Universities Press, 1958.

——. *Essays on ego psychology.* New York: International Universities Press, 1964.

Havighurst, R. J. *Developmental tasks and education.* (2nd ed.) New York: Longmans, Green, 1952.

——. *Human development and education.* New York: Longmans, Green, 1953.

Kell, B. L. & Burow, J. M. *Developmental counseling and therapy.* Boston: Houghton Mifflin, 1970.

—— & Mueller, W. J. *Impact and change.* New York: Appleton-Century-Crofts, 1966.

Kelly, G. A. *The psychology of personal constructs.* 2 Vols. New York: Norton, 1955.

Kris, E. *Psychoanalytic explorations in art.* New York: International Universities Press, 1952.

Leary, T. *Interpersonal diagnosis of personality.* New York: Ronald Press, 1957.

Lecky, P. *Self-consistency: a theory of personality.* J. F. A. Taylor and F. C. Thorne (eds.) New York: Anchor Books, 1969.

Lindzey, G. (ed.) *Assessment of human motives.* New York: Holt, Rinehart and Winston, 1958.

May, R. *Man's search for himself.* New York: Norton, 1953.

Menninger, K. *Theory of psychoanalytic technique.* New York: Basic Books, 1958.

——. *The vital balance.* New York: The Viking Press, 1963.

Mueller, W. J. Patterns of behavior and their reciprocal impact in the family and in psychotherapy. *Journal of Counseling Psychology,* 1969, *16* (Monogr. Suppl.)

—— & Dilling, C. Studying interpersonal themes in psychotherapy research. *Journal of Counseling Psychology,* 1969, *16,* 50-58.

—— & Kell, B. L. *Coping with conflict.* New York: Appleton-Century-Crofts, 1972.

Mullahy, P. (ed.) *A study of interpersonal relations.* New York: Hermitage House, 1949.

——(ed.) *The contributions of Harry Stack Sullivan: A symposium on interpersonal theory in psychiatry and social science.* New York: Hermitage House, 1952.

Pepinsky, H. B. & Pepinsky, P. N. *Counseling: theory and practice.* New York: Ronald Press, 1954.

Rogers, C. R. *Client-centered therapy.* Boston: Houghton Mifflin, 1951.

——. A theory of therapy, personality, and interpersonal relationships as developed in the client-centered framework. In S. Koch (ed.) *Psychology: a study of a science* Vol. 3. New York: McGraw Hill, 1959.

——. *On becoming a person.* Boston: Houghton Mifflin, 1961.

Solley, C. M. & Murphy, G. *Development of the perceptual world.* New York: Basic Books, 1960.

Sullivan, H.S. Psychiatry: Introduction to the study of interpersonal relations. *Psychiatry*, 1938, *1*, 121-134.

——. *Conceptions of modern psychiatry*. (2nd ed.) New York: Norton, 1953.

——.*The interpersonal theory of psychiatry*. H. S. Perry and M. L. Gawel (eds.) New York: Norton, 1953.

——. *The psychiatric interview*. H. S. Perry and M. L. Gawel (eds.) New York: Norton, 1954.

——. *Clinical studies in psychiatry*. H. S. Perry, M. L. Gawel, and M. Gibbon (eds.) New York: Norton, 1956.

Tagiuri, R. & Petrullo, L. (eds.) *Person perception and interpersonal behavior*. Stanford: Stanford University Press, 1958.

Thompson, C. *Psychoanalysis: evolution and development*. New York: Hermitage House, 1950.

Weiss, E. *Principles of psychodynamics*. New York: Grune & Stratton, 1950.

White, R. W. (ed.) *The study of lives*. New York: Atherton Press, 1963.

Wolstein, B. *Countertransference*. New York: Grune & Stratton, 1959.

——. *Transference: its structure and function in psychoanalytic therapy*. (2nd ed.) New York: Grune & Stratton, 1964.

Index